Rust Programming By Example

Enter the world of Rust by building engaging, concurrent, reactive, and robust applications

Guillaume Gomez
Antoni Boucher

BIRMINGHAM - MUMBAI

Rust Programming By Example

Commissioning Editor: Aaron Lazar
Acquisition Editor: Alok Dhuri
Content Development Editor: Akshada Iyer
Technical Editor: Mehul Singh
Copy Editor: Safis Editing
Project Coordinator: Prajakta Naik
Proofreader: Safis Editing
Indexer: Pratik Shirodkar
Graphics: Jason Monteiro
Production Coordinator: Deepika Naik

First published: January 2018

Production reference: 1090118

Published by Packt Publishing Ltd.
Livery Place
35 Livery Street
Birmingham
B3 2PB, UK.

ISBN 978-1-78839-063-7

www.packtpub.com

`mapt.io`

Mapt is an online digital library that gives you full access to over 5,000 books and videos, as well as industry leading tools to help you plan your personal development and advance your career. For more information, please visit our website.

Why subscribe?

- Spend less time learning and more time coding with practical eBooks and Videos from over 4,000 industry professionals

- Improve your learning with Skill Plans built especially for you

- Get a free eBook or video every month

- Mapt is fully searchable

- Copy and paste, print, and bookmark content

PacktPub.com

Did you know that Packt offers eBook versions of every book published, with PDF and ePub files available? You can upgrade to the eBook version at `www.PacktPub.com` and as a print book customer, you are entitled to a discount on the eBook copy. Get in touch with us at `service@packtpub.com` for more details.

At `www.PacktPub.com`, you can also read a collection of free technical articles, sign up for a range of free newsletters, and receive exclusive discounts and offers on Packt books and eBooks.

Contributors

About the authors

Guillaume Gomez is an open source lover (let's keep this simple). He's a reviewer for the Rust language and a member of the GNOME organization. Guillaume lives in Paris, France.

I would like to thank Sebastian Dröge for his review of the book. He did an amazing job in helping us improve the book.

Antoni Boucher has been enjoying programming for 10 years, especially functional and system programming. He works in the ad tech industry and strives to improve the performance and reliability of software. He contributes to multiple open source projects and is interested in system programming and compilers. Antoni lives in Montreal, Canada.

About the reviewers

Sebastian Dröge is a free software developer, currently working for Centricular Ltd. His main involvement is with the GStreamer project, a cross-platform multimedia framework. He also contributes to various other projects, such as Debian, GNOME, Rust, and WebKit. He works as a contractor on free software.

> *Thanks to the authors for making the Rust programming language accessible to more people with this book and for offering me to review this book, and to the Rust team for creating such a useful and usable language with great documentation.*

Daniel Durante is an avid coffee drinker/roaster, motorcyclist, archer, welder, and carpenter whenever he isn't programming. From the age of 12, he has been involved with web and embedded programming with PHP, Node.js, Golang, Rust, and C.

He has worked on text-based browser games that have reached over 1,000,000 active players and created bin-packing software for CNC machines. He loves working with embedded programming with cortex-m and PIC circuits, high-frequency trading applications, and he has helped contribute to one of the oldest ORMs of Node.js (SequelizeJS).

> *I would like to thank my parents, my brother, and friends who've all put up with my insanity sitting in front of a computer day in and day out. I would not be here today if it wasn't for their patience, guidance, and love.*

Packt is searching for authors like you

If you're interested in becoming an author for Packt, please visit `authors.packtpub.com` and apply today. We have worked with thousands of developers and tech professionals, just like you, to help them share their insight with the global tech community. You can make a general application, apply for a specific hot topic that we are recruiting an author for, or submit your own idea.

Table of Contents

Preface   1

Chapter 1: Basics of Rust   7

  Getting to know Rust   8

    Installing Rust   9

      Windows   9

      Linux/Mac   9

      Test your installation   11

  Documentation and reference   12

  Main function   12

    Variables   12

  Built-in data types   13

    Integer types   14

    Floating-point types   14

    Boolean type   14

    Character type   14

  Control flow   15

    Writing a condition   15

    Creating while loops   15

  Creating functions   16

  Creating structures   16

  References   18

    Clone types   19

    Copy types   20

    Mutable references   21

  Methods   21

    Constructors   22

  Tuples   23

  Enumerations   23

  Pattern matching   24

    Irrefutable patterns   26

  Traits   26

    Default methods   28

    Associated types   28

    Rules   29

Generics	30
The Option type	30
Arrays	31
Slices	31
For loops	32
Macros	34
Multiple pattern rules	35
Repetitions	36
Optional quantifier	38
Summary	39
Chapter 2: Starting with SDL	41
Understanding Rust crates	41
Installing SDL2	41
Installing SDL2 on Linux	41
Installing SDL2 on Mac	42
Installing SDL2 on Windows	42
Windows with Build Script	42
Windows (MinGW)	44
Windows (MSVC)	45
Setting up your Rust project	46
Cargo and crates.io	47
The docs.rs documentation	49
Back to our Cargo.toml file	50
Rust's modules	51
Tetris	53
Creating a window	54
Drawing	56
Playing with Options	62
Solution	63
Loading images	66
Installing SDL2_image on Mac	66
Installing SDL2_image on Linux	66
Installing SDL2_image on Windows	67
Playing with features	67
Playing with images	68
Handling files	71
Saving/loading high scores	74
Iterators	74
Reading formatted data from files	76
Summary	79

Chapter 3: Events and Basic Game Mechanisms   81

   Writing Tetris   81
      Tetrimino   82
      Creating tetriminos   86
      Generating a tetrimino   92
         Rotating a tetrimino   94
      Tetris struct   98
      Interacting with the game map   102
      SDL events   105
      Score, level, lines sent   113
         Levels and lines sent   116
         Highscores loading/overwriting   117
   Summary   131

Chapter 4: Adding All Game Mechanisms   133

   Getting started with game mechanisms   133
      Rendering UI   133
         Rendering initialization   134
         Rendering   137
      Playing with fonts   144
         Install on OS X   145
         Install on Linux   145
         Other system/package manager   145
      Loading font   146
   Summary   151

Chapter 5: Creating a Music Player   153

   Installing the prerequisite   153
      Installing GTK+ on Linux   154
      Installing GTK+ on Mac   154
      Installing GTK+ on Windows   154
   Creating your first window   154
      Closure   157
      Preventing the default behavior of an event   158
   Creating a toolbar   158
      Stock item   160
   Improving the organization of the application   161
   Adding tool button events   164
      Lifetime   166
      Ownership   170
   Containers   171

Types of containers	171
The Box container	172
Adding a playlist	174
The MVC pattern	176
Opening MP3 files	180
Reference-counting pointer	181
ID3— MP3 metadata	182
Opening files with a file dialog	183
Deleting a song	185
Displaying the cover when playing a song	186
Summary	187
Chapter 6: Implementing the Engine of the Music Player	189
Installing the dependencies	190
Installing dependencies on Linux	190
Installing dependencies on Mac	190
Installing dependencies on Windows	190
Decoding MP3 files	191
Adding dependencies	191
Implementing an MP3 decoder	191
Getting the frame samples	195
Playing music	196
Event loop	197
Atomic reference counting	198
Mutual exclusion	199
Send trait	199
Sync trait	199
Lock-free data structures	199
Playing music	202
Mutex guard	204
RAII	204
Using the music player	206
Pausing and resuming the song	207
Interior mutability	208
Showing the progression of the song	215
Improving CPU usage	219
Condition variable	220
Showing the song's current time	222
Loading and saving the playlist	226
Saving a playlist	226
Loading a playlist	229

Using gstreamer for playback	232
Summary	236
Chapter 7: Music Player in a More Rusty Way with Relm	**237**
Reasons to use relm instead of gtk-rs directly	238
State mutation	238
Asynchronous user interface	239
Creating custom widgets	239
Creating a window with relm	240
Installing Rust nightly	241
Widget	242
Model	242
Messages	242
View	243
Properties	244
Events	244
Code generation	244
Update function	245
Adding child widgets	246
One-way data binding	249
Post-initialization of the view	250
Dialogs	254
Other methods	256
Playlist	258
Model parameter	259
Adding a relm widget	265
Communicating between widgets	266
Communicating with the same widget	266
Emit	267
With different widgets	268
Handle messages from a relm widget	270
Syntax sugar to send a message to another relm widget	271
Playing music	275
Computing the song duration	285
Using relm on stable Rust	289
Relm widgets data binding	291
Summary	293
Chapter 8: Understanding FTP	**295**
File transfer protocol	295
Introduction to FTP	296

Implementing simple chunks of commands   297
   Starting with basics   299
Commands implementation   307
   Implementing the SYST command   307
   Implementing the USER command   308
   Implementing the NOOP command   310
   Implementing the PWD command   311
   Implementing the TYPE command   311
   Implementing the LIST command   312
      Implementing the PASV command   312
      Back to the LIST command   315
   Implementing the CWD command   318
   Implementing the CDUP command   322
   Full implementation of the LIST command   322
   Implementing the MKD command   325
   Implementing the RMD command   326
Testing it   327
Summary   328

Chapter 9: Implementing an Asynchronous FTP Server   329
Advantages of asynchronous IO   329
Disadvantages of asynchronous IO   329
Creating the new project   330
Using Tokio   335
Tokio event loop   336
Using futures   336
Handling errors   336
Unwrapping   336
Custom error type   337
   Displaying the error   337
   Composing error types   339
   The ? operator, revisited   341
Starting the Tokio event loop   341
Starting the server   342
Handling clients   344
Handling commands   345
FTP codec   346
   Decoding FTP commands   347
   Encoding FTP commands   348
Handling commands   349
Managing the current working directory   351
Printing the current directory   351
Changing the current directory   352

Setting the transfer type 355
Entering passive mode 357
Bytes codec 360
Decoding data bytes 360
Encoding data bytes 361
Quitting 361
Creating directories 362
Removing directories 363
Summary 364

Chapter 10: Implementing Asynchronous File Transfer 365
Listing files 365
Downloading a file 371
Uploading files 374
Going further! 376
Configuration 376
Securing the config.toml access 388
Unit tests 389
Backtraces 392
Testing failures 393
Ignoring tests 394
Integration tests 396
Teardown 397
Print output to stdout 400
Documentation 400
Documenting a crate 401
Documenting a module 401
Headers 401
Code blocks 402
Documenting an enumeration (or any type with public fields) 402
Generating the documentation 403
Warning about public items without documentation 404
Hiding items from the documentation 405
Documentation tests 405
Tags 405
ignore 406
compile_fail 407
no_run 408
should_panic 409
Combining flags? 409
About the doc blocks themselves 410

Hiding code blocks lines	410
Fuzzing tests	411
Summary	418
Appendix: Rust Best Practices	419
Rust best practices	419
Slices	419
API tips and improvements	421
Explaining the Some function	421
Using the Path function	422
Usage tips	423
Builder pattern	423
Playing with mutable borrows	424
Playing with moves	425
Code readability	425
Big number formatting	425
Specifying types	426
Matching	427
Summary	427
Other Books You May Enjoy	429
Index	433

Preface

The aim of this book is to give a little tour of some Rust basics (playing with GUIs) and advanced (async programming) features. Because interesting projects are always a huge plus in a language learning process, we wrote the book with this focus. We think this language is awesome and we hope to give you the motivation and knowledge in order to have even more rustaceans in the future!

Who this book is for

Readers only need a basic knowledge of the Rust language to follow through this book if they want to enjoy it the most, even though it's recommended to always have the documentation open alongside to answer questions this book might not provide (we, authors, aren't almighty, which is a shame, we know). For readers who don't know Rust at all, we recommend that they first read the Rust book that you can find here at `https://doc.rust-lang.org/stable/book/` and then come back to read this one!

What this book covers

`Chapter 1`, *Basics of Rust*, covers the installation of Rust and teaches the syntax and basic principles of the language so that you are ready to code projects with it.

`Chapter 2`, *Starting with SDL*, shows how to start using SDL and its main features, such as events and drawings. Once the project is created, we'll make a window displaying an image.

`Chapter 3`, *Events and Basic Game Mechanisms*, takes you deeper into how to handle events. We'll write the tetrimino objects and make them change following the received events.

`Chapter 4`, *Adding All Game Mechanisms*, completes the game's mechanisms. At the end of this chapter, we'll have a fully running Tetris game.

`Chapter 5`, *Creating a Music Player*, helps you start building a graphical music player. Only the user interface will be covered in this chapter.

`Chapter 6`, *Implementing the Engine of the Music Player*, adds the music player engine to the graphical application.

Chapter 7, *Music Player in a More Rusty Way with Relm*, improves the music player to add a playing, allowing to process the music in the list to remove the vocals.

Chapter 8, *Understanding FTP*, introduces the FTP protocol by implementing a synchronous FTP server, to prepare you to write the asynchronous version in the next chapters.

Chapter 9, *Implementing an Asynchronous FTP Server*, implements an FTP protocol with Tokio.

Chapter 10, *Implementing Asynchronous File Transfer*, implements the FTP service itself. This is where the application will be able to upload and download files.

Appendix, *Rust Best Practices*, shows how to write nice Rust APIs and how to make them as easy and nice to use as possible.

To get the most out of this book

There isn't much that you require. Besides, Rust is well supported on any operating system. Linux is the best-supported operating system here. You can also use Rust on Windows and macOS as well, you'll need a fairly recent computer; a gigabyte of RAM should be enough for the purposes of this book.

Download the example code files

You can download the example code files for this book from your account at www.packtpub.com. If you purchased this book elsewhere, you can visit www.packtpub.com/support and register to have the files emailed directly to you.

You can download the code files by following these steps:

1. Log in or register at www.packtpub.com.
2. Select the **SUPPORT** tab.
3. Click on **Code Downloads & Errata**.
4. Enter the name of the book in the **Search** box and follow the onscreen instructions.

Once the file is downloaded, please make sure that you unzip or extract the folder using the latest version of:

- WinRAR/7-Zip for Windows
- Zipeg/iZip/UnRarX for Mac
- 7-Zip/PeaZip for Linux

The code bundle for the book is also hosted on GitHub at `https://github.com/PacktPublishing/Rust-Programming-By-Example`. We also have other code bundles from our rich catalog of books and videos available at `https://github.com/PacktPublishing/`. Check them out!

Download the color images

We also provide a PDF file that has color images of the screenshots/diagrams used in this book. You can download it here: `https://www.packtpub.com/sites/default/files/downloads/RustProgrammingByExample_ColorImages.pdf`

Conventions used

There are a number of text conventions used throughout this book.

`CodeInText`: Indicates code words in text, database table names, folder names, filenames, file extensions, pathnames, dummy URLs, user input, and Twitter handles. Here is an example: "Mount the downloaded `WebStorm-10*.dmg` disk image file as another disk in your system."

A block of code is set as follows:

```
html, body, #map {
  height: 100%;
  margin: 0;
  padding: 0
}
```

When we wish to draw your attention to a particular part of a code block, the relevant lines or items are set in bold:

```
[default]
exten => s,1,Dial(Zap/1|30)
exten => s,2,Voicemail(u100)
exten => s,102,Voicemail(b100)
exten => i,1,Voicemail(s0)
```

Any command-line input or output is written as follows:

```
$ mkdir css
$ cd css
```

Bold: Indicates a new term, an important word, or words that you see onscreen. For example, words in menus or dialog boxes appear in the text like this. Here is an example: "Select **System info** from the **Administration** panel."

Warnings or important notes appear like this.

Tips and tricks appear like this.

Get in touch

Feedback from our readers is always welcome.

General feedback: Email `feedback@packtpub.com` and mention the book title in the subject of your message. If you have questions about any aspect of this book, please email us at `questions@packtpub.com`.

Errata: Although we have taken every care to ensure the accuracy of our content, mistakes do happen. If you have found a mistake in this book, we would be grateful if you would report this to us. Please visit `www.packtpub.com/submit-errata`, selecting your book, clicking on the Errata Submission Form link, and entering the details.

Piracy: If you come across any illegal copies of our works in any form on the Internet, we would be grateful if you would provide us with the location address or website name. Please contact us at `copyright@packtpub.com` with a link to the material.

If you are interested in becoming an author: If there is a topic that you have expertise in and you are interested in either writing or contributing to a book, please visit `authors.packtpub.com`.

Reviews

Please leave a review. Once you have read and used this book, why not leave a review on the site that you purchased it from? Potential readers can then see and use your unbiased opinion to make purchase decisions, we at Packt can understand what you think about our products, and our authors can see your feedback on their book. Thank you!

For more information about Packt, please visit `packtpub.com`.

1
Basics of Rust

This chapter introduces you to the basics of Rust, a systems programming language designed to be secure and fast. Rust is a good candidate to write concurrent software and it helps to prevent bugs. After reading this chapter, you'll be ready to code cool projects in the subsequent chapters. After learning about the language itself, you'll install its compiler and package manager, and you'll start programming right away. You'll also learn about the following concepts:

- Variables
- Built-in data types
- Control flow (conditions and loops)
- Functions
- Custom data types
- References
- Pattern matching
- Traits and Generics
- Arrays and Slices
- Macros

Getting to know Rust

Rust is a system programming language developed by Mozilla, whose version 1.0 appeared in 2015. A system language means that you have control over the memory used by the program—you decide whether you want to allocate the memory on the stack or the heap, and when the memory is freed. But don't worry; in Rust, the compiler is very helpful and prevents you from making the many mistakes you can make in C and C++ that lead to segmentation faults. A segmentation fault arises when the programmer tries to access some memory that is not accessible to its process. Memory unsafety leads to bugs and security flaws.

Moreover, the compiler is smart enough to know where to insert the memory deallocation instructions so that you don't need to manually free your memory, all of that without a garbage collector, which is one of its greatest features. Since Rust is safe and fast, it is the perfect candidate for writing operating systems, embedded programs, servers, and games, but you can also use it to develop desktop applications and websites. A great example of this power is the `Servo web engine`, also developed by Mozilla.

Rust is multi-paradigm: it can be used in an imperative or functional way and you can even write concurrent applications safely. It is statically typed, meaning that every type must be known at compile time, but since it uses type inference, we can omit the type for most local variables. It is also strongly typed, which means that its type system prevents the programmer from some kinds of errors, such as using the wrong type for a function parameter. And Rust is very good at writing concurrent software because it prevents data races, which is concurrent access to a variable where one is a write; this is an undefined behavior in other languages. One thing to remember when reading this book is that Rust prevents you from shooting yourself in the foot. For instance, Rust doesn't have:

- null pointers
- data races
- use after free
- use before initialization
- goto
- automatic coercion of Boolean, numbers and enumerations

Also, Rust helps to prevent memory leaks. However, all of this is possible with `unsafe` code, which is explained in `Chapter 3`, *Events and Basic Game Mechanisms*.

Without further ado, let's install the tools we'll need throughout the book.

Installing Rust

In this section we'll install `rustup`, which allows us to install different versions of the compiler and package manager.

Windows

Go to `https://rustup.rs` and follow the instructions in order to download `rustup-init.exe`, then run it.

Linux/Mac

Unless your distribution provides a package for `rustup`, you'll need to install `rustup` by typing the following command in your terminal:

```
$ curl https://sh.rustup.rs -sSf | sh
info: downloading installer

Welcome to Rust!

[...]

Current installation options:

   default host triple: x86_64-unknown-linux-gnu
     default toolchain: stable
  modify PATH variable: yes

1) Proceed with installation (default)
2) Customize installation
3) Cancel installation
```

This downloaded `rustup` and asked you whether you want to customize the installation. Unless you have particular needs, you'll be okay with the default.

 Note: The $ represents your shell prompt and should not be typed; you must type the text following it. Also, a line of text that doesn't start with $ represents the text output of the program.

To proceed with the installation, enter 1 and press *Enter*. This will install the `rustc` compiler, and the `cargo` package manager, among other things:

```
info: syncing channel updates for 'stable-x86_64-unknown-linux-gnu'
info: latest update on 2017-07-20, rust version 1.19.0 (0ade33941
2017-07-17)
info: downloading component 'rustc'

[...]

  stable installed - rustc 1.19.0 (0ade33941 2017-07-17)


Rust is installed now. Great!

To get started you need Cargo's bin directory ($HOME/.cargo/bin) in your
PATH
environment variable. Next time you log in this will be done automatically.

To configure your current shell run source $HOME/.cargo/env
```

As pointed out by the installer, you need to execute the following command in order to add the directory containing these tools in your PATH:

```
$ source $HOME/.cargo/env
# Which is the same as executing the following:
$ export PATH="$HOME/.cargo/bin:$PATH"
```

(This is only needed once because the rustup installer added it to your ~/.profile file.)

Now, test that you have both `cargo` and `rustc`, as you'll need them very soon:

```
$ cargo -V
cargo 0.23.0 (61fa02415 2017-11-22)
$ rustc -V
rustc 1.22.1 (05e2e1c41 2017-11-22)
```

Cargo is Rust's package manager and build tool: it allows you to compile and run your projects, as well as managing their dependencies.

At the time of writing this book, the stable Rust version was 1.22.0.

Test your installation

Let's try to build a Rust program. First, create a new project with `cargo`:

```
$ cargo new --bin hello_world
     Created binary (application) `hello_world` project
```

The `--bin` flag indicates that we want to create an executable project, as opposed to a library (which is the default without this flag). In the Rust world, a **crate** is a package of libraries and/or executable binaries.

This created a `hello_world` directory containing the following files and directory:

```
$ tree hello_world/
hello_world/
├────── Cargo.toml
└────── src
        └────── main.rs

1 directory, 2 files
```

The `Cargo.toml` file is where the metadata (name, version, and so on) of your project resides, as well as its dependencies. The source files of your project are in the `src` directory. It's now time to run this project:

```
$ cd hello_world/
$ cargo run
   Compiling hello_world v0.1.0
(file:///home/packtpub/projects/hello_world)
    Finished dev [unoptimized + debuginfo] target(s) in 0.39 secs
     Running `target/debug/hello_world`
Hello, world!
```

The first three lines printed after `cargo run` are lines printed by `cargo` indicating what it did: it compiled the project and ran it. The last line, `Hello, world!`, is the line printed by our project. As you can see, `cargo` generates a Rust file that prints text to `stdout` (standard output):

```
$ cat src/main.rs
fn main() {
    println!("Hello, world!");
}
```

If you only want to compile the project without running it, type the following instead:

```
$ cargo build
    Finished dev [unoptimized + debuginfo] target(s) in 0.0 secs
```

This time, we didn't see `Compiling hello_world` because `cargo` did not see any changes to the project's files, thus, there's no need to compile again.

Documentation and reference

You can find the API documentation here: `https://doc.rust-lang.org/stable/std/`. The reference can be found here: `https://doc.rust-lang.org/stable/reference/`.

Main function

Let's look again at our first project source code:

```
fn main() {
    println!("Hello, world!");
}
```

It only contains a `main` function—this is where the execution of the program begins. It is a function that takes no arguments (hence the empty parentheses) and returns a unit, also written `()`. The body of the function, between curly brackets, contains a call to the `println!()` macro—we can see this is a macro because it ends with `!`, as opposed to a function. This macro prints the text between parentheses, followed by a new line. We'll see what is a macro in the Macros section.

Variables

We'll now change the previous program to add a variable:

```
fn main() {
    let name = "world";
    println!("Hello, {}!", name);
}
```

The `{}` part in the string literal is replaced by the content of the `name` variable. Here, we see the type inference in action—we don't have to specify the type of the `name` variable and the compiler will infer it for us. We could have also written the type ourselves:

```
let name: &str = "world";
```

(From now on, I'll omit the `main` function, but this code should be written inside the function.)

In Rust, variables are immutable by default. As such, writing the following will cause a compile-time error:

```
let age = 42;
age += 1;
```

The compiler gives us a very helpful error message:

```
error[E0384]: cannot assign twice to immutable variable `age`
  --> src/main.rs:16:5
   |
15 |     let age = 42;
   |         --- first assignment to `age`
16 |     age += 1;
   |     ^^^^^^^^ cannot assign twice to immutable variable
```

To make a variable mutable, we need to use the `mut` keyword:

```
let mut age = 42;
age += 1;
```

Built-in data types

Let's look at the basic types provided by the language, such as integers, floats, Booleans, and characters.

Integer types

The following integer types are available in Rust:

Unsigned	Signed
u8	i8
u16	i16
u32	i32
u64	i64
usize	isize

The u means unsigned, while the i means signed, and the number following it is the number of bits. For instance, a number of the u8 type can be between 0 and 255, inclusive. And a number of the i16 type can be between -32768 and 32767, inclusive. The size variants are the pointer-sized integer types: usize and isize are 64-bit on a 64-bit CPU. The default integer type is i32, which means that this type will be used by the type inference when it cannot choose a more specific type.

Floating-point types

There are two floating-point types: f32 and f64, the latter being the default. The number following f represents the number of bits for the type. An example value is 0.31415e1.

Boolean type

The bool type admits two values: true and false.

Character type

The char type represents a Unicode character. An example unicode scalar value is '€'.

Control flow

We'll now look at how to write conditions and loops in Rust. Conditions are useful to execute a block of code when a certain situation happens, and loops allow you to repeat a block of code a number of times, until a condition is met.

Writing a condition

Similar to other languages, Rust conditions are expressed with the `if` and `else` keywords:

```rust
let number1 = 24;
let number2 = 42;
if number1 > number2 {
    println!("{} > {}", number1, number2);
} else {
    println!("{} <= {}", number1, number2);
}
```

However, they do not require parentheses around the conditional expression. Also, this expression must be of the `bool` type: you cannot use a number as you would in other languages.

One particularity of Rust conditions, like many other constructs, is that they are expressions. The last expression of each branch is the value of this branch. Be careful though, the type of each branch must be the same. For instance, we can get the minimum number of the two numbers and put it into a variable:

```rust
let minimum =
    if number1 < number2 {
        number1
    } else {
        number2
    }; // Don't forget the semi-colon here.
```

Creating while loops

There are multiple kinds of loop in Rust. One of them is the `while` loop.

Let's see how to compute the greatest common divisor using the Euclidean algorithm:

```rust
let mut a = 15;
let mut b = 40;
while b != 0 {
```

```
        let temp = b;
        b = a % b;
        a = temp;
    }
    println!("Greatest common divisor of 15 and 40 is: {}", a);
```

This code executes successive divisions and stops doing so when the remainder is 0.

Creating functions

We had a brief introduction to functions when we saw the `main` function. Let's see how to create functions with parameters and a return value.

Here's how to write a function that returns the maximum of two numbers:

```
fn max(a: i32, b: i32) -> i32 {
    if a > b {
        a
    } else {
        b
    }
}
```

The parameters are between parentheses and must be explicitly typed since the type inference only infers the types of local variables. This is a good thing since this acts as a documentation. Moreover, this can prevent bugs when we change how we use the parameters or change the value that is returned. The function can be defined after it is used without any issue. The return type is after `->`. When we return `()`, we can omit the `->` and type.

The last expression in the body of a function is the value returned from the function. You don't need to use `return`. The `return` keyword is only needed when you want to return early.

Creating structures

Sometimes, we have multiple values that only make sense together, such as the two coordinates of a point. Structures are a way to create new types that contains multiple members.

Here is how we would create the aforementioned `Point` structure:

```
struct Point {
    x: i32,
    y: i32,
}
```

To create a new point and access its members, we use the following syntax:

```
let point = Point {
    x: 24,
    y: 42,
};
println!("({}, {})", point.x, point.y);
```

What if we want to print the `point` as a whole?

Let's try the following:

```
println!("{}", point);
```

The compiler does not accept this:

```
error[E0277]: the trait bound `Point: std::fmt::Display` is not satisfied
  --> src/main.rs:7:20
   |
7  |      println!("{}", point);
   |                     ^^^^^ `Point` cannot be formatted with the default
formatter; try using `:?` instead if you are using a format string
   |
   = help: the trait `std::fmt::Display` is not implemented for `Point`
   = note: required by `std::fmt::Display::fmt`
```

The `{}` syntax is used to display a value to the end user of the application. Nevertheless, there's no standard way to display arbitrary structures. We can do what the compiler suggests: using the `{:?}` syntax. That requires you to add an attribute to the structure, so let's change it:

```
#[derive(Debug)]
struct Point {
    x: i32,
    y: i32,
}

println!("{:?}", point);
```

The `#[derive(Debug)]` attribute tells the compiler to automatically generate the code to be able to print a debug representation of the structure. We'll see how this works in the section about traits. It prints the following:

```
Point { x: 24, y: 42 }
```

Sometimes, the structure contains a lot of nested fields and this representation is hard to read. To remedy that, we can use the `{:#?}` syntax to pretty-print the value:

```
println!("{:#?}", point);
```

This gives the following output:

```
Point {
    x: 24,
    y: 42
}
```

The documentation describes what other formatting syntax can be used: `https://doc.rust-lang.org/stable/std/fmt/`.

References

Let's try the following code, which would work in other programming languages:

```
let p1 = Point { x: 1, y: 2 };
let p2 = p1;
println!("{}", p1.x);
```

We can see that Rust doesn't accept this. It gives the following error:

```
error[E0382]: use of moved value: `p1.x`
  --> src/main.rs:4:20
   |
3  |      let p2 = p1;
   |               -- value moved here
4  |      println!("{}", p1.x);
   |                     ^^^^ value used here after move
   |
   = note: move occurs because `p1` has type `Point`, which does not
implement the `Copy` trait
```

This means that we cannot use a value after it is moved. In Rust, values are moved by default instead of being copied, except in some cases, as we'll see in the next sub-section.

To avoid moving a value, we can take a reference to it by prefixing it with `&`:

```
let p1 = Point { x: 1, y: 2 };
let p2 = &p1;
println!("{}", p1.x);
```

This code compiles and, in this case, `p2` is a reference to `p1`, which means that it points to the same memory location. Rust ensures that it is always safe to use a reference, since references are not pointers, they cannot be NULL.

References can also be used in the type of a function parameter. This is a function that prints a `point`, without moving the value:

```
fn print_point(point: &Point) {
    println!("x: {}, y: {}", point.x, point.y);
}
```

We can use it this way:

```
print_point(&p1);
println!("{}", p1.x);
```

We can still use the `point` after calling `print_point`, because we send a reference to the function instead of moving the `point` into the function.

Clone types

An alternative to using references is to clone values. By cloning a value, we don't move it. To be able to clone a `point`, we can add `derive` to it:

```
#[derive(Clone, Debug)]
struct Point {
    x: i32,
    y: i32,
}
```

We can now call the `clone()` method to avoid moving our `p1` point:

```
fn print_point(point: Point) {
    println!("x: {}, y: {}", point.x, point.y);
}
```

```
let p1 = Point { x: 1, y: 2 };
let p2 = p1.clone();
print_point(p1.clone());
println!("{}", p1.x);
```

Copy types

Some types are not moved when we assigned a value of these types to another variable. This is the case for basic types such as integers. For instance, the following code is perfectly valid:

```
let num1 = 42;
let num2 = num1;
println!("{}", num1);
```

We can still use `num1` even thought we assigned it to `num2`. This is because the basic types implement a special marker: `Copy`. Copy types are copied instead of moved.

We can make our own types `Copy` by adding `derive` to them:

```
#[derive(Clone, Copy)]
struct Point {
    x: i32,
    y: i32,
}
```

Since `Copy` requires `Clone`, we also implement the latter for our `Point` type. We cannot derive `Copy` for a type containing a value that does not implement `Copy`. Now, we can use a `Point` without having to bother with references:

```
fn print_point(point: Point) {
    println!("x: {}, y: {}", point.x, point.y);
}

let p1 = Point { x: 1, y: 2 };
let p2 = p1;
print_point(p1);
println!("{}", p1.x);
```

Mutable references

If we want to be able to mutable thought a reference, we need a mutable reference, since everything is immutable by default in Rust. To get a mutable reference, simply replace & with &mut. Let's write a function that will increment the x field of a Point:

```
fn inc_x(point: &mut Point) {
    point.x += 1;
}
```

Here, we see that the Point type is now &mut, which allows us to update the point in the method. To use this method, our p1 variable needs to be mut and we also need to take a mutable reference for this variable:

```
let mut p1 = Point { x: 1, y: 2 };
inc_x(&mut p1);
```

Methods

We can add methods on custom types. Let's write a method to compute the distance of a point to the origin:

```
impl Point {
    fn dist_from_origin(&self) -> f64 {
        let sum_of_squares = self.x.pow(2) + self.y.pow(2);
        (sum_of_squares as f64).sqrt()
    }
}
```

There are a lot of new syntaxes here (impl Point, as, and .method()), so let's explain all of them. First of all, methods of a type are declared within the impl Type {} construct. This method takes a special parameter: &self. This parameter is the instance the method is called on, like this in other programming languages. The & operator before self means that the instance is passed by immutable reference. As we can see, it is possible to call methods on basic types in Rust—self.x.pow(2) computes the power of two of the x field. We can find this method, and many others, in the documentation, at https://doc.rust-lang.org/stable/std/primitive.i32.html#method.pow . In the last expression of the method, we cast the sum_of_squares integer to f64 before computing its square root, because the sqrt() method is defined only on floating points.

Let's create a method that will update the fields of the structure:

```
impl Point {
    fn translate(&mut self, dx: i32, dy: i32) {
        self.x += dx;
        self.y += dy;
    }
}
```

The difference with the previous method is that `self` is now a mutable reference, `&mut`.

Constructors

Rust does not provide constructors, but a common idiom is to create a `new()` static method, also called an associated function:

```
impl Point {
    fn new(x: i32, y: i32) -> Self {
        Self { x: x, y: y }
    }
}
```

The difference with a normal method is that it does not take `&self` (or one of its variations) as a parameter.

`Self` is the type of the `self` value; we could have used `Point` instead of `Self`.

When the field name is the same as the value assigned, it is possible to omit the value, as a shorthand:

```
fn new(x: i32, y: i32) -> Self {
    Self { x, y }
}
```

When we create an instance of `Point` with the call to its constructor (`let point = Point::new();`), this will allocate the value on the stack.

We can provide multiple constructors:

```
impl Point {
    fn origin() -> Self {
        Point { x: 0, y: 0 }
    }
}
```

Tuples

Tuples and structures are similar, except that tuples' fields are unnamed. Tuples are declared inside parentheses, with the element separated by a comma:

```
let tuple = (24, 42);
println!("({}, {})", tuple.0, tuple.1);
```

As you can see on the second line, we can access the elements of a tuple with `.index`, where `index` is a constant and this index starts at 0.

Tuples can be used to return multiple values from a function. For instance, the `str::split_at()` method returns two strings:

```
let (hello, world) = "helloworld".split_at(5);
println!("{}, {}!", hello, world);
```

Here, we assign the two elements of the tuple to the `hello` and `world` variables. We'll see why this works in the *Pattern matching* section.

Enumerations

While a structure allows us to get multiple values under the same variable, enumerations allow us to choose one value from different types of values.

For example, let's write a type representing an expression:

```
enum Expr {
    Null,
    Add(i32, i32),
    Sub(i32, i32),
    Mul(i32, i32),
    Div { dividend: i32, divisor: i32 },
    Val(i32),
}

let quotient = Expr::Div { dividend: 10, divisor: 2 };
let sum = Expr::Add(40, 2);
```

The `Null` variant does not have a value associated with it, `Val` has one associated value, and `Add` has two. `Div` also has two associated values, but they are named, similar to how we define a structure.

Pattern matching

So how can we know which variant is in a variable whose type is an enumeration and how to get the values out of it? For that, we need to use pattern matching. The `match` expression is one way to do pattern matching. Let's see how to use it to compute the result of an expression:

```
fn print_expr(expr: Expr) {
    match expr {
        Expr::Null => println!("No value"),
        Expr::Add(x, y) => println!("{}", x + y),
        Expr::Sub(x, y) => println!("{}", x - y),
        Expr::Mul(x, y) => println!("{}", x * y),
        Expr::Div { dividend: x, divisor: 0 } => println!("Divisor
         is zero"),
        Expr::Div { dividend: x, divisor: y } => println!("{}",
        x/y),
        Expr::Val(x) => println!("{}", x),
    }
}
```

A `match` expression is a way to check whether a value follows a certain pattern and executes different codes for different patterns. In this case, we match over an enumerated type, so we check for each variant. If the expression is `Expr::Add`, the code on the right of `=>` is executed: `println!("{}", x + y)`. By writing variable names inside the parentheses next to `Expr::Add`, we specify that the actual values of this variant are bound to these names. By doing so, we can use these variable names on the right side of `=>`.

Figure 1.1 is a diagram showing how pattern matching works:

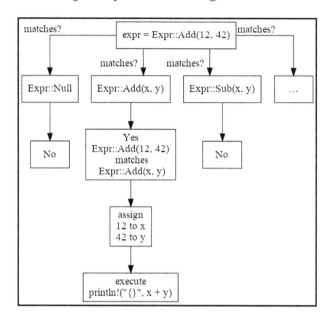

Figure 1.1

A `match` can also be used to check whether a number is within a range. This function converts an ASCII character (represented by `u8` in Rust) to uppercase:

```
fn uppercase(c: u8) -> u8 {
    match c {
        b'a'...b'z' => c - 32,
        _ => c,
    }
}
```

Here, the . . . syntax represents an inclusive range. And the underscore (_) is used to mean literally everything else, this is very useful in Rust because `match` needs to be exhaustive.

You can convert `u8` to `char` using the `as` syntax, as shown earlier:

```
println!("{}", uppercase(b'a') as char);
```

It is also possible to match against different patterns in a `match` by using the `|` operator:

```
fn is_alphanumeric(c: char) -> bool {
    match c {
```

```
                'a'...'z' | 'A'...'Z' | '0'...'9' => true,
                _ => false,
            }
        }
```

There are alternative syntaxes to do pattern matching. One of them is the `if let` construct. Let's rewrite our `uppercase` function using `if let`:

```
fn uppercase(c: u8) -> u8 {
    if let b'a'...b'z' = c {
        c - 32
    } else {
        c
    }
}
```

Unlike a `match`, `if let` does not need to be exhaustive. It does not even require an `else` branch, the rules used for the normal `if` expression also applies to `if let`. This construct can be more appropriate than `match` when you only want to match against one or two patterns.

Irrefutable patterns

Another form of pattern matching is **irrefutable patterns**. A pattern is irrefutable when there's only one way to match it and it always succeeds. For instance, another way to get the elements of a tuple is with an irrefutable pattern:

```
let tuple = (24, 42);
let (a, b) = tuple;
println!("{}, {}", a, b);
```

In the second line, we assign the first element of the tuple to a and the second to b.

Traits

Traits are a way to specify that a type must implement some methods and/or some types. They are similar to interfaces in Java. We can implement a trait on a type and we'll be able to use the methods of this trait on this type as long as this trait is imported. This is how we can add methods to types defined in other crates or even the standard library.

Let's write a trait representing a bit set:

```
trait BitSet {
    fn clear(&mut self, index: usize);
    fn is_set(&self, index: usize) -> bool;
    fn set(&mut self, index: usize);
}
```

Here, we don't write the body of the methods, as they will be defined when we implement this trait for a type.

Now, let's implement this trait for the u64 type:

```
impl BitSet for u64 {
    fn clear(&mut self, index: usize) {
        *self &= !(1 << index);
    }

    fn is_set(&self, index: usize) -> bool {
        (*self >> index) & 1 == 1
    }

    fn set(&mut self, index: usize) {
        *self |= 1 << index;
    }
}
```

As you can see, the bitwise not operator is ! in Rust, as opposed to ~ in other languages. With this code, we can call these methods on u64:

```
let mut num = 0;
num.set(15);
println!("{}", num.is_set(15));
num.clear(15);
```

Remember the #[derive(Debug)] attribute? This actually implements the Debug trait on the following type. We could also manually implement the Debug trait on our type, using the same impl syntax, if the default implement does not suit our use case.

Default methods

Traits can contain default methods, which can be convenient for the implementor of the trait since fewer methods will need to be implemented. Let's add a `toggle()` default method in the trait:

```
trait BitSet {
    fn clear(&mut self, index: usize);
    fn is_set(&self, index: usize) -> bool;
    fn set(&mut self, index: usize);

    fn toggle(&mut self, index: usize) {
        if self.is_set(index) {
            self.clear(index);
        } else {
            self.set(index);
        }
    }
}
```

Since the new method has a body, we don't need to update our previous implementation. However, we could do it to provide a more efficient implementation, for instance:

```
impl BitSet for u64 {
    // The other methods are the same as before.

    fn toggle(&mut self, index: usize) {
        *self ^= 1 << index;
    }
}
```

Associated types

We can also have types in a trait that need to be specified. For instance, let's implement the `Add` trait from the standard library on our `Point` type that we declared earlier, which allows us to use the + operator on our own types:

```
use std::ops::Add;

impl Add<Point> for Point {
    type Output = Point;

    fn add(self, point: Point) -> Self::Output {
        Point {
            x: self.x + point.x,
```

```
            y: self.y + point.y,
        }
    }
}
```

The first line is to import the `Add` trait from the standard library so that we can implement it on our type. Here we specify that the associated `Output` type is `Point`. Associated types are most useful for return types. Here, the `Output` of the `add()` method is the associated `Self::Output` type.

Now, we can use the + operator on `Point`s:

```
let p1 = Point { x: 1, y: 2 };
let p2 = Point { x: 3, y: 4 };
let p3 = p1 + p2;
```

Having to specify the output parameter with an associated type (instead of setting it to `Self`) gives us more flexibility. For instance, we could implement the scalar product for the * operator, which takes two `Point`s and returns a number.

You can find all the operators that can be overloaded on this page, at `https://doc.rust-lang.org/stable/std/ops/index.html`.

Since Rust 1.20, Rust also supports associated constants in addition to associated types.

Rules

There are some rules that must be followed in order to use traits. The compiler will throw an error if they are not respected:

- The trait must be imported in order to use its methods
- The implementation of a trait must be in the same crate as the trait or the type

The second rule is to avoid conflicts that could otherwise happen when using multiple libraries. We can have such a conflict when two imported traits provide the same method for the same type.

Generics

Generics are a way to make a function or a type work for multiple types to avoid code duplication. Let's rewrite our `max` function to make it generic:

```
fn max<T: PartialOrd>(a: T, b: T) -> T {
    if a > b {
        a
    } else {
        b
    }
}
```

The first thing to note is that there's a new part after the function name: this is where we declare the generic types. We declare a generic `T` type, `: PartialOrd` after it means that this `T` type must implement the `PartialOrd` trait. This is called a trait bound. We then use this `T` type for both of our parameters and the return type. Then, we see the same function body as the one from our non-generic function. We needed to add the trait bound because, by default, no operation is allowed on a generic type. The `PartialOrd` trait allows us to use the comparison operators.

We can then use this function with any type that implements `PartialOrd`:

```
println!("{}", max('a', 'z'));
```

This is using static dispatch as opposed to dynamic dispatch, meaning that the compiler will generate a `max` function specific to `char` in the resulting binary. Dynamic dispatch is another approach that resolves the right function to call at runtime, which is less efficient.

The Option type

Generics can also be used in a type. The `Option` type from the standard library is a generic type, defined as such:

```
enum Option<T> {
    Some(T),
    None,
}
```

This type is useful to encode the possibility of the absence of a value. `None` means no value, while `Some(value)` is used when there's a value.

Arrays

An array is a fixed-size collection of elements of the same type. We declare them with square brackets:

```
let array = [1, 2, 3, 4];
let array: [i16; 4] = [1, 2, 3, 4];
```

The second line shows how to specify the type of an array. An alternative way to do that is to use a literal suffix:

```
let array = [1u8, 2, 3, 4];
```

A literal suffix is the composition of a literal (that is, a constant) and a type suffix, so with the 1 constant and the u8 type, we get 1u8. Literal suffixes can only be used on numbers. This declares an array of 4 elements of the u8 type. Array indexing starts at 0 and bounds checking is done at runtime. Bounds checking is used to prevent accessing memory that is out of bounds, for instance, trying to access the element after the end of an array. While this can slow down the software a bit, it can be optimized in many cases. The following code will trigger a panic because the 4 index is one past the end of the array:

```
println!("{}", array[4]);
```

At runtime, we see the following message:

```
thread 'main' panicked at 'index out of bounds: the len is 4 but
the index is 4', src/main.rs:5:20
note: Run with `RUST_BACKTRACE=1` for a backtrace.
```

Another way to declare an array is:

```
let array = [0u8; 100];
```

This declares an array of 100 elements, where all of them are 0.

Slices

Arrays are fixed-size, but if we want to create a function that works with arrays of any size, we need to use another type: a slice.

A slice is a view into a contiguous sequence: it can be a view of the whole array, or a part of it. Slices are fat pointers, in addition to the pointer to the data, they contain a size. Here's a function that returns a reference to the first element of a slice:

```
fn first<T>(slice: &[T]) -> &T {
    &slice[0]
}
```

Here, we use a generic type without bound since we don't use any operation on values of the T type. The `&[T]` parameter type is a slice of T. The return type is `&T`, which is a reference on values of the T type. The body of the function is `&slice[0]`, which returns a reference to the first element of the slice. Here's how to call this function with an array:

```
println!("{}", first(&array));
```

We can create `slice` for only a portion of an array, as shown in the following example:

```
println!("{}", first(&array[2..]));
```

`&array[2..]` creates a slice that starts at the 2 index until the end of the array (hence no index after `..`). Both indices are optional, so we could also write `&array[..10]` for the first 10 elements of the array, `&array[5..10]` for the elements with the 5 to 9 index (inclusive), or `&array[..]` for all the elements.

For loops

The for loop is another form of loops that can be used in Rust. It is used to loop over elements of an iterator. An iterator is a structure that produces a sequence of value: it could produce the same value indefinitely or produce the elements of a collection. We can get an iterator from a slice, so let's do that to compute the sum of the elements in a slice:

```
let array = [1, 2, 3, 4];
let mut sum = 0;
for element in &array {
    sum += *element;
}
println!("Sum: {}", sum);
```

The only surprising part here is `*` in `sum += *element`. Since we get a reference to the elements of the slice, we need to dereference them in order to access the integers. We used `&` in front of `array` to avoid moving it, indeed, we may still want to use this variable after the loop.

Let's write a function that returns the index of an element in a slice, or None if it is not in the slice:

```
fn index<T: PartialEq>(slice: &[T], target: &T) -> Option<usize> {
    for (index, element) in slice.iter().enumerate() {
        if element == target {
            return Some(index);
        }
    }
    None
}
```

 Note: A partial equivalence relation is both symmetric and transitive, but not reflexive. The Eq trait is used when these three properties are satisfied.

Here, we use again a generic type, but this time we use the PartialEq trait bound to be able to use the == operator on values of the T type. This function returns Option<usize>, meaning that it can either return no value (None) or the index (Some(index)). In the first line of the body, we use slice.iter().enumerate() to get the index in addition to the element of the slice. We use pattern matching right after the for keyword in order to assign the index and the element to variables. Inside the condition, we use the return keyword to return a value early. So if the value is found, it will return the index; otherwise, the loop will end and the None value is returned afterward.

Let's write another function that uses a for loop. It returns the minimum and the maximum of a slice, or None if the slice is empty:

```
fn min_max(slice: &[i32]) -> Option<(i32, i32)> {
    if slice.is_empty() {
        return None;
    }
    let mut min = slice[0];
    let mut max = slice[0];
    for &element in slice {
        if element < min {
            min = element;
        }
        if element > max {
            max = element;
        }
    }
    Some((min, max))
}
```

Here we return multiple values from a function by using a tuple. This time, `&` is on the left side of `in`, while previously it was on the right side of it; this is because this `for` loop is pattern matching against a reference by using `&element`. This is something we can do in Rust, thus we don't need to dereference the element anymore with `*`.

Macros

Macro rules, also called macros by example, are a way to avoid code duplication by generating code at compile time. We will implement a simple macro to implement our `BitSet` trait for integer types:

```
macro_rules! int_bitset {
    ($ty:ty) => {
        impl BitSet for $ty {
            fn clear(&mut self, index: usize) {
                *self &= !(1 << index);
            }

            fn is_set(&self, index: usize) -> bool {
                (*self >> index) & 1 == 1
            }

            fn set(&mut self, index: usize) {
                *self |= 1 << index;
            }
        }
    };
}
```

The name of the `int_bitset` macro is written after `macro_rules!`. A macro can have multiple rules, similar to match arms, but it matches on Rust syntactic elements instead, with types, expressions, blocks of code, and so on. Here we only have one rule and it matches against a single type since we use `:ty`. The part before `:ty` (`$ty`) is the name for the element that was matched. Inside the curly brackets, after the `=>` symbol, we see the actual code that will be generated. It is the same as our previous implementation of `BitSet` for `u64`, except that it uses the meta-variable `$ty` instead of `u64`.

To avoid a lot of boilerplate code, we can then use this macro as follows:

```
int_bitset!(i32);
int_bitset!(u8);
int_bitset!(u64);
```

Multiple pattern rules

Let's write a macro that will simplify the implementation of the traits to overload operators. This macro will have two rules: one for the + and one for the – operators. Here's the first rule of the macro:

```
macro_rules! op {
    (+ $_self:ident : $self_type:ty, $other:ident $expr:expr) => {
        impl ::std::ops::Add for $self_type {
            type Output = $self_type;

            fn add($_self, $other: $self_type) -> $self_type {
                $expr
            }
        }
    };
    // ...
```

In this pattern, we use other types of syntactic elements: ident, which is an identifier, and <span>expr, which is an expression. The trait (::std::ops::Add) is fully qualified so that the code using this macro won't need to import the Add trait.

And here's the rest of the macro:

```
    (- $_self:ident : $self_type:ty, $other:ident $expr:expr) => {
        impl ::std::ops::Sub for $self_type {
            type Output = $self_type;

            fn sub($_self, $other: $self_type) -> $self_type {
                $expr
            }
        }
    };
}
```

We can then use this macro with our Point type, like this:

```
op!(+ self:Point, other {
    Point {
        x: self.x + other.x,
        y: self.y + other.y,
    }
});

op!(- self:Point, other {
    Point {
        x: self.x - other.x,
```

```
                y: self.y - other.y,
            }
    });
```

Let's see how the matching works:

For the first macro call, we start with +, so the first branch is taken because it matches +, which is the start of this branch. Next we have `self`, which is an identifier, so it matches the `ident` pattern and this is assigned to the `$_self` meta-variable. Then, we have : which matches the colon in the pattern. After that, we have `Point`, which matches the `$self_type` meta-variable of the `ty` type (for matching on a type). Then we have `,` which matches the comma in the pattern. Next, we have `other`, which matches the next item in the pattern, which is the `$other` meta-variable of the `ident` type. Finally, we have `{ Point { ... } }`, which matches the expression required at the end of the pattern. This is why these macros are called macros by example, we write what the call should look like and the user must match the example (or pattern).

As an exercise to the reader, try the following:

- Add the missing operators: * and /
- Add the ability to specify the types of `$other` and the return type in the pattern
- If you haven't already done this in the previous point, add more tokens so that it looks more like a function declaration: `+(self: Point, other: Point) -> Point { ... }`
- Try moving the operator in the pattern after the `$self_type` meta-variable to see the limitations of `macro_rules`

Repetitions

In a macro pattern, it is also possible to match against an unlimited number of patterns, using the repetition operators + and *. They behave exactly like the same operators in regular expressions:

- + matches 1 or more times.
- * matches 0, 1, or more times.

Let's write a very useful macro, a macro to provide syntactic sugar to create `HashMap`s:

 Note: A `HashMap` is a data structure from Rust's standard library that maps keys to values.

```
macro_rules! hash {
    ($( $key:expr => $value:expr ),*) => {{
        let mut hashmap = ::std::collections::HashMap::new();
        $(hashmap.insert($key, $value);)*
        hashmap
    }};
}
```

As we can see, we use the `*` operator here. The comma before it specify the separator token: this token must be present between each occurrence of the pattern between parentheses (which is the pattern that can be repeated). Don't forget the leading `$` before the opening parenthesis; without it, the macro will match the literal `(`. Inside the parentheses, we see a normal pattern, an expression, followed by the `=>` operator, followed by another expression. The body of this rule is particular, since it uses two pairs of curly brackets instead of only one.

First, let's look at how we use this macro, and we'll go back to this peculiarity right after:

```
let hashmap = hash! {
    "one" => 1,
    "two" => 2
};
```

If we were to use only one pair of curly brackets, like this:

```
macro_rules! hash {
    ($( $key:expr => $value:expr ),*) => {
        let mut hashmap = ::std::collections::HashMap::new();
        $(hashmap.insert($key, $value);)*
        hashmap
    };
}
```

The compiler will try to generate the following code, which doesn't compile:

```
let hashmap = let mut hashmap = ::std::collections::HashMap::new();
    hashmap.insert("one", 1);
    hashmap.insert("two", 2);
    hashmap;
```

It doesn't compile because Rust wants an expression on the right-hand side of =. To transform this code into an expression, we simply need to add the curly brackets:

```
let hashmap = {
    let mut hashmap = ::std::collections::HashMap::new();
    hashmap.insert("one", 1);
    hashmap.insert("two", 2);
    hashmap
};
```

Hence the second pair of curly brackets.

There's one remaining line that requires an explanation in the body of the macro:

```
$(hashmap.insert($key, $value);)*
```

This means that the statement will be repeated as many times as there are pairs of key/values. Notice that ; is inside the parentheses; and there's no separator before * because every statement needs to end with a semicolon. But it's still possible to specify a separator here, as shown in the following example:

```
let keys = [$($key),*];
```

This will expand all the $keys, separating them by a comma. For instance, with a call like:

```
hash! {
    "one" => 1,
    "two" => 2
}
```

It will results in:

```
let keys = ["one", "two"];
```

Optional quantifier

In the macro_rules system, there's no way to specify that a pattern is optional, like with the ? quantifier in regular expressions. If we wanted to allow the user of our hash macro to use a trailing comma, we could change the rule by moving the comma inside the parentheses: ($($key:expr => $value:expr,)*).

However, it will force the user to write a trailing macro. If we want to allow both variants, we can use the following trick, which uses the * operator: `($( $key:expr =>`
`$value:expr ),* $(,)* )`.

This means that a comma must be used between each pattern and we can use any number of commas after the last pattern, including no comma at all.

Summary

This chapter introduced you to the basics of Rust by showing you how to use variables, functions, control flow structures, and types. You also learned more advanced concepts such as references and ownership to manage the memory, and you saw how you can use traits, generics, and macros to avoid code repetition.

In the next chapter, you'll practise what you've just learned by creating a video game.

2
Starting with SDL

Before starting to write the Tetris, a few things remain to be talked about, such as crates, which we'll be using a lot (and you'll be using a lot as well once you're *rusting* on your own!). Let's start with crates!

Understanding Rust crates

In Rust, packages (both binaries and libraries) are named crates. You can find a lot of them on `crates.io`. Today, we'll use the SDL2 crate in order to make our tetris, but before even thinking about this, we need to install the `SDL2` library that is used by the `SDL2` crate!

Installing SDL2

Before going any further, we need to install the SDL library.

Installing SDL2 on Linux

Depending on your package management tool, run the following to install SDL2 on Linux:

```
apt package mananger:
```

```
$ sudo apt-get install libsdl2-dev
```

```
dnf package manager:
```

```
$ sudo dnf install SDL2-devel
```

yum package manager:

```
$ yum install SDL2-devel
```

Once done, your SDL2 installation is ready!

Installing SDL2 on Mac

To install SDL2 on Mac, Simply run the following:

```
$ brew install sdl2
```

You're good to go!

Installing SDL2 on Windows

All these installation instructions come directly from the Rust SDL2 crate.

Windows with Build Script

A few steps will be required in order to make all of it work. Follow the guide!

1. Download the `mingw` and `msvc` development libraries from `http://www.libsdl.org/` (`SDL2-devel-2.0.x-mingw.tar.gz` and `SDL2-devel-2.0.x-VC.zip`).
2. Unpack to folders of your choice. (You can delete it afterward.)
3. Create the following folder structure in the same folder as your `Cargo.toml`:

   ```
   gnu-mingw\dll\32
   gnu-mingw\dll\64
   gnu-mingw\lib\32
   gnu-mingw\lib\64
   msvc\dll\32
   msvc\dll\64
   msvc\lib\32
   msvc\lib\64
   ```

4. Copy the `lib` and `dll` files from the source archive to the directories we created in step 3 as follows:

```
SDL2-devel-2.0.x-mingw.tar.gz\SDL2-2.0.x\i686-w64-mingw32\bin    ->
gnu-mingw\dll\32
```

```
SDL2-devel-2.0.x-mingw.tar.gz\SDL2-2.0.x\x86_64-w64-mingw32\bin  ->
gnu-mingw\dll\64
SDL2-devel-2.0.x-mingw.tar.gz\SDL2-2.0.x\i686-w64-mingw32\lib    ->
gnu-mingw\lib\32
SDL2-devel-2.0.x-mingw.tar.gz\SDL2-2.0.x\x86_64-w64-mingw32\lib  ->
gnu-mingw\lib\64
SDL2-devel-2.0.5-VC.zip\SDL2-2.0.x\lib\x86\*.dll                 ->
msvc\dll\32
SDL2-devel-2.0.5-VC.zip\SDL2-2.0.x\lib\x64\*.dll                 ->
msvc\dll\64
SDL2-devel-2.0.5-VC.zip\SDL2-2.0.x\lib\x86\*.lib                 ->
msvc\lib\32
SDL2-devel-2.0.5-VC.zip\SDL2-2.0.x\lib\x64\*.lib                 ->
msvc\lib\64
```

5. Create a Build Script. If you don't already have one, put this in your `Cargo.toml` file under `[package]`:

    ```
    build = "build.rs"
    ```

6. Create a file in the same directory as `Cargo.toml` called `build.rs` and write this into it:

    ```
    use std::env;
    use std::path::PathBuf;

    fn main() {
      let target = env::var("TARGET").unwrap();
      if target.contains("pc-windows") {
        let manifest_dir =
          PathBuf::from(env::var("CARGO_MANIFEST_DIR").unwrap());
        let mut lib_dir = manifest_dir.clone();
      let mut dll_dir = manifest_dir.clone();
      if target.contains("msvc") {
          lib_dir.push("msvc");
          dll_dir.push("msvc");
      } else {
          lib_dir.push("gnu-mingw");
          dll_dir.push("gnu-mingw");
      }
      lib_dir.push("lib");
      dll_dir.push("dll");
      if target.contains("x86_64") {
          lib_dir.push("64");
          dll_dir.push("64");
      } else {
          lib_dir.push("32");
    ```

```
        dll_dir.push("32");
    }
    println!("cargo:rustc-link-search=all={}",
      lib_dir.display());
    for entry in std::fs::read_dir(dll_dir).expect("Can't
      read DLL dir")  {
     let entry_path = entry.expect("Invalid fs entry").path();
     let file_name_result = entry_path.file_name();
     let mut new_file_path = manifest_dir.clone();
     if let Some(file_name) = file_name_result {
       let file_name = file_name.to_str().unwrap();
       if file_name.ends_with(".dll") {
         new_file_path.push(file_name);
       std::fs::copy(&entry_path,
       new_file_path.as_path()).expect("Can't copy
         from DLL dir");
       }
     }
    }
   }
}
```

7. On build, the Build Script will copy the needed DLLs into the same directory as your `Cargo.toml` file. You probably don't want to commit these to any Git repositories though, so add the following line to your `.gitignore` file:

   /*.dll

8. When you're shipping your game, make sure that you copy the corresponding `SDL2.dll` to the same directory that your compiled `exe` is in; otherwise, the game won't launch.

And now your project should build and run on any Windows computer!

Windows (MinGW)

A few steps will be required in order to make all of it work. Follow the guide!

1. Download `mingw` development libraries from `http://www.libsdl.org/` (SDL2-devel-2.0.x-mingw.tar.gz).

2. Unpack to a folder of your choice. (You can delete it afterward.)

3. Copy all `lib` files from the following path:

   `SDL2-devel-2.0.x-mingw\SDL2-2.0.x\x86_64-w64-mingw32\lib`

   Next, copy it to this path:

   `C:\Program Files\Rust\lib\rustlib\x86_64-pc-windows-gnu\lib`

   Alternately, you can copy to your library folder of choice and ensure that you have a system environment variable as follows:

   `LIBRARY_PATH = C:\your\rust\library\folder`

   For Rustup users, this folder will be at the following location:

   `C:\Users\{Your Username}.multirust\toolchains\{current toolchain}\lib\rustlib\{current toolchain}\lib`

   Here, the current toolchain is probably `stable-x86_64-pc-windows-gnu`.

4. Copy `SDL2.dll` from the following:

   `SDL2-devel-2.0.x-mingw\SDL2-2.0.x\x86_64-w64-mingw32\bin`

   The copied `SDL2.dll` is pasted into your cargo project, right next to your `Cargo.toml`.

5. When you're shipping your game, make sure that you copy `SDL2.dll` to the same directory that your compiled `exe` is in; otherwise, the game won't launch.

Windows (MSVC)

A few steps will be required in order to make all of it work. Follow the guide!

1. Download MSVC development libraries from `http://www.libsdl.org/` `SDL2-devel-2.0.x-VC.zip`.
2. Unpack `SDL2-devel-2.0.x-VC.zip` to a folder of your choice. (You can delete it afterward.)
3. Copy all `lib` files from the following path:

   `SDL2-devel-2.0.x-VC\SDL2-2.0.x\lib\x64\`

   The `lib` files will be pasted here:

```
C:\Program Files\Rust\lib\rustlib\x86_64-pc-windows-msvc\lib
```

Alternatively, they'll be pasted to your library folder of choice. Ensure that you have a system environment variable with the following:

```
LIB = C:\your\rust\library\folder
```

Here, the current toolchain is probably `stable-x86_64-pc-windows-msvc`.

4. Copy `SDL2.dll` from the following code snippet:

```
SDL2-devel-2.0.x-VC\SDL2-2.0.x\lib\x64\
```

The copied `SDL2.dll` is pasted into your cargo project, right next to your `Cargo.toml`.

5. When you're shipping your game, make sure that you copy `SDL2.dll` to the same directory that your compiled `exe` is in; otherwise, the game won't launch.

Setting up your Rust project

The Rust package manager, `cargo`, allows us to create a new project very easily with just one command, `cargo new`. Let's run it as follow:

```
cargo new tetris --bin
```

You should have a new folder `tetris` containing the following:

```
tetris/
|
|- Cargo.toml
|- src/
    |
    |- main.rs
```

Note that if you ran `cargo new` without the `--bin` flag, then you will have a `lib.rs` file instead of `main.rs`.

Now write this into your `Cargo.toml` file:

```
[package]
name = "tetris"
version = "0.0.1"

[dependencies]
sdl2 = "0.30.0"
```

Here, we declare that our project's name is `tetris`, its version is `0.0.1` (it isn't really important at the moment), and that it has a dependency on the `sdl2` crate.

For the versioning, `Cargo` follows **SemVer** (**Semantic Versioning**). It works as follows:

`[major].[minor].[path]`

So here's exactly what every part means:

- Update the `[major]` number version when you make incompatible API changes
- Update the `[minor]` number version when adding functionalities that don't break backward compatibility
- Update the `[patch]` number version when you make bug fixes that don't break backward compatibility

It's not vital to know this, but it's always nice to be aware of it in case you intend to write crates in the future.

Cargo and crates.io

A very important thing to note with Rust's ecosystem is that `Cargo` is really important if not central. It makes things much easier and all Rust projects are using it.

Cargo isn't only a build tool, it's also Rust's default package manager. If you need to download a dependency, `Cargo` will do it. You can find all available published crates on `https://crates.io/`. Consider the following screenshot:

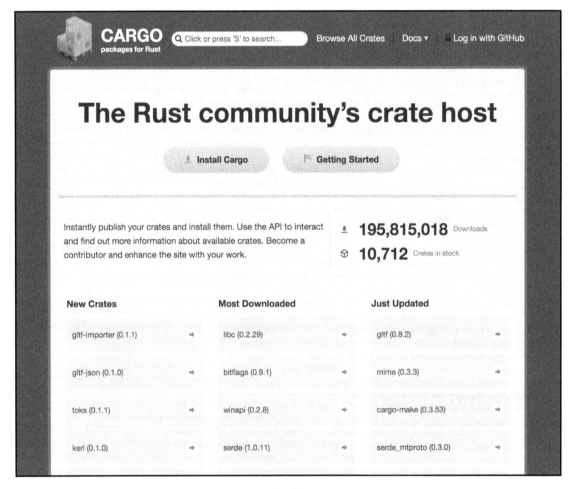

Figure 2.1

In the case of the `sdl2` crate, we can see on its page (`https://crates.io/crates/sdl2`) some interesting and useful information:

Links	Dependencies	Versions
Documentation	bitflags ^0.7	0.30.0 May 14, 2017
Repository	lazy_static ^0.2	0.30.0-beta May 5, 2017
Dependent crates	libc ^0.2	0.29.1 Apr 5, 2017
	num ^0.1	0.29.0 Feb 14, 2017
	rand ^0.3	0.28.0 Jan 17, 2017
	sdl2-sys ^0.30.0	
	c_vec 1.0." optional	show all 79 versions

Figure 2.2

On the right-hand side, you can see the version history. It can be useful to check whether you have the last version or not and whether the crate is still maintained.

In the middle, you have the crate's dependencies. It's always interesting to know what you'll need to install in addition to your crate if something is missing.

And finally on the left-hand side, you have a few links that might be very useful (not always those ones, it depends on what has been put into the `Cargo.toml` file):

- **Documentation**: This is where the documentation is hosted (even though I generally recommend `docs.rs`, I'll talk about it in a moment)
- **Repository**: This is where this crate's repository is hosted
- **Dependent crates**: This is the list of the crates depending on this one
- **Homepage**: If the crate has a website, you can go to its link

Time to go back to `docs.rs` for a bit.

The docs.rs documentation

Every published crate on `crates.io` gets its documentation generated and hosted on `https://docs.rs/`. If the crate's documentation hasn't been published by anyone anywhere online, you'll find it there as long as it has been published. With `crates.io` and `rust-lang.org`, it's one of the most known places of the Rust ecosystem, so bookmark it and doesn't lose it!

Here's a screenshot of what `docs.rs` looks like:

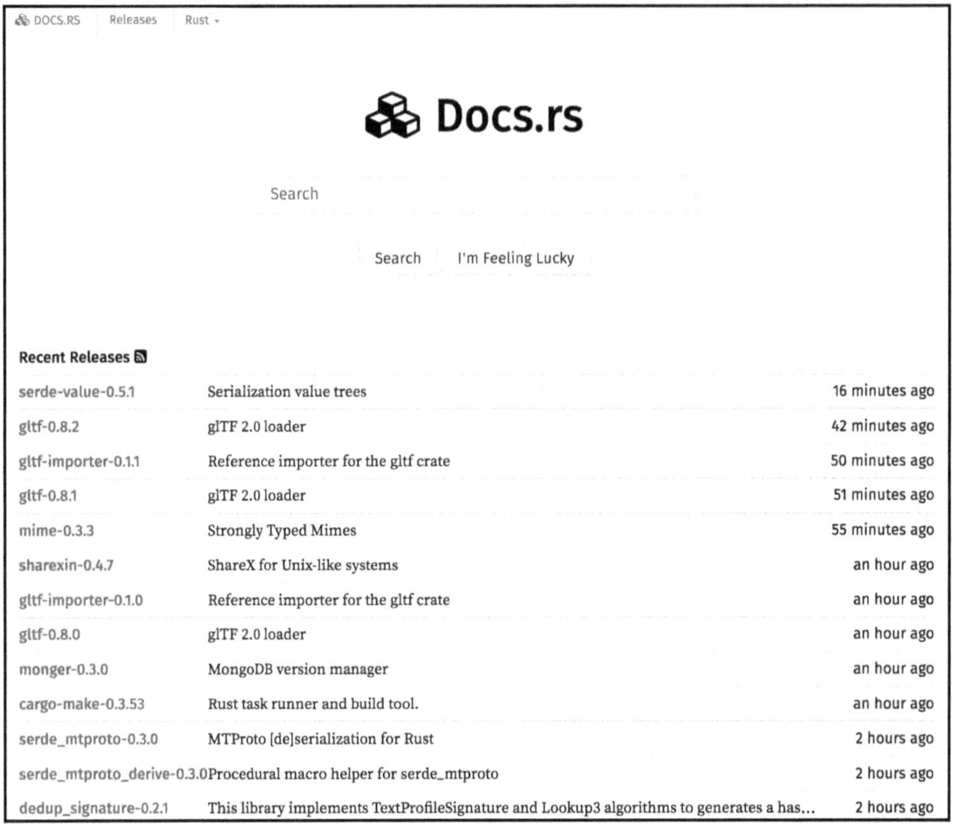

Figure 2.3

Back to our Cargo.toml file

To go back to our `Cargo.toml` file, it's also possible to use crates directly from their repositories; you just have to specify this when adding the dependency in your `Cargo.toml` file. Generally, the published version is less advanced than the one on the corresponding repository but will be more stable.

So for example, if we want to use the repository version for the `sdl2` crate, we need to write in our `Cargo.toml` file:

```
[dependencies]
sdl2 = { git = "https://github.com/Rust-SDL2/rust-sdl2" }
```

Easy right? `Cargo` can also start tests or benchmarks, install binaries, handle special builds through a build file (by default in `build.rs`), or handle features (we'll come back to this point later in this part).

To put it simply, it's a complete tool, and explaining most of its features would take a lot of time and space, so we'll just stick to the basics for the moment.

 You can find a very good documentation/tutorial on Cargo at `http://doc. crates.io/index.html`.

Rust's modules

Before going any further, we need to talk about how file hierarchy works in Rust through its modules.

The first thing to know is that files and folders are handled as modules in Rust. Consider the following:

```
|- src/
    |
    |- main.rs
    |- another_file.rs
```

If you want to declare that a module is in the `another_file.rs` file, you'll need to add to your `main.rs` file:

```
mod another_file;
```

You will now have access to everything contained in `another_file.rs` (as long as it's public).

Another thing to know: you can only declare modules whose files are on the same level as your current module/file. Here's a short example to sum this up:

```
|- src/
    |
    |- main.rs
    |- subfolder/
        |- another_file.rs
```

If you try to declare a module referring to `another_file.rs` directly into `main.rs`, as shown preceding, it'll fail because there are no `another_file.rs` in `src/`. In this case, you'll need to do three things:

1. Add a `mod.rs` file into the `subfolder` folder.
2. Declare `another_file` into `mod.rs`.
3. Declare `subfolder` into `main.rs`.

You certainly wonder, why `mod.rs`? It's the norm in Rust—when you import a module, which is a folder, the compiler will look for a file named `mod.rs` into it. The `mod.rs` files are mainly used for re-exporting modules' content outside.

Let's now write down the code to do this:

Inside `mod.rs`:

```
pub mod another_file;
```

Inside `main.rs`:

```
mod subfolder;
```

Now, you can use everything that is in `another_file` (as long as it's public!). Consider the following example:

```
use subfolder::another_file::some_function;
```

You will certainly have noticed that we declared `another_file` publicly in `mod.rs`. It's simply because `main.rs` won't be able to access its content otherwise, as it's not at the same module level. However, a child module can access a parent's private items.

To conclude this small part, let's talk about the third type of modules: the module blocks (yes, as simple as that).

Just like you import a file or a folder, you can create a module block by using the same keyword:

```
mod a_module {
    pub struct Foo;
}
```

And you now created a new module named `a_module` containing a public structure. The rules described previously are applied the same way to this last kind of module.

You now know how to use modules to import files and folders. Let's start writing down our game!

Tetris

Okay, we're now ready to start writing down our tetris!

First, let's fulfill our `main.rs` file in order to check whether everything is working as expected:

```
extern crate sdl2;

use sdl2::pixels::Color;
use sdl2::event::Event;
use sdl2::keyboard::Keycode;
use std::time::Duration;
use std::thread::sleep;

pub fn main() {
    let sdl_context = sdl2::init().expect("SDL initialization
    failed");
    let video_subsystem = sdl_context.video().expect("Couldn't get
     SDL video subsystem");

    let window = video_subsystem.window("rust-sdl2 demo: Video", 800,
          600)
      .position_centered()
      .opengl()
      .build()
      .expect("Failed to create window");

    let mut canvas = window.into_canvas().build().expect("Failed to
      convert window into canvas");

    canvas.set_draw_color(Color::RGB(255, 0, 0));
    canvas.clear();
    canvas.present();
    let mut event_pump = sdl_context.event_pump().expect("Failed to
      get SDL event pump");

    'running: loop {
        for event in event_pump.poll_iter() {
            match event {
                Event::Quit { .. } |
                Event::KeyDown { keycode: Some(Keycode::Escape), .. } =>
```

```
            {
                break 'running
            },
            _ => {}
        }
    }
    sleep(Duration::new(0, 1_000_000_000u32 / 60));
    }
}
```

You'll note the following line:

```
::std::thread::sleep(Duration::new(0, 1_000_000_000u32 / 60));
```

It allows you to avoid using all your computer CPU time needlessly and only rendering 60 times every second at most.

Now run the following in your terminal:

```
$ cargo run
```

If you have a window filled with red (just as shown in the following screenshot), then everything's fine!

Figure 2.4

Creating a window

The previous example created a window and drew into it. Now let's see how it did that!

Before going any further, we need to import the SDL2 crate, as follows:

```
extern crate sdl2;
```

With this, we now have access to everything it contains.

Now that we've imported `sdl2`, we need to initialize an SDL context:

```
let sdl_context = sdl2::init().expect("SDL initialization failed");
```

Once done, we need to get the video subsystem:

```
let video_subsystem = sdl_context.video().expect("Couldn't get SDL
    video subsystem");
```

We can now create the window:

```
let window = video_subsystem.window("Tetris", 800, 600)
                        .position_centered()
                        .opengl()
                        .build()
                        .expect("Failed to create window");
```

A few notes on these methods:

- The parameters for the `window` method are title, width, height
- `.position_centered()` gets the window in the middle of the screen
- `.opengl()` makes the SDL use `opengl` to render
- `.build()` creates the window by applying all previously received parameters
- `.expect` panics with the given message if an error occurred

If you try to run this sample of code, it'll display a window and close it super quickly. We now need to add an event loop in order to keep it running (and then to manage user inputs).

At the top of the file, you need to add this:

```
use sdl2::event::Event;
use sdl2::keyboard::Keycode;

use std::thread::sleep;
use std::time::Duration;
```

Now let's actually write our event manager. First, we need to get the event handler as follows:

```
let mut event_pump = sdl_context.event_pump().expect("Failed to
    get SDL event pump");
```

Then, we create an infinite loop to loop over events:

```
'running: loop {
  for event in event_pump.poll_iter() {
    match event {
        Event::Quit { .. } |
        Event::KeyDown { keycode: Some(Keycode::Escape), .. } => {
            break 'running // We "break" the infinite loop.
        },
        _ => {}
    }
  }
  sleep(Duration::new(0, 1_000_000_000u32 / 60));
}
```

To go back on these two lines:

```
'running: loop {
  break 'running
```

`loop` is a keyword that allows creating an infinite loop in Rust. An interesting feature though is that you can add a label to your loops (so, `while` and `for` as well). In this case, we added the label `running` to the main loop. The point is to be able to break directly an upper loop without having to set a variable.

Now, if we receive a `quit` event (pressing the cross of the window) or if you press the *Esc* key, the program quits.

Now you can run this code and you'll have a window.

Drawing

We now have a working window; it'd be nice to draw into it. First, we need to get the window's canvas before starting the main loop:

```
let mut canvas = window.into_canvas()
                    .target_texture()
                    .present_vsync()
                    .build()
```

```
                            .expect("Couldn't get window's canvas");
```

A few explanations for the preceding code:

- `into_canvas` transforms the window into a canvas so that we can manipulate it more easily
- `target_texture` activates texture rendering support
- `present_vsync` enables the v-sync (also known as vertical-synchronization) limit
- `build` creates the canvas by applying all previously set parameters

Then we'll create a texture that we'll paste onto the window's canvas. First, let's get the texture creator, but before that, add this include at the top of the file:

```
use sdl2::render::{Canvas, Texture, TextureCreator};
```

Now we can get the texture creator:

```
let texture_creator: TextureCreator<_> = canvas.texture_creator();
```

OK! Now we need to create a rectangle. To make things easier to read, we'll create a constant that will be the texture's size (better to put it at the head of the file, just after the imports, for readability reasons):

```
const TEXTURE_SIZE: u32 = 32;
```

Let's create a texture with a 32x32 size:

```
let mut square_texture: Texture =
    texture_creator.create_texture_target(None, TEXTURE_SIZE,
        TEXTURE_SIZE)
    .expect("Failed to create a texture");
```

Good! Now let's color it. First, add this import at the top of the file:

```
use sdl2::pixels::Color;
```

We use the canvas to draw our square texture:

```
canvas.with_texture_canvas(&mut square_texture, |texture| {
    texture.set_draw_color(Color::RGB(0, 255, 0));
    texture.clear();
});
```

An explanation of the preceding code is as follows:

- `set_draw_color` sets the color to be used when drawing occurs. In our case, it's green.
- `clear` washes/clears the texture so it'll be filled with green.

Now, we just have to draw this square texture onto our window. In order to make it work, we need it to be drawn into the main loop but right after the event loop.

One thing to note before we continue: when drawing with the SDL2, the (0, 0) coordinates are at the top-left of a window, not at the bottom-left. The same goes for all shapes.

Add this import at the top of your file:

```
use sdl2::rect::Rect;
```

Now let's draw. In order to be able to update the rendering of your window, you need to draw inside the main loop (and after the event loop). So firstly, let's fill our window with red:

```
canvas.set_draw_color(Color::RGB(255, 0, 0));
canvas.clear();
```

Next, we copy our texture into the window in the top-left corner with a 32x32 size:

```
canvas.copy(&square_texture,
        None,
        Rect::new(0, 0, TEXTURE_SIZE, TEXTURE_SIZE))
    .expect("Couldn't copy texture into window");
```

Finally, we update the window's display:

```
canvas.present();
```

So if we take a look at the full code, we now have the following:

```
extern crate sdl2;

use sdl2::event::Event;
use sdl2::keyboard::Keycode;
use sdl2::pixels::Color;
use sdl2::rect::Rect;
use sdl2::render::{Texture, TextureCreator};

use std::thread::sleep;
use std::time::Duration;
```

```rust
fn main() {
  let sdl_context = sdl2::init().expect("SDL initialization
  failed");
  let video_subsystem = sdl_context.video().expect("Couldn't get
    SDL video subsystem");

  // Parameters are: title, width, height
  let window = video_subsystem.window("Tetris", 800, 600)
    .position_centered() // to put it in the middle of the screen
    .build() // to create the window
    .expect("Failed to create window");

  let mut canvas = window.into_canvas()
    .target_texture()
    .present_vsync() // To enable v-sync.
    .build()
    .expect("Couldn't get window's canvas");

  let texture_creator: TextureCreator<_> =
   canvas.texture_creator();
   // To make things easier to read, we'll create a constant
      which will be the texture's size.
  const TEXTURE_SIZE: u32 = 32;

  // We create a texture with a 32x32 size.
  let mut square_texture: Texture =
    texture_creator.create_texture_target(None, TEXTURE_SIZE,
        TEXTURE_SIZE)
      .expect("Failed to create a texture");

  // We use the canvas to draw into our square texture.
  canvas.with_texture_canvas(&mut square_texture, |texture| {
    // We set the draw color to green.
    texture.set_draw_color(Color::RGB(0, 255, 0));
    // We "clear" our texture so it'll be fulfilled with green.
    texture.clear();
  }).expect("Failed to color a texture");

  // First we get the event handler:
  let mut event_pump = sdl_context.event_pump().expect("Failed
    to get SDL event pump");

  // Then we create an infinite loop to loop over events:
  'running: loop {
    for event in event_pump.poll_iter() {
      match event {
      // If we receive a 'quit' event or if the user press the
          'ESC' key, we quit.
```

```
        Event::Quit { .. } |
        Event::KeyDown { keycode: Some(Keycode::Escape), .. } => {
            break 'running // We "break" the infinite loop.
        },
        _ => {}
    }
}

// We set fulfill our window with red.
canvas.set_draw_color(Color::RGB(255, 0, 0));
// We draw it.
canvas.clear();
// Copy our texture into the window.
canvas.copy(&square_texture,
    None,
    // We copy it at the top-left of the window with a 32x32 size.
    Rect::new(0, 0, TEXTURE_SIZE, TEXTURE_SIZE))
    .expect("Couldn't copy texture into window");
// We update window's display.
canvas.present();

// We sleep enough to get ~60 fps. If we don't call this,
    the program will take
// 100% of a CPU time.
sleep(Duration::new(0, 1_000_000_000u32 / 60));
    }
}
```

If you run this code, you should have a red window with a small green rectangle at the top-left (just as shown in the following screenshot):

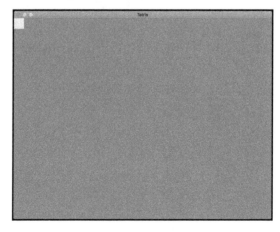

Figure 2.5

Now, what about switching the color of our small rectangle every second? Alright, first thing, we need to create another rectangle. To make things easier, we'll write a small function that will create texture.

As usual, add the following import at the top of your file:

```
use sdl2::video::{Window, WindowContext};
```

For convenience, we'll create a small enum to indicate the color as well:

```
#[derive(Clone, Copy)]
enum TextureColor {
  Green,
  Blue,
}
```

To make our lives easier, we'll handle errors outside of the next function, so no need to handle them directly here:

```
fn create_texture_rect<'a>(canvas: &mut Canvas<Window>,
    texture_creator: &'a TextureCreator<WindowContext>,
    color: TextureColor, size: u32) -> Option<Texture<'a>> {
    // We'll want to handle failures outside of this function.
    if let Ok(mut square_texture) =
        texture_creator.create_texture_target(None, size, size) {
          canvas.with_texture_canvas(&mut square_texture, |texture| {
            match color {
                TextureColor::Green =>
                  texture.set_draw_color(Color::RGB(0, 255, 0)),
                TextureColor::Blue =>
                  texture.set_draw_color(Color::RGB(0, 0, 255)),
            }
            texture.clear();
          }).expect("Failed to color a texture");
          Some(square_texture)
    } else {
        None
        }
    }
```

You'll note that the function returns an Option type, wrapping a texture. Option is an enum containing two variants: Some and None.

Playing with Options

To explain briefly how it works, when the `Option` type is `Some`, it simply means it contains a value whereas `None` doesn't. It has already been explained in Chapter 1, *Basics of Rust*, but here's a little recap just in case you need one. We can compare this mechanism with pointers in C-like languages; when the pointer is null, there is no data to access. The same goes for `None`.

Here's a short example:

```
fn divide(nb: u32, divider: u32) -> Option<u32> {
  if divider == 0 {
    None
  } else {
      Some(nb / divider)
    }
}
```

So here, if the divider is 0, we can't divide or we'll get an error. Instead of setting an error or returning a complicated type, we just return an `Option`:

```
let x = divide(10, 3);
let y = divide(10, 0);
```

Here, x is equal to `Some(3)` and y is equal to `None`.

The biggest advantage of this type compared to `null` is that if we have `Some`, you're sure that the data is valid. And in addition, when it's `None`, you can't accidentally read its content, it's simply impossible in Rust (and if you try to `unwrap` it, your program will panic immediately, but at least, you'll know what failed and why—no magical segmentation fault).

You can take a look at its documentation at `https://doc.rust-lang.org/std/option/enum.Option.html`.

Let's explain what happens here:

1. We create a texture or return `None` if the creation fails.
2. We set the color and then fulfill the texture with it.
3. We return the texture.

If we return `None`, it simply means an error occurred. Also, for now, this function only handles two colors, but it's pretty easy to add more if you want.

It might look a bit complicated at the moment, but it'll make our life easier afterward. Now, let's call this function by creating a blue square of size 32x32:

```
let mut blue_square = create_texture_rect(&mut canvas,
    &texture_creator,
    TextureColor::Blue,
    TEXTURE_SIZE).expect("Failed to create a texture");
```

Easy, right?

> Now we can just put pieces together. I'll let you try to handle the color switch. A small tip: take a look at the SystemTime struct. You can refer to its documentation at https://doc.rust-lang.org/stable/std/time/struct.SystemTime.html.

Solution

I guess you did it without any issues, but in any case, here's the code:

```
extern crate sdl2;

use sdl2::event::Event;
use sdl2::keyboard::Keycode;
use sdl2::pixels::Color;
use sdl2::rect::Rect;
use sdl2::render::{Canvas, Texture, TextureCreator};
use sdl2::video::{Window, WindowContext};

use std::thread::sleep;
use std::time::{Duration, SystemTime};

// To make things easier to read, we'll create a constant which
    will be the texture's size.
const TEXTURE_SIZE: u32 = 32;

#[derive(Clone, Copy)]
enum TextureColor {
  Green,
  Blue,
}

fn create_texture_rect<'a>(canvas: &mut Canvas<Window>,
  texture_creator: &'a TextureCreator<WindowContext>,
  color: TextureColor,
  size: u32) -> Option<Texture<'a>> {
```

```
        // We'll want to handle failures outside of this function.
    if let Ok(mut square_texture) =
        texture_creator.create_texture_target(None, size, size) {
            canvas.with_texture_canvas(&mut square_texture, |texture| {
                match color {
                    // For now, TextureColor only handles two colors.
                    TextureColor::Green => texture.set_draw_color(Color::RGB(0,
                        255, 0)),
                    TextureColor::Blue => texture.set_draw_color(Color::RGB(0,
                        0, 255)),
                }
                texture.clear();
            }).expect("Failed to color a texture");
            Some(square_texture)
        }
        else {
         // An error occured so we return nothing and let the function
            caller handle the error.
         None
        }
    }

    fn main() {
        let sdl_context = sdl2::init().expect("SDL initialization
         failed");
        let video_subsystem = sdl_context.video().expect("Couldn't get
            SDL video subsystem");

        // Parameters are: title, width, height
        let window = video_subsystem.window("Tetris", 800, 600)
            .position_centered() // to put it in the middle of the screen
            .build() // to create the window
            .expect("Failed to create window");

        let mut canvas = window.into_canvas()
            .target_texture()
            .present_vsync() // To enable v-sync.
            .build()
            .expect("Couldn't get window's canvas");

        let texture_creator: TextureCreator<_> =
         canvas.texture_creator();

        // We create a texture with a 32x32 size.
        let green_square = create_texture_rect(&mut canvas,
            &texture_creator,
            TextureColor::Green,
            TEXTURE_SIZE).expect("Failed to create a texture");
```

```
let blue_square = create_texture_rect(&mut canvas,
    &texture_creator,
    TextureColor::Blue,
    TEXTURE_SIZE).expect("Failed to create a texture");

let timer = SystemTime::now();

// First we get the event handler:
let mut event_pump = sdl_context.event_pump().expect("Failed
  to get SDL event pump");

// Then we create an infinite loop to loop over events:
'running: loop {
  for event in event_pump.poll_iter() {
    match event {
        // If we receive a 'quit' event or if the user press the
            'ESC' key, we quit.
        Event::Quit { .. } |
        Event::KeyDown { keycode: Some(Keycode::Escape), .. } => {
          break 'running // We "break" the infinite loop.
        },
        _ => {}
    }
  }

  // We fill our window with red.
  canvas.set_draw_color(Color::RGB(255, 0, 0));
  // We draw it.
  canvas.clear();

  // The rectangle switch happens here:
  let display_green = match timer.elapsed() {
      Ok(elapsed) => elapsed.as_secs() % 2 == 0,
      Err(_) => {
          // In case of error, we do nothing...
          true
      }
  };
  let square_texture = if display_green {
      &green_square
  } else {
      &blue_square
  };
  // Copy our texture into the window.
  canvas.copy(square_texture,
    None,
      // We copy it at the top-left of the window with a 32x32
        size.
```

```
                Rect::new(0, 0, TEXTURE_SIZE, TEXTURE_SIZE))
                .expect("Couldn't copy texture into window");
            // We update window's display.
            canvas.present();

        // We sleep enough to get ~60 fps. If we don't call this,
            the program will take
        // 100% of a CPU time.
        sleep(Duration::new(0, 1_000_000_000u32 / 60));
    }
}
```

You can now see the small rectangle at the top-left switching color every second.

Loading images

Uptill now, we've only created simple textures, but what about loading images instead?

Before trying to go through this, check whether you have installed the SDL2_image library (it's not included by default with the SDL2 library!). If not, you can install it by following the upcoming sections.

Installing SDL2_image on Mac

Just run the following:

```
$ brew install SDL2_image
```

And you're good to go!

Installing SDL2_image on Linux

Depending on your package management tool, run the following to install SDL2_image on Linux:

For apt package manager use the following command:

```
$ sudo apt-get install libsdl2-image-2.0-0-dev
```

For dnf package manager use the following command:

```
$ sudo dnf install SDL2_image-devel
```

For `yum package manager` use the following command:

```
$ yum install SDL2_image-devel
```

And you're good to go!

Installing SDL2_image on Windows

For the Windows platform, the simplest way is to go to `https://www.libsdl.org/ projects/SDL_image/` and download it.

Playing with features

By default, you can't use the `image` module with `sdl2`, we need to activate it. To do so, we need to update our `Cargo.toml` file by adding a new section as follows:

```
[features]
default = ["sdl2/image"]
```

`default` means that by default, the following features (`"sdl2/image"`) will be enabled. Now, let's explain what `"sdl2/image"` means; `sdl2` refers to the crate where we want to enable a feature and `image` is the feature we want to enable.

Of course, if you want to enable a feature on the current project, you don't need the `sdl2/` part. Consider the following example:

```
[features]
network = []
default = ["network"]
```

As I am sure you understood, it's absolutely possible to chain features activation and even to activate multiple features at once! If you want to enable features depending on a version number, for example:

```
[features]
network_v1 = []
network_v2 = ["network_v1"]
network_v3 = ["network_v2"]
v1 = ["network_v1"]
v2 = ["v1", "network_v2"]
v3 = ["v2", "network_v3"]
```

So if you enable the v3 feature, all the others will be activated as well! It can be incredibly useful when you need to handle multiple versions at once.

Now let's go back to our images.

Playing with images

Just like textures, we need to initialize the image context. Now that we've activated the image feature, we can call the linked functions and import them. Let's add some new imports:

```
use sdl2::image::{LoadTexture, INIT_PNG, INIT_JPG};
```

Then we create the image context:

```
sdl2::image::init(INIT_PNG | INIT_JPG).expect("Couldn't initialize
    image context");
```

Now that the context has been initialized, let's actually load the image:

```
let image_texture =
 texture_creator.load_texture("assets/my_image.png")
    .expect("Couldn't load image");
```

A few explanations for the preceding code:

load_texture takes a file path as an argument. Be very careful with paths, even more when they're relative!

After that, it's just like we did with other textures. Let's put our image into our Window's background:

```
canvas.copy(&Image_texture, None, None).expect("Render failed");
```

To sum everything up, here's what your project's folder should look like now:

```
|- your_project/
   |
   |- Cargo.toml
   |- src/
   |   |
   |   |- main.rs
   |- assets/
      |
      |- my_image.png
```

And that's it!

Here's the full code in case you missed a step:

```
extern crate sdl2;
use sdl2::pixels::Color;
use sdl2::event::Event;
use sdl2::keyboard::Keycode;
use sdl2::render::TextureCreator;
use sdl2::image::{LoadTexture, INIT_PNG, INIT_JPG};
use std::time::Duration;

pub fn main() {
  let sdl_context = sdl2::init().expect("SDL initialization
    failed");
  let video_subsystem = sdl_context.video().expect("Couldn't
      get SDL video subsystem");

  sdl2::image::init(INIT_PNG | INIT_JPG).expect("Couldn't
  initialize
    image context");

  let window = video_subsystem.window("rust-sdl2 image demo", 800,
    600)
    .position_centered()
    .opengl()
    .build()
    .expect("Failed to create window");

  let mut canvas = window.into_canvas().build().expect("Failed to
    convert window into canvas");


  let texture_creator: TextureCreator<_> =
   canvas.texture_creator();
  let image_texture =
    texture_creator.load_texture("assets/my_image.png")
     .expect("Couldn't load image");

  let mut event_pump = sdl_context.event_pump().expect("Failed to
      get SDL event pump");

  'running: loop {
    for event in event_pump.poll_iter() {
        match event {
            Event::Quit { .. } |
            Event::KeyDown { keycode: Some(Keycode::Escape), .. }
          => {
```

```
                    break 'running
            },
            _ => {}
        }
    }
    canvas.set_draw_color(Color::RGB(0, 0, 0));
    canvas.clear();
    canvas.copy(&image_texture, None, None).expect("Render
      failed");
    canvas.present();
    ::std::thread::sleep(Duration::new(0, 1_000_000_000u32 / 60));
    }
}
```

In my case, it gives the following output:

Figure 2.6

Now that we know how to make Windows and play with events and textures, let's see how to save and load high scores from files!

Handling files

Let's start with the basics. First, let's open and write into a file:

```
use std::fs::File;
use std::io::{self, Write};

fn write_into_file(content: &str, file_name: &str) -> io::Result<()> {
    let mut f = File::create(file_name)?;
    f.write_all(content.as_bytes())
}
```

Now let's explain this code:

```
use std::fs::File;
```

Nothing fancy, we just import the `File` type:

```
use std::io::{self, Write};
```

This set of imports is more interesting: we import the `io` module (`self`) and the `Write` trait. For the second, if we didn't import it, we wouldn't be able to use the `write_all` method (because you need to import a trait to use its methods):

```
fn write_into_file(content: &str, file_name: &str) -> io::Result<()> {
```

We declared a function named `write_into_file` that takes a filename and the content you want to write into the file as arguments. (Note that the file will be overwritten by this content!) It returns an `io::Result` type. It is an alias over the normal `Result` type (its documentation is at `https://doc.rust-lang.org/stable/std/result/enum.Result.html`) declared as follows:

```
type Result<T> = Result<T, Error>;
```

The only difference is that in case of error, the error type is already defined.

> I recommend that you to take a look at its documentation in case you want to go further, at `https://doc.rust-lang.org/stable/std/io/type.Result.html`.

So if our function worked without errors, it'll return `Ok(())`; it's the `Ok` variant containing an empty tuple which is considered the Rust equivalent of the `void` type. In case of error, it'll contain an `io::Error`, and it'll be up to you to handle it (or not). We'll come back to error handling a bit later.

Now let's look at the next line:

```
let mut f = File::create(file_name)?;
```

Here, we call the static method `create` of the `File` type. If the file exists, it'll be truncated and if it doesn't, it'll be created. More information about this method can be found at `https://doc.rust-lang.org/stable/std/fs/struct.File.html#method.create`.

Now let's look at this strange `?` symbol. It's a syntactic sugar over the `try!` macro. The `try!` macro is very simple to understand and its code can be resumed as this:

```
match result {
    Ok(value) => value,
  Err(error) => return Err(error),
  }
```

So that's pretty easy, but annoying to rewrite over and over, so the Rust teams decided to first introduce the `try!` macro and then after a long consensus, decided to add the `?` syntactic sugar over it (it also works with the `Option` type). However, both code pieces are still working, so you can perfectly do as well:

```
use std::fs::File;
use std::io::{self, Write};

fn write_into_file(content: &str, file_name: &str) ->
io::Result<()> {
  let mut f = try!(File::create(file_name));
  f.write_all(content.as_bytes())
}
```

It's exactly the same. Alternatively, you can write the full version too:

```
use std::fs::File;
use std::io::{self, Write};

fn write_into_file(content: &str, file_name: &str) -> io::Result<()>
{
  let mut f = match File::create(file_name) {
     Ok(value) => value,
     Err(error) => return Err(error),
  };
```

```
   f.write_all(content.as_bytes())
}
```

It's up to you, but now you know what options you have!

Now let's check the last line:

```
f.write_all(content.as_bytes())
```

Nothing fancy here; we write all our data into the file. We just need to convert (it's not really a conversion in this case, more like getting internal data) our &str into a slice of u8 (so a &[u8]).

Now that we have a function to write a file, it'd be nice to be able to read from a file as well:

```
use std::fs::File;
use std::io::{self, Read};

fn read_from_file(file_name: &str) -> io::Result<String> {
   let mut f = File::open(file_name)?;
   let mut content = String::new();
   f.read_to_string(&mut content)?;
   Ok(content)
}
```

Now let's go over what this function does quickly:

```
fn read_from_file(file_name: &str) -> io::Result<String> {
```

This time, it only takes a filename as an argument and returns a String if the reading was successful:

```
let mut f = File::open(file_name)?;
let mut content = String::new();
f.read_to_string(&mut content)?;
```

Just like before, we open the file. Then we create a mutable String where the file content will be stored and finally we read all the file content at once with the read_to_string method (the String is reallocated as many times as needed). This method will fail if the string isn't proper UTF-8.

And to finish, if everything went fine, we return our content:

```
Ok(content)
```

So now, let's see how we can use this in our future tetris.

Saving/loading high scores

To keep things simple, we'll have a very simple file format:

- On the first line, we store the best scores
- On the second line, we store the highest number of lines

Let's start by writing the `save` function:

```
fn slice_to_string(slice: &[u32]) -> String {
    slice.iter().map(|highscore| highscore.to_string()).
      collect::<Vec<String>>().join(" ")
}

fn save_highscores_and_lines(highscores: &[u32],
    number_of_lines: &[u32]) -> bool {
    let s_highscores = slice_to_string(highscores);
    let s_number_of_lines = slice_to_string(number_of_lines);
    write_into_file(format!("{}\n{}\n", s_highscores,
      s_number_of_lines)).is_ok()
}
```

It was a small lie: there are actually two functions. The first one is just here to make the code smaller and easier to read even though we need to explain what it does, because we're about to talk about a big feature from Rust—**iterators**!

Iterators

The Rust documentation describes an iterator as *Composable external iteration.*

They're used a lot in idiomatic Rust code on collection types (`slice`, `Vec`, `HashMap`, and so on) so it's very important to learn to master them. This code will allow us to have a nice introduction. Let's look at the code now:

```
slice.iter().map(|highscore| highscore.to_string()).
  collect::<Vec<String>>().join(" ")
```

This is quite difficult to read and understand for the moment, so let's rewrite it as follows:

```
slice.iter()
    .map(|highscore| highscore.to_string())
```

```
    .collect::<Vec<String>>()
    .join(" ")
```

Better (or at least more readable!). Now let's go step by step, as follows:

```
    slice.iter()
```

Here, we create an iterator from our slice. A really important and fundamental thing to note about iterators in Rust; they're lazy. Creating an iterator doesn't cost anything more than the size of the type (generally a structure containing a pointer and an index). Until the `next()` method is called, nothing happens.

So now we have an iterator, awesome! Let's check the next step:

```
    .map(|highscore| highscore.to_string())
```

We call the iterator's `map` method. What it does is simple: it converts the current type into another one. So here, we convert a `u32` into a `String`.

Really important to note: at this point, the iterator still hasn't done anything. Keep in mind that nothing is done until the `next()` method is called!

```
    .collect::<Vec<String>>()
```

And now we call the `collect()` method. It'll call the `next()` method of our iterator as long as it didn't get all elements and store them into a `Vec`. This is where the `map()` method will be called on every element of our iterator.

And finally the last step:

```
    .join(" ")
```

This method (as its name indicates) joins all the elements of the `Vec` into a `String` separated by the given `&str` (so, " " in our case).

Finally, if we give `&[1, 14, 5]` to the `slice_to_string` function, it'll return a `String` containing `"1 14 5"`. Pretty convenient, right?

> If you want to go a bit deeper with the iterators, you can take a look at the blog post at `https://blog.guillaume-gomez.fr/articles/2017-03-09+Little+tour+of+multiple+iterators+implementation+in+Rust` or directly take a look at the iterator official documentation at `https://doc.rust-lang.org/stable/std/iter/index.html`.

It's time to go back to our saving function:

```
fn save_highscores_and_lines(highscores: &[u32],
    number_of_lines: &[u32]) -> bool {
  let s_highscores = slice_to_string(highscores);
  let s_number_of_lines = slice_to_string(number_of_lines);
  write_into_file(format!("{}\n{}\n", s_highscores,
    s_number_of_lines), "scores.txt").is_ok()
}
```

Once we have converted our slices to `String`, we write them into the `scores.txt` file. The `is_ok()` method call just informs the caller of the `save_highscores_and_lines()` function if everything has been saved as expected or not.

Now that we can save scores, it'd be nice to be able to get them back when the tetris game is starting!

Reading formatted data from files

As you will certainly have guessed at this point, we'll use iterators once again. This is what the loading function will look like:

```
fn line_to_slice(line: &str) -> Vec<u32> {
    line.split(" ").filter_map(|nb|
nb.parse::<u32>().ok()).collect()
}

fn load_highscores_and_lines() -> Option<(Vec<u32>, Vec<u32>)> {
    if let Ok(content) = read_from_file("scores.txt") {
        let mut lines = content.splitn(2, "\n").map(|line|
            line_to_slice(line)).collect::<Vec<_>>();
        if lines.len() == 2 {
            let (number_lines, highscores) = (lines.pop().unwrap(),
                lines.pop().unwrap());
            Some((highscores, number_lines))
        } else {
          None
          }
    } else {
        None
    }
}
```

Once again, not easy to understand, at first sight. So let's explain all this!

```
fn line_to_slice(line: &str) -> Vec<u32> {
```

Our `line_to_slice()` function does the opposite of `slice_to_string()`; it transforms a `&str` into a slice of `u32` (or `&[u32]`). Let's see the iterator now:

```
line.split(" ").filter_map(|nb| nb.parse::<u32>().ok()).collect()
```

Just like last time, let's split the calls:

```
line.split(" ")
  .filter_map(|nb| nb.parse::<u32>().ok())
  .collect()
```

A bit better! Now let's explain:

```
line.split(" ")
```

We create an iterator that will contain all strings between spaces. So `a  b` will contain `a` and `b`:

```
.filter_map(|nb| nb.parse::<u32>().ok())
```

This method is particularly interesting since it's the merge of two others: `filter()` and `map()`. We already know `map()` but what about `filter()`? If the condition isn't verified (so if the returned value of the closure is `false`), the iterator won't pass the value to the next method call. `filter_map()` works the same at this point: if the closure returns `None`, the value won't be passed to the next method call.

Now let's focus on this part:

```
nb.parse::<u32>().ok()
```

Here, we try to convert `&str` into `u32`. The `parse()` method returns a `Result` but the `filter_map()` expects an `Option` so we need to convert it. That's what the `ok()` method is for! If your `Result` is an `Ok(value)`, then it'll convert it into a `Some(value)`. However, if it's an `Err(err)`, it'll convert it into a `None` (but you'll lose the error value).

To sum this up, this whole line tries to convert a `&str` into a number and ignores it if the conversion fails so it's not added to our final `Vec`. Amazing how much we can do with such small code!

And finally:

```
.collect()
```

We `collect` all the successful conversions into a `Vec` and return it.

That's it for this function, now let's look at the other one:

```
fn load_highscores_and_lines() -> Option<(Vec<u32>, Vec<u32>)> {
```

Here, if everything went fine (if the file exists and has two lines), we return an `Option` containing in the first position the highest scores and in the second position the highest number of lines:

```
if let Ok(content) = read_from_file("scores.txt") {
```

So if the file exists and we can get its content, we parse the data:

```
let mut lines = content.splitn(2, "\n").map(|line|
    line_to_slice(line)).collect::<Vec<_>>();
```

Another iterator! As usual, let's rewrite it a bit:

```
let mut lines = content.splitn(2, "\n")
    .map(|line| line_to_slice(line))
    .collect::<Vec<_>>();
```

I think you're starting to get how they work, but just in case you don't know, here's how:

```
content.splitn(2, "\n")
```

We make an iterator containing at most two entries (because of the 2 as the first argument) splitting lines:

```
.map(|line| line_to_slice(line))
```

We transform each line into a `Vec<u32>` by using the function described in the preceding code:

```
.collect::<Vec<_>>();
```

And finally, we collect those `Vec`s into a `Vec<Vec<u32>>`, which should only contain two entries.

Let's look at the next line now:

```
if lines.len() == 2 {
```

As said before, if we don't have two entries inside our `Vec`, it means something is wrong with the file:

```
let (number_lines, highscores) = (lines.pop().unwrap(),
     lines.pop().unwrap());
```

In case our `Vec` has two entries, we can get the corresponding values. Since the `pop` method removes the last entry of the `Vec`, we get them in reverse (even though we return high scores first then the highest number of lines):

```
Some((highscores, number_lines))
```

Then everything else is just the error handling. As we said previously, if any error occurs, we return `None`. In this case, it's not really important to handle the error since it's just high scores. If we have errors with the `sdl` libraries, nothing will work as expected, so we need to handle them to avoid a panic.

It's now time to really start the game!

Summary

In this chapter, we saw a lot of important things like how to use `Cargo` (through the `Cargo.toml` file), how to import new crates into a project, thanks to `Cargo`, and the basics for Rust modules handling. We even covered how to use iterators and read and write files, `SDL2` basics like how to create a window and fill it with colors, and loading/creating new textures and images (thanks to the `SDL2-image` library!).

In `Chapter 3`, *Events and Basic Game Mechanisms*, we'll start the implementation of the tetris game, so be sure to master everything explained in this chapter before starting the next one!

3
Events and Basic Game Mechanisms

In the last chapter, we saw how to add dependencies into a project thanks to `Cargo` and the basics of the `SDL2` library.

We now have all the Rust basics in order to write the Tetris game. Time to look at how we will actually write Tetris.

In this chapter, we will cover the following topics:

- Tetrimino
- Creating tetriminos
- Generating a tetrimino
- Tetris struct
- Interacting with the game map
- SDL events
- Score, level, lines sent

Writing Tetris

First, let's review the Tetris rules (just in case):

- There is a grid with a height of 16 blocks and a width of 10 blocks.
- You have seven different `tetrimino` (a tetris piece) that are all composed of four blocks.

- A new `tetrimino` appears at the top of the game's grid every time the previous one cannot descend any more (because the block below is already occupied or because you've reached the game's floor).
- The game is over when a new `tetrimino` cannot appear anymore (because there is already a tetrimino at the top of the grid).
- Every time a line is *full* (all blocks are occupied by a `tetrimino` part), it disappears and all lines above descend by one line.

Now that we all agree on the game rules, let's see how to actually write those mechanisms.

First, we need to actually create those `tetriminos`.

Tetrimino

As said previously, every `tetrimino` has four blocks. Another thing to note is that they can rotate. So for example you have this `tetrimino`:

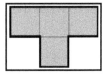

Figure 3.1

It can also rotate in the three following positions:

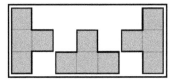

Figure 3.2

Theoretically, every `tetrimino` should have four states, but in reality, not all of them do. For example, this one has no transformation so to speak:

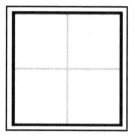

Figure 3.3

And these three only have two states:

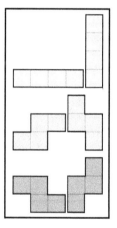

Figure 3.4

We have two ways of handling these rotations: using matrix rotation or storing the different states. To have a code that's easy to read and update, I picked the second option, but don't hesitate to try using matrix on your own, it could help you learn a lot of new things!

So first, let's write down a `struct` for `tetriminos`:

```
struct Tetrimino {
    states: Vec<Vec<Vec<u8>>>,
    x: isize,
    y: usize,
    current_state: u8,
}
```

Everything seems fine except this line:

```
states: Vec<Vec<Vec<u8>>>,
```

Pretty ugly, right? Let's make it look a bit better by using type aliasing!

So what is our `states` field representing? Simply a list of states. Each state represents a piece's transformation. I suppose it's a bit hard to understand all of this. Let's write an example:

```
vec![vec![1, 1, 0, 0],
     vec![1, 1, 0, 0],
     vec![0, 0, 0, 0],
     vec![0, 0, 0, 0]]
```

In here, 0 means the block is empty, otherwise, it's a `tetrimino` block. So from reading this code, I suppose you could guess that we were representing the square:

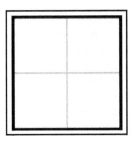

Figure 3.5

In case you wondered, we have four lines with four blocks because the *biggest* `tetrimino` has a height (or a width, depending the transformation) of four:

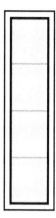

Figure 3.6

This isn't mandatory (we could make it fit the form of each `tetrimino`), but it makes our lives easier, so why not?

Coming back to our type aliasing: a piece is basically a vector or vector of numbers. It's long to write it down every time, so let's alias it as follows:

```
type Piece = Vec<Vec<u8>>;
```

Now we can rewrite the `states` field declaration as follows:

```
states: Vec<Piece>,
```

Way better and more explicit, right? But since we'll be using those states as well, why not alias them too?

```
type States = Vec<Piece>;
```

And now our `states` field declaration becomes:

```
states: States,
```

Let's explain the other fields (just in case):

```
struct Tetrimino {
    states: States,
    x: isize,
    y: usize,
    current_state: u8,
}
```

A little explanation of this struct:

- `states` (if you didn't already understand it) is the list of possible states of the `tetrimino`
- `x` is the *x* position of the `tetrimino`
- `y` is the *y* position of the `tetrimino`
- `current_state` is the state in which the `tetrimino` is currently

Ok, so far so good. Now how should we handle the creation of this type generically? We don't want to rewrite this for every `tetrimino`. This is where `traits` kick in!

Creating tetriminos

We wrote the type that will be used in our game, but we didn't write its initialization/creation yet. This is where Rust `traits` will be useful.

Let's start by writing a generator trait that will be implemented on all `tetriminos`:

```
trait TetriminoGenerator {
    fn new() -> Tetrimino;
}
```

And that's it. This `trait` just provides a function that creates a new `Tetrimino` instance. It maybe doesn't like this very much, but thanks to this `trait`, we'll be able to easily create all our `tetriminos`.

Time to write our first `tetrimino`:

```
struct TetriminoI;
```

No need to look for more code, this is what a `tetrimino` really looks like. It's an empty structure. The interesting part comes just after:

```
impl TetriminoGenerator for TetriminoI {
    fn new() -> Tetrimino {
        Tetrimino {
            states: vec![vec![vec![1, 1, 1, 1],
                              vec![0, 0, 0, 0],
                              vec![0, 0, 0, 0],
                              vec![0, 0, 0, 0]],
                         vec![vec![0, 1, 0, 0],
                              vec![0, 1, 0, 0],
                              vec![0, 1, 0, 0],
```

```
                                  vec![0, 1, 0, 0]]],
            x: 4,
            y: 0,
            current_state: 0,
        }
      }
    }
```

Which is:

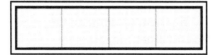

Figure 3.7

In here, a number represents a color and 0 means no color (because there is no block).

And that's it. Now you can create this tetrimino just by calling:

```
let tetrimino = TetriminoI::new();
```

It'll return an instance of the Tetrimino structure and that's the one you'll be using in the game. The other tetrimino structures (such as TetriminoI in here) are just used to generically create the Tetrimino structure with the related information.

We now need to create all the other tetrimino as well, so let's do it:

```
struct TetriminoJ;

impl TetriminoGenerator for TetriminoJ {
    fn new() -> Tetrimino {
        Tetrimino {
            states: vec![vec![vec![2, 2, 2, 0],
                              vec![2, 0, 0, 0],
                              vec![0, 0, 0, 0],
                              vec![0, 0, 0, 0]],
                         vec![vec![2, 2, 0, 0],
                              vec![0, 2, 0, 0],
                              vec![0, 2, 0, 0],
                              vec![0, 0, 0, 0]],
                         vec![vec![0, 0, 2, 0],
                              vec![2, 2, 2, 0],
                              vec![0, 0, 0, 0],
                              vec![0, 0, 0, 0]],
                         vec![vec![2, 0, 0, 0],
```

```
                                        vec![2, 0, 0, 0],
                                        vec![2, 2, 0, 0],
                                        vec![0, 0, 0, 0]]],
                    x: 4,
                    y: 0,
                    current_state: 0,
                }
            }
        }
```

In case you're wondering why the blocks have 2 as values, it's simply so that we can differentiate them when displaying them (having all tetrimino with the same color wouldn't be very pretty...). It has no other meaning.

This tetrimino looks like this:

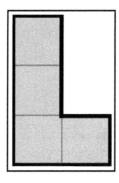

Figure 3.8

Let's go for the next one:

```
        struct TetriminoL;

        impl TetriminoGenerator for TetriminoL {
            fn new() -> Tetrimino {
                Tetrimino {
                    states: vec![vec![vec![3, 3, 3, 0],
                                      vec![0, 0, 3, 0],
                                      vec![0, 0, 0, 0],
                                      vec![0, 0, 0, 0]],
                                 vec![vec![0, 3, 0, 0],
                                      vec![0, 3, 0, 0],
                                      vec![3, 3, 0, 0],
                                      vec![0, 0, 0, 0]],
                                 vec![vec![3, 0, 0, 0],
                                      vec![3, 3, 3, 0],
```

```
                                    vec![0, 0, 0, 0],
                                    vec![0, 0, 0, 0]],
                            vec![vec![3, 3, 0, 0],
                                    vec![3, 0, 0, 0],
                                    vec![3, 0, 0, 0],
                                    vec![0, 0, 0, 0]]],
                x: 4,
                y: 0,
                current_state: 0,
            }
        }
    }
```

This `tetrimino` looks like this:

Figure 3.9

Another `tetrimino`:

```
        struct TetriminoO;

        impl TetriminoGenerator for TetriminoO {
            fn new() -> Tetrimino {
                Tetrimino {
                    states: vec![vec![vec![4, 4, 0, 0],
                                    vec![4, 4, 0, 0],
                                    vec![0, 0, 0, 0],
                                    vec![0, 0, 0, 0]]],
                x: 5,
                y: 0,
                current_state: 0,
            }
        }
    }
```

This `tetrimino` looks like this:

Figure 3.10

Another `tetrimino` (will it ever end?!):

```
struct TetriminoS;

impl TetriminoGenerator for TetriminoS {
    fn new() -> Tetrimino {
        Tetrimino {
            states: vec![vec![vec![0, 5, 5, 0],
                              vec![5, 5, 0, 0],
                              vec![0, 0, 0, 0],
                              vec![0, 0, 0, 0]],
                         vec![vec![0, 5, 0, 0],
                              vec![0, 5, 5, 0],
                              vec![0, 0, 5, 0],
                              vec![0, 0, 0, 0]]],
            x: 4,
            y: 0,
            current_state: 0,
        }
    }
}
```

This `tetrimino` looks like this:

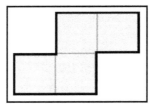

Figure 3.11

Guess what? Another `tetrimino`:

```
struct TetriminoZ;

impl TetriminoGenerator for TetriminoZ {
    fn new() -> Tetrimino {
        Tetrimino {
            states: vec![vec![vec![6, 6, 0, 0],
                              vec![0, 6, 6, 0],
                              vec![0, 0, 0, 0],
                              vec![0, 0, 0, 0]],
                         vec![vec![0, 0, 6, 0],
                              vec![0, 6, 6, 0],
                              vec![0, 6, 0, 0],
                              vec![0, 0, 0, 0]]],
            x: 4,
            y: 0,
            current_state: 0,
        }
    }
}
```

This `tetrimino` looks like this:

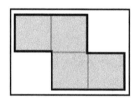

Figure 3.12

And the last one (finally!):

```
struct TetriminoT;

impl TetriminoGenerator for TetriminoT {
    fn new() -> Tetrimino {
        Tetrimino {
            states: vec![vec![vec![7, 7, 7, 0],
                              vec![0, 7, 0, 0],
                              vec![0, 0, 0, 0],
                              vec![0, 0, 0, 0]],
                         vec![vec![0, 7, 0, 0],
                              vec![7, 7, 0, 0],
                              vec![0, 7, 0, 0],
```

```
                                     vec![0, 0, 0, 0]],
                        vec![vec![0, 7, 0, 0],
                             vec![7, 7, 7, 0],
                             vec![0, 0, 0, 0],
                             vec![0, 0, 0, 0]],
                        vec![vec![0, 7, 0, 0],
                             vec![0, 7, 7, 0],
                             vec![0, 7, 0, 0],
                             vec![0, 0, 0, 0]]],
            x: 4,
            y: 0,
            current_state: 0,
        }
      }
    }
```

And finally, this `tetrimino` looks like this:

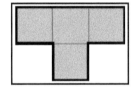

Figure 3.13

Phew... That was quite a lot of code! Easy code, but still a lot!

It's now time to see how we can generate a new `tetrimino` randomly.

Generating a tetrimino

In order to do so, we'll need to import another `crate`—`rand`. This `crate` is used to generate random numbers and that is exactly what we need here.

First, add the following line to your `Cargo.toml` file (in the `[dependencies]` section):

```
rand = "0.3"
```

Next, add the following line to your `main.rs` file:

```
extern crate rand;
```

And we're done! Now we can write the generation function of the `tetrimino`:

```
fn create_new_tetrimino() -> Tetrimino {
    let rand_nb = rand::random::<u8>() % 7;
    match rand_nb {
        0 => TetriminoI::new(),
        1 => TetriminoJ::new(),
        2 => TetriminoL::new(),
        3 => TetriminoO::new(),
        4 => TetriminoS::new(),
        5 => TetriminoZ::new(),
        6 => TetriminoT::new(),
        _ => unreachable!(),
    }
}
```

Pretty easy, right? Though, please note that this is a bit too random. It'd be problematic if we had the same `tetrimino` generated more than twice in a row (which is already a lot!), so let's improve this function a bit by adding a `static` variable:

```
fn create_new_tetrimino() -> Tetrimino {
    static mut PREV: u8 = 7;
    let mut rand_nb = rand::random::<u8>() % 7;
    if unsafe { PREV } == rand_nb {
        rand_nb = rand::random::<u8>() % 7;
    }
    unsafe { PREV = rand_nb; }
    match rand_nb {
        0 => TetriminoI::new(),
        1 => TetriminoJ::new(),
        2 => TetriminoL::new(),
        3 => TetriminoO::new(),
        4 => TetriminoS::new(),
        5 => TetriminoZ::new(),
        6 => TetriminoT::new(),
        _ => unreachable!(),
    }
}
```

A bit of explanation might be helpful here. First, what is a `static` variable? It's a variable that will keep its value and won't be destroyed when the scope it has been created inside has been left. An example:

```
fn foo() -> u32 {
    static mut VALUE: u32 = 12;
    unsafe {
        VALUE += 1;
```

```
            VALUE
        }
    }

    for _ in 0..5 {
        println!("{}", foo());
    }
```

If you execute this code, it'll print out:

```
13
14
15
16
17
```

Here are the other properties of the `static` variable:

- It cannot have a destructor (it's possible to avoid this limitation by using the `lazy_static` crate though, but we won't talk about it here) so only *simple* types that don't implement the `Drop` trait can be used as `static`
- Changing the value of a `static` variable is unsafe (that's why there are `unsafe` blocks) for the simple reason that the `static` is shared between all threads in the program and can be modified and read at the same time
- Reading the value of a mutable `static` is unsafe (for the reason mentioned previously)

We now have a function that can generate a `tetrimino`. We now need to add the following functionalities:

- Rotating
- Changing position

Let's start with the rotation part!

Rotating a tetrimino

Thanks to how we created the `Tetrimino` type, it's quite easy to do:

```
impl Tetrimino {
    fn rotate(&mut self) {
        self.current_state += 1;
        if self.current_state as usize >= self.states.len() {
            self.current_state = 0;
```

```
              }
          }
      }
```

And we're done. However, we don't check anything: what happens if there is a block already used by another `tetrimino`? We'll just overwrite it. Such a thing cannot be accepted!

In order to perform this check, we'll need the game *map* as well. It's simply a vector line and a line is a vector of `u8`. Or, more simply:

```
Vec<Vec<u8>>
```

Considering that it isn't too hard to read, we'll just keep it this way. Now let's write the method:

```
fn test_position(&self, game_map: &[Vec<u8>],
                 tmp_state: usize, x: isize, y: usize) -> bool {
    for decal_y in 0..4 {
      for decal_x in 0..4 {
        let x = x + decal_x;
        if self.states[tmp_state][decal_y][decal_x as usize] != 0
          &&
                (y + decal_y >= game_map.len() ||
                 x < 0 ||
                 x as usize >= game_map[y + decal_y].len() ||
                 game_map[y + decal_y][x as usize] != 0) {
                 return false;
          }
      }
    }
    return true;
}
```

Before explaining this function, it seems important to explain why the game map became a `&[Vec<u8>]`. When you send a non-mutable reference over a vector (`Vec<T>`), it is then dereferenced into a `&[T]` slice, which is a constant *view* over the vector's content.

And we're done (for this method)! Now time for explanations: we loop over every block of our `tetrimino` and check whether the block is free in the game map (by checking whether it is equal to `0`) and if it isn't going out of the game map.

Now that we have our `test_position` method, we can update the `rotate` method:

```
fn rotate(&mut self, game_map: &[Vec<u8>]) {
    let mut tmp_state = self.current_state + 1;
    if tmp_state as usize >= self.states.len() {
        tmp_state = 0;
    }
    let x_pos = [0, -1, 1, -2, 2, -3];
    for x in x_pos.iter() {
        if self.test_position(game_map, tmp_state as usize,
                              self.x + x, self.y) == true {
            self.current_state = tmp_state;
            self.x += *x;
            break
        }
    }
}
```

A bit longer, indeed. Since we can't be sure that the piece will be put where we want it to go, we need to make temporary variables and then check the possibilities. Let's go through the code:

```
let mut tmp_state = self.current_state + 1;
if tmp_state as usize >= self.states.len() {
    tmp_state = 0;
}
```

This is *exactly* what our `rotate` method did before, except that now, we use temporary variables before going further:

```
let x_pos = [0, -1, 1, -2, 2, -3];
```

This line on its own doesn't make much sense but it'll be very useful next: in case the piece cannot be placed where we want, we try to move it on the x axis to see if it'd work in some other place. It allows you to have a Tetris that is much more flexible and comfortable to play:

```
for x in x_pos.iter() {
    if self.test_position(game_map, tmp_state as usize,
                          self.x + x, self.y) == true {
        self.current_state = tmp_state;
        self.x += *x;
        break
    }
}
```

With the explanations given previously, this loop should be really easy to understand. For each x shift, we check whether the piece can be placed there. If it works, we change the values of our tetrimino, otherwise we just continue.

If no x shift worked, we just leave the function without doing anything.

Now that we can rotate and test the position of a tetrimino, it'd be nice to actually move it as well (when the timer goes to 0 and the tetrimino needs to go down, for example). The main difference with the rotate method will be that, if the tetrimino cannot move, we'll return a Boolean value to allow the caller to be aware of it.

So the method looks like this:

```
fn change_position(&mut self, game_map: &[Vec<u8>], new_x: isize,
new_y: usize) -> bool {
    if self.test_position(game_map, self.current_state as usize,
    new_x, new_y) == true {
        self.x = new_x as isize;
        self.y = new_y;
        true
    } else {
        false
    }
}
```

Another difference that you have certainly already spotted is that we don't check multiple possible positions, just the one received. The reason is simple; contrary to a rotation, we can't move the tetrimino around when it receives a move instruction. Imagine asking the tetrimino to move to the right and it doesn't move, or worse, it moves to the left! We can't allow it and so we're not doing it.

Now about the method's code: it's very simple. If we can put the tetrimino in a place, we update the position of the tetrimino and return true, otherwise, we do nothing other than return false.

Most of the work is performed in the test_position method, allowing our method to be really small.

With these three methods, we have almost everything we need. But for even more simplicity in the future, let's add one more:

```
fn test_current_position(&self, game_map: &[Vec<u8>]) -> bool {
    self.test_position(game_map, self.current_state as usize,
    self.x, self.y)
}
```

We'll use it when we generate a new `tetrimino`: if it cannot be placed where it appeared because another `tetrimino` is already there, it means the game is over.

We can now say that our `Tetrimino` type is fully implemented. Congratulations! Time to start the game type!

Tetris struct

This type will be the one holding all the game's information:

- Game map
- Current level
- Score
- Number of lines
- The current `tetrimino`
- Some potential other information (such as a ghost, or the preview of the next `tetrimino`!)

Let's write down this type:

```
struct Tetris {
    game_map: Vec<Vec<u8>>,
    current_level: u32,
    score: u32,
    nb_lines: u32,
    current_piece: Option<Tetrimino>,
}
```

Once again, pretty simple. I don't think any additional information is required so let's continue!

Let's start by writing the `new` method for this new type:

```
impl Tetris {
    fn new() -> Tetris {
        let mut game_map = Vec::new();
        for _ in 0..16 {
            game_map.push(vec![0, 0, 0, 0, 0, 0, 0, 0, 0, 0]);
        }
        Tetris {
            game_map: game_map,
            current_level: 1,
            score: 0,
```

```
                nb_lines: 0,
                current_piece: None,
            }
        }
    }
```

Nothing really complicated except maybe the loop. Let's look at how it works:

```
let mut game_map = Vec::new();
for _ in 0..16 {
    game_map.push(vec![0, 0, 0, 0, 0, 0, 0, 0, 0, 0]);
}
```

We know that a `tetris` map has a width of 10 blocks and a height of 16 blocks. This loop creates our game map by looping over the number of lines and generating an empty vector of 10 blocks, which will be a line.

Apart from this, everything else is very straightforward:

- You start at level 1
- With your score at 0
- With 0 lines sent
- No current `tetrimino`

Let's start by generating a new `tetrimino` randomly. For this, you'll require the `rand` crate. Add the following to your `Cargo.toml` file:

```
rand = "0.3"
```

Then add this at the top of your `main` file:

```
extern crate rand;
```

Then we can write the method:

```
fn create_new_tetrimino(&self) -> Tetrimino {
    static mut PREV: u8 = 7;
    let mut rand_nb = rand::random::<u8>() % 7;
    if unsafe { PREV } == rand_nb {
        rand_nb = rand::random::<u8>() % 7;
    }
    unsafe { PREV = rand_nb; }
    match rand_nb {
        0 => TetriminoI::new(),
        1 => TetriminoJ::new(),
        2 => TetriminoL::new(),
```

```
        3 => TetriminoO::new(),
        4 => TetriminoS::new(),
        5 => TetriminoZ::new(),
        6 => TetriminoT::new(),
        _ => unreachable!(),
    }
}
```

Explanations:

```
static mut PREV: u8 = 7;
```

The `static` keyword is the same in Rust as it is in C and C++ for variables: the value set to the variable will be kept between the function calls. So for example, if you write the following function:

```
fn incr() -> u32 {
    static mut NB: u32 = 0;
    unsafe {
        NB += 1;
        NB
    }
}
```

And you then call it, as follows:

```
for _ in 0..5 {
    println!("{}", incr());
}
```

You'll get the following output:

```
1
2
3
4
5
```

So now, why do we have these `unsafe` blocks? The reason is quite simple: in case the static variable is accessed and modified from different threads, you can't be *sure* that you won't have data race, concurrency errors, or even memory errors.

In this case, since we don't have threads, it's fine. However, keep in mind that you should ALWAYS try to avoid unsafe at all costs and use it ONLY when nothing else can be done.

However, if our static variable wasn't mutable, then we could access its value without needing the `unsafe` blocks. The reason once again is simple: even if multiple threads try to access its value at the same time, since this value cannot change, you can't have data race and therefore it is safe.

Let's continue with our function's code explanations:

```
let mut rand_nb = rand::random::<u8>() % 7;
```

This line generates a random `u8` and then limits its value between 0 (included) and 6 (included) because we have seven different `tetrimino`:

```
if unsafe { PREV } == rand_nb {
    rand_nb = rand::random::<u8>() % 7;
}
```

If the generated `tetrimino` is the same as the previous one, we generate another one. It enables you to prevent having the same `tetrimino` too many times at once. It isn't the best way to do it, having a specific balancing for each `tetrimino` would be better, but this solution is acceptable enough (and a lot easier to write!):

```
unsafe { PREV = rand_nb; }
```

We now set the generated `tetrimino` *ID* to our `static` variable:

```
match rand_nb {
    0 => TetriminoI::new(),
    1 => TetriminoJ::new(),
    2 => TetriminoL::new(),
    3 => TetriminoO::new(),
    4 => TetriminoS::new(),
    5 => TetriminoZ::new(),
    6 => TetriminoT::new(),
    _ => unreachable!(),
}
```

Nothing much to say about this pattern matching. Every *ID* matches a `tetrimino` and then we call the corresponding constructor. The only really interesting thing about this construction is the following line:

```
_ => unreachable!(),
```

This macro is really useful. It allows us to add a security over the matched value. If the code ever enters this pattern matching, it'll panic right away (because, as the macro's name suggests, it's not supposed to happen).

Interacting with the game map

Ok, we can now move all the tetrimino and generate them. Two mechanisms are still missing: checking lines to see whether one can be sent (that is, removed since complete) and making a tetrimino *permanent* (that is, not movable anymore).

Let's start with the line check:

```
fn check_lines(&mut self) {
    let mut y = 0;

    while y < self.game_map.len() {
        let mut complete = true;

        for x in &self.game_map[y] {
            if *x == 0 {
                complete = false;
                break
            }
        }
        if complete == true {
            self.game_map.remove(y);
            y -= 1;
            // increase the number of self.lines
        }
        y += 1;
    }
    while self.game_map.len() < 16 {
        self.game_map.insert(0, vec![0, 0, 0, 0, 0, 0, 0, 0, 0,
0]);
    }
}
```

For now, I didn't add the score, lines sent counting, nor level handling but this is here that'll do it later.

Now time to explain this method a bit. Its purpose is to remove lines when they're full (meaning when every block is occupied by a tetrimino block). So we just go through the game map line by line and run the check on each.

The code itself doesn't use much of the Rust-specific syntax, but you might wonder why we did it like this. I'm talking about this loop:

```
while y < self.game_map.len() {
```

When we could have just used:

```
for line in self.game_map {
```

This is actually a good question and the answer is simple, but maybe hard to understand, if you're used to how Rust ownership works.

All the problems actually come from this line:

```
self.game_map.remove(y);
```

In here, we mutably borrow `self.game_map` in order to remove a line. However, `self.game_map` would already be non-mutably borrowed by the `for` loop! A quick reminder on how the borrowing rules work:

- You can non-mutably borrow a variable as many times as you want
- You can mutably borrow a variable only if there are no other borrows (either mutable or non-mutable)

So in our case, the `for` loop would break the second rule since we'd have a non-mutable borrow when trying to get mutable access to `self.game_map`.

In this case, we have two solutions:

- Iterate over the game map "by hand" (with an index variable)
- Store lines to remove into a second vector and then remove them after we get out of the loop

Both solutions are more or less equivalent in this case so I just picked the first one.

Once the first loop is finished, we have filled the game map with empty lines to replace the one(s) we deleted:

```
while self.game_map.len() < 16 {
    self.game_map.insert(0, vec![0, 0, 0, 0, 0, 0, 0, 0, 0, 0]);
}
```

And we're done with this method! Let's write the other one.

So now it's time to write the `make_permanent` method. Just like the previous one, it won't be a complete version, but in the future, this is where we'll update the score (we update it when a `tetrimino` is made permanent).

So let's write it:

```
fn make_permanent(&mut self) {
    if let Some(ref mut piece) = self.current_piece {
        let mut shift_y = 0;

        while shift_y < piece.states[piece.current_state as
        usize].len() &&
            piece.y + shift_y < self.game_map.len() {
            let mut shift_x = 0;

            while shift_x < piece.states[piece.current_state as
            usize][shift_y].len() &&
                (piece.x + shift_x as isize) <
                self.game_map[piece.y +
                shift_y].len() as isize {
                if piece.states[piece.current_state as usize]
                [shift_y][shift_x] != 0 {
                    let x = piece.x + shift_x as isize;
                    self.game_map[piece.y + shift_y][x as usize] =
                        piece.states[piece.current_state as usize]
                        [shift_y][shift_x];
                }
                shift_x += 1;
            }
            shift_y += 1;
        }
    }
    self.check_lines();
    self.current_piece = None;
}
```

This code doesn't seem very encouraging... Brace yourselves, explanations are coming:

```
if let Some(ref mut piece) = self.current_piece {
```

It's simple pattern matching. If `self.current_piece` is `Some`, then we enter the condition and the value contained by `Some` that is bound into the `piece` variable:

```
while shift_y < piece.states[piece.current_state as usize].len() &&
    piece.y + shift_y < self.game_map.len() {
```

This loop and its condition allow us to avoid a buffer overflow error by checking whether we're not outside of the game map limit for the current rotation (that is, `self.current_state`).

The same goes for the inner loop (which iterates over the blocks of a line):

```
while shift_x < piece.states[piece.current_state as
usize][shift_y].len() &&
      (piece.x + shift_x as isize) < self.game_map[piece.y +
shift_y].len() as isize {
```

It is in this loop that we write the blocks of the current `tetrimino` into the game map:

```
if piece.states[piece.current_state as usize][shift_y][shift_x] !=
0 {
    let x = piece.x + shift_x as isize;
    self.game_map[piece.y + shift_y][x as usize] =
        piece.states[piece.current_state as
usize][shift_y][shift_x];
}
```

If the current block of the current `tetrimino` isn't empty, then we put it into the game map (it's as simple as that).

Once done, this is where we call the `check_lines` method. But now you'll certainly wonder why we don't call it directly inside the `if let` condition. Well, it's for the exact same reason that we didn't use the `for` loop inside the `check_lines` method, `self` is already mutably borrowed by the following line:

```
if let Some(ref mut piece) = self.current_piece {
```

That's right: if an element of a type is borrowed, then its parent is mutably borrowed as well!

With these two methods, our `Tetris` type is now fully implemented (minus the small required modifications that will come later). Time to add the SDL events handling!

SDL events

There aren't many different events to handle:

- *Left* and *right arrow* keys to move the `tetrimino` to the right or the left
- *Up arrow* key to make the `tetrimino` rotate
- *Down arrow* key to make the `tetrimino` descend one block
- *Spacebar* to make the `tetrimino` descend to the bottom instantly
- *Escape* to quit the game

It's still possible to add some later on (such as pausing the game with the *return* key, for example) but for now, let's focus on these ones. For this, go back inside the main loop of the game (inside the `main` function) and replace the current event handling with the following function:

```
fn handle_events(tetris: &mut Tetris, quit: &mut bool, timer: &mut
SystemTime,
                 event_pump: &mut sdl2::EventPump) -> bool {
    let mut make_permanent = false;
    if let Some(ref mut piece) = tetris.current_piece {
        let mut tmp_x = piece.x;
        let mut tmp_y = piece.y;

        for event in event_pump.poll_iter() {
            match event {
            Event::Quit { .. } |
            Event::KeyDown { keycode: Some(Keycode::Escape), .. } =>
                {
                    *quit = true;
                    break
                }
            Event::KeyDown { keycode: Some(Keycode::Down), .. } =>
                {
                    *timer = SystemTime::now();
                    tmp_y += 1;
                }
            Event::KeyDown { keycode: Some(Keycode::Right), .. } =>
                {
                    tmp_x += 1;
                }
            Event::KeyDown { keycode: Some(Keycode::Left), .. } =>
                {
                    tmp_x -= 1;
                }
            Event::KeyDown { keycode: Some(Keycode::Up), .. } =>
                {
                    piece.rotate(&tetris.game_map);
                }
            Event::KeyDown { keycode: Some(Keycode::Space), .. } =>
                {
                    let x = piece.x;
                    let mut y = piece.y;
                    while piece.change_position(&tetris.game_map, x, y + 1)
                    == true {
                        y += 1;
                    }
                    make_permanent = true;
```

```
                    }
                    _ => {}
                }
            }
            if !make_permanent {
                if piece.change_position(&tetris.game_map, tmp_x, tmp_y)
                    ==
                    false &&
                        tmp_y != piece.y {
                            make_permanent = true;
                    }
                }
            }
        }
        if make_permanent {
            tetris.make_permanent();
            *timer = SystemTime::now();
        }
        make_permanent
    }
```

Quite a big one:

```
    let mut make_permanent = false;
```

This variable will tell us whether the current tetrimino is still falling. If not, then it becomes true, the tetrimino is then put into the game map and we generate a new one. Luckily for us, we already wrote all the needed functions to perform these operations:

```
    if let Some(ref mut piece) = tetris.current_piece {
```

This is simple pattern binding. If our game doesn't have a current piece (for some reason), then we don't do anything and just leave:

```
        let mut tmp_x = piece.x;
        let mut tmp_y = piece.y;
```

If there is a move on the x or on the y axis, we'll write it into these variables and then we'll test whether the tetrimino can actually go there:

```
        for event in event_pump.poll_iter() {
```

As there can be multiple events that happened since the last time we came into this function, we need to loop over all of them.

Now we're arriving at the interesting part:

```
match event {
    Event::Quit { .. } |
    Event::KeyDown { keycode: Some(Keycode::Escape), .. } => {
        *quit = true;
        break
    }
    Event::KeyDown { keycode: Some(Keycode::Down), .. } => {
        *timer = SystemTime::now();
        tmp_y += 1;
    }
    Event::KeyDown { keycode: Some(Keycode::Right), .. } => {
        tmp_x += 1;
    }
    Event::KeyDown { keycode: Some(Keycode::Left), .. } => {
        tmp_x -= 1;
    }
    Event::KeyDown { keycode: Some(Keycode::Up), .. } => {
        piece.rotate(&tetris.game_map);
    }
    Event::KeyDown { keycode: Some(Keycode::Space), .. } => {
        let x = piece.x;
        let mut y = piece.y;
        while piece.change_position(&tetris.game_map, x, y + 1) ==
        true {
            y += 1;
        }
        make_permanent = true;
    }
    _ => {}
}
```

We can almost consider this small code as the core of our application, without it, no interaction with the program is possible. If you want more interactions, this is where you'll add them:

```
Event::Quit { .. } |
Event::KeyDown { keycode: Some(Keycode::Escape), .. } => {
    *quit = true;
    break
}
```

If we receive a *quit* event from `sdl` or if we receive an `Escape`, `KeyDown` event, we set the `quit` variable to `true`. It'll be used outside of this function to then leave the main loop--and therefore leave the program itself. Then we *break;* no need to go further since we know that we're leaving the game:

```
Event::KeyDown { keycode: Some(Keycode::Down), .. } => {
    *timer = SystemTime::now();
    tmp_y += 1;
}
```

If the *down arrow* is pressed, we need to make our `tetrimino` descend by one block and also put the `timer` value to now. `timer` is used to know at what speed the `tetrimino` blocks are falling. The shorter the time, the faster they'll descend.

For now, it isn't used in this function, so we'll see how to handle it outside of it:

```
Event::KeyDown { keycode: Some(Keycode::Right), .. } => {
    tmp_x += 1;
}
Event::KeyDown { keycode: Some(Keycode::Left), .. } => {
    tmp_x -= 1;
}
```

In here, we handle the *right* and *left arrow* keys. It's just like the *down arrow* key, except we don't need to change the `timer` variable:

```
Event::KeyDown { keycode: Some(Keycode::Up), .. } => {
    piece.rotate(&tetris.game_map);
}
```

If we receive an *up arrow* key pressed event, we rotate the `tetrimino`:

```
Event::KeyDown { keycode: Some(Keycode::Space), .. } => {
    let x = piece.x;
    let mut y = piece.y;
    while piece.change_position(&tetris.game_map, x, y + 1) == true {
        y += 1;
    }
    make_permanent = true;
}
```

And finally the last of our events: the *spacebar* key pressed event. Here, we move the `tetrimino` down as much as we can and then set the `make_permanent` variable to `true`.

With this, that's it for our events. However, like we said before if you want to add more events, this is where you should put them.

Time to put all this into our main loop:

```rust
fn print_game_information(tetris: &Tetris) {
    println!("Game over...");
    println!("Score:              {}", tetris.score);
    // println!("Number of lines: {}", tetris.nb_lines);
    println!("Current level:    {}", tetris.current_level);
    // Check highscores here and update if needed
}

let mut tetris = Tetris::new();
let mut timer = SystemTime::now();

loop {
    if match timer.elapsed() {
        Ok(elapsed) => elapsed.as_secs() >= 1,
        Err(_) => false,
    } {
        let mut make_permanent = false;
        if let Some(ref mut piece) = tetris.current_piece {
            let x = piece.x;
            let y = piece.y + 1;
            make_permanent =
             !piece.change_position(&tetris.game_map,
             x, y);
        }
        if make_permanent {
            tetris.make_permanent();
        }
        timer = SystemTime::now();
    }

    // We need to draw the tetris "grid" in here.

    if tetris.current_piece.is_none() {
        let current_piece = tetris.create_new_tetrimino();
        if !current_piece.test_current_position(&tetris.game_map) {
            print_game_information(&tetris);
            break
        }
        tetris.current_piece = Some(current_piece);
    }
    let mut quit = false;
    if !handle_events(&mut tetris, &mut quit, &mut timer, &mut
```

```
event_pump) {
    if let Some(ref mut piece) = tetris.current_piece {
        // We need to draw our current tetrimino in here.
    }
}
if quit {
    print_game_information(&tetris);
    break
}

// We need to draw the game map in here.

sleep(Duration::new(0, 1_000_000_000u32 / 60));
}
```

Doesn't seem that long, right? Just a few comments where we're supposed to draw our `Tetris`, but otherwise everything is in there, which means that our `Tetris` is now fully functional (even though it isn't displayed).

Let's explain what's happening in there:

```
let mut tetris = Tetris::new();
let mut timer = SystemTime::now();
```

In here, we initialize both our `Tetris` object and the `timer`. The timer will be used to let us know when the `tetrimino` is supposed to descend by one block:

```
if match timer.elapsed() {
    Ok(elapsed) => elapsed.as_secs() >= 1,
    Err(_) => false,
} {
    let mut make_permanent = false;
    if let Some(ref mut piece) = tetris.current_piece {
        let x = piece.x;
        let y = piece.y + 1;
        make_permanent = !piece.change_position(&tetris.game_map,
            x, y);
    }
    if make_permanent {
        tetris.make_permanent();
    }
    timer = SystemTime::now();
}
```

This code checks whether it's been one second or more since the last time the `tetrimino` descended by one block. If we want to handle levels, we'll need to replace the following line:

```
Ok(elapsed) => elapsed.as_secs() >= 1,
```

Its replacement will need to be something more generic and we'll add an array to store the different levels' speed of descent.

So coming back to the code, if it's been one second or more then we try to make the `tetrimino` descend by one block. If it cannot, then we put it into the game map and re-initialize the `timer` variable.

Once again, you might wonder why we had to create the `make_permanent` variable instead of directly checking the output of:

```
!piece.change_position(&tetris.game_map, x, y)
```

It has an `if` condition, right? Well, just like the previous times, it's because of the borrow checker. We borrow `tetris` here:

```
if let Some(ref mut piece) = tetris.current_piece {
```

So as long as we're in this condition, we can't use `tetris` mutably, which is why we store the result of the condition in `make_permanent` so we can use the `make_permanent` method after:

```
if tetris.current_piece.is_none() {
    let current_piece = tetris.create_new_tetrimino();
    if !current_piece.test_current_position(&tetris.game_map) {
        print_game_information(&tetris);
        return
    }
    tetris.current_piece = Some(current_piece);
}
```

If there is no current `tetrimino`, we need to generate a new one, which we do by calling the `create_new_tetrimino` method. Then we check whether it can be put into the game on the top line by calling the `test_current_position` method. If not, then it means the game is over and we quit. Otherwise, we store the newly-generated `tetrimino` in `tetris.current_piece` and we move on.

Two things are missing here:

- Since we don't handle the increase of lines sent, nor the score, nor the level, there's no need to print them
- We didn't add yet the highscores loading/overwrite

Of course, we'll add all this later on:

```
let mut quit = false;
if !handle_events(&mut tetris, &mut quit, &mut timer, &mut
event_pump) {
    if let Some(ref mut piece) = tetris.current_piece {
        // We need to draw our current tetrimino in here.
    }
}
if quit {
    print_game_information(&tetris);
    break
}
```

This code calls the `handle_events` function and acts according to its output. It returns whether the current `tetrimino` has been put into the game map or not. If it is the case, then there is no need to draw it.

We now need to do the following remaining things:

- Add the score, levels, and number of lines sent
- Load/overwrite the highscores if needed
- Actually draw the `Tetris`

Seems like we're getting very close to the end! Let's start by adding the score, number of lines sent, and levels!

Score, level, lines sent

The biggest required change will be the level handling. You need to create an array with different times to increase the `tetrimino`'s speed of descent and to check whether the level needs to be changed or not (based on the number of lines).

The score will be updated in the following cases:

- When the tetrimino is made permanent
- When a line is sent
- When the player makes a Tetris (no more blocks in the game map)

Let's start with the easiest change—the score.

First, let's add the following method into our Tetris type:

```
fn update_score(&mut self, to_add: u32) {
    self.score += to_add;
}
```

We can suppose that no additional explanations are required here.

Next, let's update a few methods:

```
fn check_lines(&mut self) {
    let mut y = 0;
    let mut score_add = 0;

    while y < self.game_map.len() {
        let mut complete = true;

        for x in &self.game_map[y] {
            if *x == 0 {
                complete = false;
                break
            }
        }
        if complete == true {
            score_add += self.current_level;
            self.game_map.remove(y);
            y -= 1;
        }
        y += 1;
    }
    if self.game_map.len() == 0 {
        // A "tetris"!
        score_add += 1000;
    }
    self.update_score(score_add);
    while self.game_map.len() < 16 {
        // we'll add this method just after!
        self.increase_line();
```

```
            self.game_map.insert(0, vec![0, 0, 0, 0, 0, 0, 0, 0, 0,
            0]);
        }
    }
```

As usual, we create a temporary variable (here, `score_add`) and once the borrow of `self` is over, we call the `update_score` method. There is also the usage of the `increase_line` method. We haven't defined it yet; it'll come just after.

The second method is `make_permanent`:

```
fn make_permanent(&mut self) {
    let mut to_add = 0;
    if let Some(ref mut piece) = self.current_piece {
        let mut shift_y = 0;

        while shift_y < piece.states[piece.current_state as
          usize].len() &&
              piece.y + shift_y < self.game_map.len() {
            let mut shift_x = 0;

            while shift_x < piece.states[piece.current_state as usize]
              [shift_y].len() &&
                  (piece.x + shift_x as isize) < self.game_map[piece.y
                  + shift_y].len() as isize {
                if piece.states[piece.current_state as usize][shift_y]
                  [shift_x] != 0 {
                    let x = piece.x + shift_x as isize;
                    self.game_map[piece.y + shift_y][x as usize] =
                        piece.states[piece.current_state as usize]
                        [shift_y][shift_x];
                }
                shift_x += 1;
            }
            shift_y += 1;
        }
        to_add += self.current_level;
    }
    self.update_score(to_add);
    self.check_lines();
    self.current_piece = None;
}
```

Include this just above the `self.check_lines` call.

With these two methods updated, we now have the score handling fully implemented.

Levels and lines sent

The next two being strongly bound (the level depends directly on the number of lines sent), we'll implement them at the same time.

Before doing anything else, let's define the two following const:

```
const LEVEL_TIMES: [u32; 10] = [1000, 850, 700, 600, 500, 400, 300,
250, 221, 190];
const LEVEL_LINES: [u32; 10] = [20,   40,  60,  80,  100, 120, 140,
160, 180, 200];
```

The first one corresponds to the times before the current tetrimino descends by one block. Each case being a different level.

The second one corresponds to how many lines the player needs before getting to the next level.

Next, let's add the following method in our Tetris type:

```
fn increase_line(&mut self) {
    self.nb_lines += 1;
    if self.nb_lines > LEVEL_LINES[self.current_level as usize - 1]
{
        self.current_level += 1;
    }
}
```

Nothing complicated. Just be careful when reading the LEVEL_LINES const because our current_level variable starts at 1 and not 0.

Next, we'll need to update how we determine whether the time is up or not. To do so, let's write another function:

```
fn is_time_over() {
    match timer.elapsed() {
        Ok(elapsed) => {
            let millis = elapsed.as_secs() as u32 * 1000 +
            elapsed.subsec_nanos() / 1_000_000;
            millis > LEVEL_TIMES[tetris.current_level as usize - 1]
        }
        Err(_) => false,
    }
}
```

A small but tricky one. The problem is that the type returned by `timer.elapsed` (which is `Duration`) doesn't provide a method to get the number of milliseconds, so we need to get it ourselves.

First, we get the number of seconds elapsed and then multiply it by 1,000 (because 1 second = 1,000 milliseconds). Finally, we get the number of nanoseconds (in the current second) and divide it by 1,000,000 (because 1 millisecond = 1 million nanoseconds).

We can now compare the results to see whether the `tetrimino` should descend or not and return the result:

```
if is_time_over(&tetris, &timer) {
    let mut make_permanent = false;
    if let Some(ref mut piece) = tetris.current_piece {
        let x = piece.x;
        let y = piece.y + 1;
        make_permanent = !piece.change_position(&tetris.game_map,
            x, y);
    }
    if make_permanent {
        tetris.make_permanent();
    }
    timer = SystemTime::now();
}
```

And with this, we've finished this part. Let's make the last one now: the highscore loading/overwriting!

Highscores loading/overwriting

We already saw how to perform the I/O operations in the previous chapter, so it'll be very quick to do:

```
const NB_HIGHSCORES: usize = 5;

fn update_vec(v: &mut Vec<u32>, value: u32) -> bool {
    if v.len() < NB_HIGHSCORES {
        v.push(value);
        v.sort();
        true
    } else {
        for entry in v.iter_mut() {
            if value > *entry {
                *entry = value;
                return true;
```

```
                }
            }
            false
        }
    }

    fn print_game_information(tetris: &Tetris) {
        let mut new_highest_highscore = true;
        let mut new_highest_lines_sent = true;
        if let Some((mut highscores, mut lines_sent)) =
          load_highscores_and_lines() {
            new_highest_highscore = update_vec(&mut highscores,
              tetris.score);
            new_highest_lines_sent = update_vec(&mut lines_sent,
              tetris.nb_lines);
            if new_highest_highscore || new_highest_lines_sent {
                save_highscores_and_lines(&highscores, &lines_sent);
            }
        } else {
            save_highscores_and_lines(&[tetris.score], &
              [tetris.nb_lines]);
        }
        println!("Game over...");
        println!("Score:              {}{}",
                tetris.score,
                if new_highest_highscore { " [NEW HIGHSCORE]"} else {
                "" });
        println!("Number of lines: {}{}",
                tetris.nb_lines,
                if new_highest_lines_sent { " [NEW HIGHSCORE]"} else {
                "" });
        println!("Current level:    {}", tetris.current_level);
    }
```

Not much to explain with this code. For the moment, we limited the number of each highscore to 5. Just update it as you want.

And with this code, all the mechanisms are implemented. All that's left is to actually draw the game!

Here is the full code for this chapter:

```rust
extern crate rand;
extern crate sdl2;

use sdl2::event::Event;
use sdl2::keyboard::Keycode;
use sdl2::pixels::Color;
use sdl2::rect::Rect;
use sdl2::render::{Canvas, Texture, TextureCreator};
use sdl2::video::{Window, WindowContext};

use std::fs::File;
use std::io::{self, Read, Write};
use std::thread::sleep;
use std::time::{Duration, SystemTime};

const TETRIS_HEIGHT: usize = 40;
const HIGHSCORE_FILE: &'static str = "scores.txt";
const LEVEL_TIMES: [u32; 10] = [1000, 850, 700, 600, 500, 400, 300,
250, 221, 190];
const LEVEL_LINES: [u32; 10] = [20,   40,  60,  80,  100, 120, 140,
160, 180, 200];
const NB_HIGHSCORES: usize = 5;

type Piece = Vec<Vec<u8>>;
type States = Vec<Piece>;

trait TetriminoGenerator {
    fn new() -> Tetrimino;
}

struct TetriminoI;

impl TetriminoGenerator for TetriminoI {
    fn new() -> Tetrimino {
        Tetrimino {
            states: vec![vec![vec![1, 1, 1, 1],
                              vec![0, 0, 0, 0],
                              vec![0, 0, 0, 0],
                              vec![0, 0, 0, 0]],
                         vec![vec![0, 1, 0, 0],
                              vec![0, 1, 0, 0],
                              vec![0, 1, 0, 0],
                              vec![0, 1, 0, 0]]],
            x: 4,
            y: 0,
            current_state: 0,
```

```rust
                        }
                    }
                }

        struct TetriminoJ;

        impl TetriminoGenerator for TetriminoJ {
            fn new() -> Tetrimino {
                Tetrimino {
                    states: vec![vec![vec![2, 2, 2, 0],
                                      vec![2, 0, 0, 0],
                                      vec![0, 0, 0, 0],
                                      vec![0, 0, 0, 0]],
                                 vec![vec![2, 2, 0, 0],
                                      vec![0, 2, 0, 0],
                                      vec![0, 2, 0, 0],
                                      vec![0, 0, 0, 0]],
                                 vec![vec![0, 0, 2, 0],
                                      vec![2, 2, 2, 0],
                                      vec![0, 0, 0, 0],
                                      vec![0, 0, 0, 0]],
                                 vec![vec![2, 0, 0, 0],
                                      vec![2, 0, 0, 0],
                                      vec![2, 2, 0, 0],
                                      vec![0, 0, 0, 0]]],
                    x: 4,
                    y: 0,
                    current_state: 0,
                }
            }
        }

        struct TetriminoL;

        impl TetriminoGenerator for TetriminoL {
            fn new() -> Tetrimino {
                Tetrimino {
                    states: vec![vec![vec![3, 3, 3, 0],
                                      vec![0, 0, 3, 0],
                                      vec![0, 0, 0, 0],
                                      vec![0, 0, 0, 0]],
                                 vec![vec![0, 3, 0, 0],
                                      vec![0, 3, 0, 0],
                                      vec![3, 3, 0, 0],
                                      vec![0, 0, 0, 0]],
                                 vec![vec![3, 0, 0, 0],
                                      vec![3, 3, 3, 0],
                                      vec![0, 0, 0, 0],
```

```
                                  vec![0, 0, 0, 0]],
                       vec![vec![3, 3, 0, 0],
                            vec![3, 0, 0, 0],
                            vec![3, 0, 0, 0],
                            vec![0, 0, 0, 0]]],
            x: 4,
            y: 0,
            current_state: 0,
        }
    }
}

struct TetriminoO;

impl TetriminoGenerator for TetriminoO {
    fn new() -> Tetrimino {
        Tetrimino {
            states: vec![vec![vec![4, 4, 0, 0],
                              vec![4, 4, 0, 0],
                              vec![0, 0, 0, 0],
                              vec![0, 0, 0, 0]]],
            x: 5,
            y: 0,
            current_state: 0,
        }
    }
}

struct TetriminoS;

impl TetriminoGenerator for TetriminoS {
    fn new() -> Tetrimino {
        Tetrimino {
            states: vec![vec![vec![0, 5, 5, 0],
                              vec![5, 5, 0, 0],
                              vec![0, 0, 0, 0],
                              vec![0, 0, 0, 0]],
                       vec![vec![0, 5, 0, 0],
                            vec![0, 5, 5, 0],
                            vec![0, 0, 5, 0],
                            vec![0, 0, 0, 0]]],
            x: 4,
            y: 0,
            current_state: 0,
        }
    }
}
```

```rust
struct TetriminoZ;

impl TetriminoGenerator for TetriminoZ {
    fn new() -> Tetrimino {
        Tetrimino {
            states: vec![vec![vec![6, 6, 0, 0],
                              vec![0, 6, 6, 0],
                              vec![0, 0, 0, 0],
                              vec![0, 0, 0, 0]],
                         vec![vec![0, 0, 6, 0],
                              vec![0, 6, 6, 0],
                              vec![0, 6, 0, 0],
                              vec![0, 0, 0, 0]]],
            x: 4,
            y: 0,
            current_state: 0,
        }
    }
}

struct TetriminoT;

impl TetriminoGenerator for TetriminoT {
    fn new() -> Tetrimino {
        Tetrimino {
            states: vec![vec![vec![7, 7, 7, 0],
                              vec![0, 7, 0, 0],
                              vec![0, 0, 0, 0],
                              vec![0, 0, 0, 0]],
                         vec![vec![0, 7, 0, 0],
                              vec![7, 7, 0, 0],
                              vec![0, 7, 0, 0],
                              vec![0, 0, 0, 0]],
                         vec![vec![0, 7, 0, 0],
                              vec![7, 7, 7, 0],
                              vec![0, 0, 0, 0],
                              vec![0, 0, 0, 0]],
                         vec![vec![0, 7, 0, 0],
                              vec![0, 7, 7, 0],
                              vec![0, 7, 0, 0],
                              vec![0, 0, 0, 0]]],
            x: 4,
            y: 0,
            current_state: 0,
        }
    }
}
```

```rust
struct Tetrimino {
    states: States,
    x: isize,
    y: usize,
    current_state: u8,
}

impl Tetrimino {
    fn rotate(&mut self, game_map: &[Vec<u8>]) {
        let mut tmp_state = self.current_state + 1;
        if tmp_state as usize >= self.states.len() {
            tmp_state = 0;
        }
        let x_pos = [0, -1, 1, -2, 2, -3];
        for x in x_pos.iter() {
            if self.test_position(game_map, tmp_state as usize,
                                  self.x + x, self.y) == true {
                self.current_state = tmp_state;
                self.x += *x;
                break
            }
        }
    }

    fn test_position(&self, game_map: &[Vec<u8>],
                     tmp_state: usize, x: isize, y: usize) -> bool
{
        for shift_y in 0..4 {
            for shift_x in 0..4 {
                let x = x + shift_x;
                if self.states[tmp_state][shift_y][shift_x as
usize] != 0 &&
                    (y + shift_y >= game_map.len() ||
                     x < 0 ||
                     x as usize >= game_map[y + shift_y].len() ||
                     game_map[y + shift_y][x as usize] != 0) {
                    return false;
                }
            }
        }
        return true;
    }

    fn test_current_position(&self, game_map: &[Vec<u8>]) -> bool {
        self.test_position(game_map, self.current_state as usize,
self.x, self.y)
    }
```

```
        fn change_position(&mut self, game_map: &[Vec<u8>], new_x:
isize, new_y: usize) -> bool {
            if self.test_position(game_map, self.current_state as
usize, new_x, new_y) == true {
                self.x = new_x as isize;
                self.y = new_y;
                true
            } else {
                false
            }
        }
    }

    struct Tetris {
        game_map: Vec<Vec<u8>>,
        current_level: u32,
        score: u32,
        nb_lines: u32,
        current_piece: Option<Tetrimino>,
    }

    impl Tetris {
        fn new() -> Tetris {
            let mut game_map = Vec::new();
            for _ in 0..16 {
                game_map.push(vec![0, 0, 0, 0, 0, 0, 0, 0, 0, 0]);
            }
            Tetris {
                game_map: game_map,
                current_level: 1,
                score: 0,
                nb_lines: 0,
                current_piece: None,
            }
        }

        fn update_score(&mut self, to_add: u32) {
            self.score += to_add;
        }

        fn increase_level(&mut self) {
            self.current_level += 1;
        }

        fn increase_line(&mut self) {
            self.nb_lines += 1;
            if self.nb_lines > LEVEL_LINES[self.current_level as usize
- 1] {
```

```
                self.increase_level();
            }
        }

    fn check_lines(&mut self) {
        let mut y = 0;
        let mut score_add = 0;

        while y < self.game_map.len() {
            let mut complete = true;

            for x in &self.game_map[y] {
                if *x == 0 {
                    complete = false;
                    break
                }
            }
            if complete == true {
                score_add += self.current_level;
                self.game_map.remove(y);
                y -= 1;
            }
            y += 1;
        }
        if self.game_map.len() == 0 {
            // A "tetris"!
            score_add += 1000;
        }
        self.update_score(score_add);
        while self.game_map.len() < 16 {
            self.increase_line();
            self.game_map.insert(0, vec![0, 0, 0, 0, 0, 0, 0, 0, 0,
0]);
        }
    }

    fn create_new_tetrimino(&self) -> Tetrimino {
        static mut PREV: u8 = 7;
        let mut rand_nb = rand::random::<u8>() % 7;
        if unsafe { PREV } == rand_nb {
            rand_nb = rand::random::<u8>() % 7;
        }
        unsafe { PREV = rand_nb; }
        match rand_nb {
            0 => TetriminoI::new(),
            1 => TetriminoJ::new(),
            2 => TetriminoL::new(),
            3 => TetriminoO::new(),
```

```
                    4 => TetriminoS::new(),
                    5 => TetriminoZ::new(),
                    6 => TetriminoT::new(),
                    _ => unreachable!(),
            }
        }

    fn make_permanent(&mut self) {
        let mut to_add = 0;
        if let Some(ref mut piece) = self.current_piece {
            let mut shift_y = 0;

            while shift_y < piece.states[piece.current_state as
usize].len() &&
                    piece.y + shift_y < self.game_map.len() {
                let mut shift_x = 0;

                while shift_x < piece.states[piece.current_state as
usize]
                    [shift_y].len() &&
                        (piece.x + shift_x as isize) <
self.game_map[piece.y +
                        shift_y].len() as isize {
                    if piece.states[piece.current_state as
usize][shift_y][shift_x]
                        != 0 {
                        let x = piece.x + shift_x as isize;
                        self.game_map[piece.y + shift_y][x as
usize] =
                            piece.states[piece.current_state as
usize][shift_y]
                            [shift_x];
                    }
                    shift_x += 1;
                }
                shift_y += 1;
            }
            to_add += self.current_level;
        }
        self.update_score(to_add);
        self.check_lines();
        self.current_piece = None;
    }
}

fn handle_events(tetris: &mut Tetris, quit: &mut bool, timer: &mut
SystemTime,
                event_pump: &mut sdl2::EventPump) -> bool {
```

```
    let mut make_permanent = false;
    if let Some(ref mut piece) = tetris.current_piece {
        let mut tmp_x = piece.x;
        let mut tmp_y = piece.y;

        for event in event_pump.poll_iter() {
            match event {
                Event::Quit { .. } |
                Event::KeyDown { keycode: Some(Keycode::Escape), ..
} => {
                    *quit = true;
                    break
                }
                Event::KeyDown { keycode: Some(Keycode::Down), .. }
=> {
                    *timer = SystemTime::now();
                    tmp_y += 1;
                }
                Event::KeyDown { keycode: Some(Keycode::Right), ..
} => {
                    tmp_x += 1;
                }
                Event::KeyDown { keycode: Some(Keycode::Left), .. }
=> {
                    tmp_x -= 1;
                }
                Event::KeyDown { keycode: Some(Keycode::Up), .. }
=> {
                    piece.rotate(&tetris.game_map);
                }
                Event::KeyDown { keycode: Some(Keycode::Space), ..
} => {
                    let x = piece.x;
                    let mut y = piece.y;
                    while piece.change_position(&tetris.game_map,
x, y + 1) == true
                    {
                        y += 1;
                    }
                    make_permanent = true;
                }
                _ => {}
            }
        }
        if !make_permanent {
            if piece.change_position(&tetris.game_map, tmp_x,
tmp_y) == false &&
                tmp_y != piece.y {
```

```
                    make_permanent = true;
                }
            }
        }
        if make_permanent {
            tetris.make_permanent();
            *timer = SystemTime::now();
        }
        make_permanent
    }

    fn write_into_file(content: &str, file_name: &str) ->
    io::Result<()> {
        let mut f = File::create(file_name)?;
        f.write_all(content.as_bytes())
    }

    fn read_from_file(file_name: &str) -> io::Result<String> {
        let mut f = File::open(file_name)?;
        let mut content = String::new();
        f.read_to_string(&mut content)?;
        Ok(content)
    }

    fn slice_to_string(slice: &[u32]) -> String {
        slice.iter().map(|highscore|
    highscore.to_string()).collect::<Vec<String>>().join(" ")
    }

    fn save_highscores_and_lines(highscores: &[u32], number_of_lines:
    &[u32]) -> bool {
        let s_highscores = slice_to_string(highscores);
        let s_number_of_lines = slice_to_string(number_of_lines);
        write_into_file(&format!("{}\n{}\n", s_highscores,
    s_number_of_lines), HIGHSCORE_FILE).is_ok()
    }

    fn line_to_slice(line: &str) -> Vec<u32> {
        line.split(" ").filter_map(|nb|
    nb.parse::<u32>().ok()).collect()
    }

    fn load_highscores_and_lines() -> Option<(Vec<u32>, Vec<u32>)> {
        if let Ok(content) = read_from_file(HIGHSCORE_FILE) {
            let mut lines = content.splitn(2, "\n").map(|line|
    line_to_slice(line)).collect::<Vec<_>>();
            if lines.len() == 2 {
                let (lines_sent, highscores) = (lines.pop().unwrap(),
```

```
lines.pop().unwrap());
            Some((highscores, lines_sent))
        } else {
            None
        }
    } else {
        None
    }
}

fn update_vec(v: &mut Vec<u32>, value: u32) -> bool {
    if v.len() < NB_HIGHSCORES {
        v.push(value);
        true
    } else {
        for entry in v.iter_mut() {
            if value > *entry {
                *entry = value;
                return true;
            }
        }
        false
    }
}

fn print_game_information(tetris: &Tetris) {
    let mut new_highest_highscore = true;
    let mut new_highest_lines_sent = true;
    if let Some((mut highscores, mut lines_sent)) =
load_highscores_and_lines() {
        new_highest_highscore = update_vec(&mut highscores,
tetris.score);
        new_highest_lines_sent = update_vec(&mut lines_sent,
tetris.nb_lines);
        if new_highest_highscore || new_highest_lines_sent {
            save_highscores_and_lines(&highscores, &lines_sent);
        }
    } else {
        save_highscores_and_lines(&[tetris.score],
&[tetris.nb_lines]);
    }
    println!("Game over...");
    println!("Score:          {}{}",
            tetris.score,
            if new_highest_highscore { " [NEW HIGHSCORE]"} else {
"" });
    println!("Number of lines: {}{}",
            tetris.nb_lines,
```

```rust
                    if new_highest_lines_sent { " [NEW HIGHSCORE]"} else {
"" });
    println!("Current level:   {}", tetris.current_level);
}

fn is_time_over(tetris: &Tetris, timer: &SystemTime) -> bool {
    match timer.elapsed() {
        Ok(elapsed) => {
            let millis = elapsed.as_secs() as u32 * 1000 +
elapsed.subsec_nanos() /
                1_000_000;
            millis > LEVEL_TIMES[tetris.current_level as usize - 1]
        }
        Err(_) => false,
    }
}

fn main() {
    let sdl_context = sdl2::init().expect("SDL initialization
failed");
    let mut tetris = Tetris::new();
    let mut timer = SystemTime::now();

    let mut event_pump = sdl_context.event_pump().expect("Failed to
get SDL event
     pump");

    let grid_x = (width - TETRIS_HEIGHT as u32 * 10) as i32 / 2;
    let grid_y = (height - TETRIS_HEIGHT as u32 * 16) as i32 / 2;

    loop {
        if is_time_over(&tetris, &timer) {
            let mut make_permanent = false;
            if let Some(ref mut piece) = tetris.current_piece {
                let x = piece.x;
                let y = piece.y + 1;
                make_permanent =
!piece.change_position(&tetris.game_map, x, y);
            }
            if make_permanent {
                tetris.make_permanent();
            }
            timer = SystemTime::now();
        }

        // We need to draw the tetris "grid" in here.

        if tetris.current_piece.is_none() {
```

```
        let current_piece = tetris.create_new_tetrimino();
        if
!current_piece.test_current_position(&tetris.game_map) {
            print_game_information(&tetris);
            break
        }
        tetris.current_piece = Some(current_piece);
    }
    let mut quit = false;
    if !handle_events(&mut tetris, &mut quit, &mut timer, &mut
event_pump) {
        if let Some(ref mut piece) = tetris.current_piece {
            // We need to draw our current tetrimino in here.
        }
    }
    if quit {
        print_game_information(&tetris);
        break
    }

    // We need to draw the game map in here.

    sleep(Duration::new(0, 1_000_000_000u32 / 60));
    }
}
```

Summary

Phew! That was quite the chapter! But now, all the game's mechanisms are here so adding the last remaining parts (such as the drawing) will be a piece of cake.

Once again, be sure to understand this chapter before starting to read the next one.

4

Adding All Game Mechanisms

In the previous chapters, Chapter 1, *Basics of Rust*, Chapter 2, *Starting with SDL*, and Chapter 3, *Events and Basic Game Mechanisms*, we wrote all the mechanisms that we needed. The only missing parts are the UI rendering and the font management. In short, the easy parts So in this chapter, we'll add the drawing of the game and some fonts handling as well.

Let's go!

Getting started with game mechanisms

Let's start with the UI rendering first and then add the font management in order to display the game information in real time.

Rendering UI

With the current code base, very few changes are required in order to be able to have a fully working Tetris.

Rendering initialization

For now, the `main` function is very small. First, let's add the following lines at the top of the function:

```
let sdl_context = sdl2::init().expect("SDL initialization
    failed");
let video_subsystem = sdl_context.video().expect("Couldn't get
    SDL video subsystem");
let width = 600;
let height = 800;
```

No need for explanations, we've already explained everything in the previous chapters, so let's continue.

Just after the following lines:

```
let sdl_context = sdl2::init().expect("SDL initialization
    failed");
let mut tetris = Tetris::new();
let mut timer = SystemTime::now();

let mut event_pump = sdl_context.event_pump().expect("Failed to
    get SDL event pump");

let grid_x = (width - TETRIS_HEIGHT as u32 * 10) as i32 / 2;
let grid_y = (height - TETRIS_HEIGHT as u32 * 16) as i32 / 2;
```

Let's add the following ones:

```
let window = video_subsystem.window("Tetris", width, height)
    .position_centered() // to put it in the middle of the screen
    .build() // to create the window
    .expect("Failed to create window");

let mut canvas = window.into_canvas()
    .target_texture()
    .present_vsync() // To enable v-sync.
    .build()
    .expect("Couldn't get window's canvas");

let texture_creator: TextureCreator<_> = canvas.texture_creator();

let grid = create_texture_rect(&mut canvas,
    &texture_creator,
    0, 0, 0,
    TETRIS_HEIGHT as u32 * 10,
```

```
        TETRIS_HEIGHT as u32 * 16).expect("Failed to create
            a texture");

    let border = create_texture_rect(&mut canvas,
        &texture_creator,
        255, 255, 255,
        TETRIS_HEIGHT as u32 * 10 + 20,
        TETRIS_HEIGHT as u32 * 16 + 20).expect("Failed to create
            a texture");

macro_rules! texture {
    ($r:expr, $g:expr, $b:expr) => (
        create_texture_rect(&mut canvas,
            &texture_creator,
            $r, $g, $b,
            TETRIS_HEIGHT as u32,
            TETRIS_HEIGHT as u32).unwrap()
    )
}

    let textures = [texture!(255, 69, 69), texture!(255, 220, 69),
        texture!(237, 150, 37),texture!(171, 99, 237), texture!(77, 149,
        239), texture!(39, 218, 225), texture!(45, 216, 47)];
```

There's even a macro in the middle, so yes, a few explanations are required!

```
    let window = video_subsystem.window("Tetris", width, height)
        .position_centered()
        .build()
        .expect("Failed to create window");

    let mut canvas = window.into_canvas()
        .target_texture()
        .present_vsync()
        .build()
        .expect("Couldn't get window's canvas");

    let texture_creator: TextureCreator<_> = canvas.texture_creator();
```

We've already seen all this, so we'll just go very quickly through each:

1. We create the window.
2. We initialize the area where we'll draw.
3. We initialize the texture engine.

The two next calls are more interesting and are the start of the actual UI rendering:

```
let grid = create_texture_rect(&mut canvas,
    &texture_creator,
    0, 0, 0,
    TETRIS_HEIGHT as u32 * 10,
    TETRIS_HEIGHT as u32 * 16).expect("Failed to create a texture");

let border = create_texture_rect(&mut canvas,
    &texture_creator,
    255, 255, 255,
    TETRIS_HEIGHT as u32 * 10 + 20,
    TETRIS_HEIGHT as u32 * 16 + 20).expect("Failed to create a
texture");
```

They both call a function defined in Chapter 2, *Starting with SDL*. grid is where we'll draw the tetriminoes and border to represent the borders of the game area. The first one is black, whereas the other one is white. The following is a screenshot of what they'll look like:

Figure 4.1

So now let's write down the code to load more easily:

```
macro_rules! texture {
  ($r:expr, $g:expr, $b:expr) => (
    create_texture_rect(&mut canvas,
      &texture_creator,
      $r, $g, $b,
      TETRIS_HEIGHT as u32,
      TETRIS_HEIGHT as u32).unwrap()
  )
}
```

We already introduced macros in `Chapter 1`, *Basics of Rust*, so we will assume you'll understand pretty easily what this one is doing. (It calls the `create_texture_rect` function with $r, $g, and $b being the color we want the texture to be.)

```
let textures = [texture!(255, 69, 69), texture!(255, 220, 69),
    texture!(237, 150, 37), texture!(171, 99, 237), texture!(77, 149,
    239), texture!(39, 218, 225), texture!(45, 216, 47)];
```

In here, we create the textures for our tetriminoes blocks. So seven textures for seven types of tetrimino blocks.

We initialized everything we needed for the rendering. So now, let's render!

Rendering

Still in the `main` function, but this time we're going into the main loop (no wordplay!). Just after the `is_time_over` if condition, let's add:

```
canvas.set_draw_color(Color::RGB(255, 0, 0));
canvas.clear();
canvas.copy(&border,
    None,
    Rect::new((width - TETRIS_HEIGHT as u32 * 10) as i32 / 2 - 10,
    (height - TETRIS_HEIGHT as u32 * 16) as i32 / 2 - 10,
    TETRIS_HEIGHT as u32 * 10 + 20, TETRIS_HEIGHT as u32 * 16 + 20))
    .expect("Couldn't copy texture into window");
    canvas.copy(&grid,
    None,
    Rect::new((width - TETRIS_HEIGHT as u32 * 10) as i32 / 2,
    (height - TETRIS_HEIGHT as u32 * 16) as i32 / 2,
    TETRIS_HEIGHT as u32 * 10, TETRIS_HEIGHT as u32 * 16))
    .expect("Couldn't copy texture into window");
```

If we want to change the background depending on the player's actual level, we can just change the first line. No sweat.

About the following formulas:

```
Rect::new((width - TETRIS_HEIGHT as u32 * 10) as i32 / 2 - 10,
    (height - TETRIS_HEIGHT as u32 * 16) as i32 / 2 - 10,
    TETRIS_HEIGHT as u32 * 10 + 20, TETRIS_HEIGHT as u32 * 16 + 20)
```

I think a small explanation might come in handy here. As you certainly remember, `Rect::new` takes the four following arguments:

- *x* position
- *y* position
- width
- height

For the first two, we center our game map. For example, for the *x* position, we need to first compute how much width it'll take (so a width of 10 tetriminoes):

```
TETRIS_HEIGHT as u32 * 10
```

Then we subtract this from the total width:

```
width - TETRIS_HEIGHT as u32 * 10
```

What remains is what isn't the game map. So if we use it as *x* position, the game map will be fully on the left. Not pretty. Luckily, centering is quite easy, we just have to divide this result by 2, which is shown as follows:

```
(width - TETRIS_HEIGHT as u32 * 10) as i32 / 2
```

And here we go! Now, about the subtraction of 10; it's because of the borders. It has a width of 10, so we need to subtract it as well to be *really* centered:

```
(width - TETRIS_HEIGHT as u32 * 10) as i32 / 2 - 10
```

Not very complicated, but it can be hard to read the first time. The same goes for the height, so we won't make the same explanations twice. Time to speak about the width and height computation! I think that you already got it from the previous explanations, but just in case:

```
TETRIS_HEIGHT as u32 * 10
```

A `Tetris` has a width of ten blocks. Therefore, our game map must have the same as well.

```
TETRIS_HEIGHT as u32 * 10 + 20
```

We've now added the width of the total borders as well (since there is a border on each side and a border has a width of 10 pixels, `10 * 2 = 20`).

The same goes for the height.

Once you get how these formulas work, you'll get how all the others are working as well.

Since we've drawn the game environment, it's time to draw the tetriminoes. First, let's draw the current one! In order to do this, we need to update the `for` loop inside the `handle_events` condition:

```
if !handle_events(&mut tetris, &mut quit, &mut timer, &mut
    event_pump) {
    if let Some(ref mut piece) = tetris.current_piece {
        for (line_nb, line) in piece.states[piece.current_state
            as usize].iter().enumerate() {
            for (case_nb, case) in line.iter().enumerate() {
                if *case == 0 {
                    continue
                }
                // The new part is here:
                canvas.copy(&textures[*case as usize - 1],
                    None,
                    Rect::new(grid_x + (piece.x + case_nb as isize) as
                        i32 * TETRIS_HEIGHT as i32, grid_y + (piece.y +
                        line_nb) as i32 * TETRIS_HEIGHT as i32, TETRIS_HEIGHT
                        as u32, TETRIS_HEIGHT as u32))
                        .expect("Couldn't copy texture into window");
            }
        }
    }
}
```

For each block of the current tetrimino, we paste a texture corresponding to its ID. From the explanations of the preceding formulas, we can suppose it's not necessary to go back on those *new* ones.

With this, only the last part is remaining; drawing all the other tetriminoes blocks:

```
for (line_nb, line) in tetris.game_map.iter().enumerate() {
    for (case_nb, case) in line.iter().enumerate() {
        if *case == 0 {
            continue
        }
        canvas.copy(&textures[*case as usize - 1],
            None, Rect::new(grid_x + case_nb as i32 * TETRIS_HEIGHT
            as i32, grid_y + line_nb as i32 * TETRIS_HEIGHT as i32,
            TETRIS_HEIGHT as u32, TETRIS_HEIGHT as u32))
            .expect("Couldn't copy texture into window");
    }
}
canvas.present();
```

In this code, we iterate over a block of each line of the game map and paste the corresponding texture, if the game map's *occupied*.

Once done, we apply all the changes to the display, with:

```
canvas.present();
```

With this, our `Tetris` is now complete! You can now play by launching the command:

```
cargo run --release
```

The `--release` is for starting the program in non-debug mode.

The full code of the `main` function is now the following:

```
fn main() {
    let sdl_context = sdl2::init().expect("SDL initialization failed");
    let video_subsystem = sdl_context.video().expect("Couldn't get
        SDL video subsystem");
    let width = 600;
    let height = 800;
    let mut timer = SystemTime::now();
    let mut event_pump = sdl_context.event_pump().expect("Failed to get
        SDL event pump");

    let grid_x = (width - TETRIS_HEIGHT as u32 * 10) as i32 / 2;
    let grid_y = (height - TETRIS_HEIGHT as u32 * 16) as i32 / 2;
    let mut tetris = Tetris::new();

    let window = video_subsystem.window("Tetris", width, height)
                            .position_centered()
                            .build()
```

```
                              .expect("Failed to create window");

let mut canvas = window.into_canvas()
                    .target_texture()
                    .present_vsync()
                    .build()
                    .expect("Couldn't get window's canvas");

let texture_creator: TextureCreator<_> = canvas.texture_creator();

let grid = create_texture_rect(&mut canvas,
        &texture_creator,
        0, 0, 0,
        TETRIS_HEIGHT as u32 * 10,
        TETRIS_HEIGHT as u32 * 16).expect("Failed to create
          a texture");

let border = create_texture_rect(&mut canvas,
        &texture_creator,
        255, 255, 255,
        TETRIS_HEIGHT as u32 * 10 + 20,
        TETRIS_HEIGHT as u32 * 16 + 20).expect("Failed to create
          a texture");

macro_rules! texture {
  ($r:expr, $g:expr, $b:expr) => (
      create_texture_rect(&mut canvas,
                          &texture_creator,
                          $r, $g, $b,
                          TETRIS_HEIGHT as u32,
                          TETRIS_HEIGHT as u32).unwrap()
  )
}

let textures = [texture!(255, 69, 69), texture!(255, 220, 69),
    texture!(237, 150, 37), texture!(171, 99, 237),
    texture!(77, 149, 239), texture!(39, 218, 225),
    texture!(45, 216, 47)];

loop {
  if is_time_over(&tetris, &timer) {
    let mut make_permanent = false;
    if let Some(ref mut piece) = tetris.current_piece {
      let x = piece.x;
      let y = piece.y + 1;
      make_permanent = !piece.change_position(&tetris.game_map,
          x, y);
    }
```

```
      if make_permanent {
        tetris.make_permanent();
      }
      timer = SystemTime::now();
    }

    canvas.set_draw_color(Color::RGB(255, 0, 0));
    canvas.clear();

    canvas.copy(&border,
        None,
        Rect::new((width - TETRIS_HEIGHT as u32 * 10) as i32 / 2 - 10,
        (height - TETRIS_HEIGHT as u32 * 16) as i32 / 2 - 10,
        TETRIS_HEIGHT as u32 * 10 + 20, TETRIS_HEIGHT as u32 * 16 + 20))
        .expect("Couldn't copy texture into window");
    canvas.copy(&grid,
        None,
        Rect::new((width - TETRIS_HEIGHT as u32 * 10) as i32 / 2,
        (height - TETRIS_HEIGHT as u32 * 16) as i32 / 2,
        TETRIS_HEIGHT as u32 * 10, TETRIS_HEIGHT as u32 * 16))
        .expect("Couldn't copy texture into window");


    if tetris.current_piece.is_none() {
        let current_piece = tetris.create_new_tetrimino();
        if !current_piece.test_current_position(&tetris.game_map) {
            print_game_information(&tetris);
            break
        }
        tetris.current_piece = Some(current_piece);
    }
    let mut quit = false;
    if !handle_events(&mut tetris, &mut quit, &mut timer,
        &mut event_pump) {
     if let Some(ref mut piece) = tetris.current_piece {
        for (line_nb, line) in piece.states[piece.current_state
            as usize].iter().enumerate() {
          for (case_nb, case) in line.iter().enumerate() {
            if *case == 0 {
              continue
            }
            canvas.copy(&textures[*case as usize - 1],
                None,
                Rect::new(grid_x + (piece.x + case_nb as isize)
                  as i32 * TETRIS_HEIGHT as i32,
                grid_y + (piece.y + line_nb) as i32 * TETRIS_HEIGHT
                  as i32,
                  TETRIS_HEIGHT as u32, TETRIS_HEIGHT as u32))
```

```
                    .expect("Couldn't copy texture into window");
            }
        }
    }
}
if quit {
  print_game_information(&tetris);
    break
}

for (line_nb, line) in tetris.game_map.iter().enumerate() {
    for (case_nb, case) in line.iter().enumerate() {
        if *case == 0 {
            continue
        }
        canvas.copy(&textures[*case as usize - 1],
            None,
            Rect::new(grid_x + case_nb as i32 * TETRIS_HEIGHT as i32,
            grid_y + line_nb as i32 * TETRIS_HEIGHT as i32,
            TETRIS_HEIGHT as u32, TETRIS_HEIGHT as u32))
            .expect("Couldn't copy texture into window");
    }
}
canvas.present();

sleep(Duration::new(0, 1_000_000_000u32 / 60));
  }
}
```

And here is an example of the current output of this code:

Figure 4.2

It's now working, but what about displaying the game information, such as the current score, level, or the number of lines sent?

Playing with fonts

To display these pieces of information, we'll need to use fonts. No additional external dependencies are required, however, we'll need to use a feature, so we need to update our `Cargo.toml`:

```
[features]
default = ["sdl2/ttf"]
```

By default, the `sdl2` crate doesn't provide the `ttf` module, you need to enable it by adding the `ttf` feature to the compilation process. That's what we did by saying to `cargo`: *by default, I want the* `ttf` *feature of the* `sdl2` *crate enabled.* You can try with and without it to see the difference, after adding this new context initialization:

```
let ttf_context = sdl2::ttf::init().expect("SDL TTF initialization
    failed");
```

 If you get a missing library compilation error, it means you didn't install the corresponding library. To fix this issue, you need to install it through your favorite package manager.

Install on OS X

Run the following command:

```
brew install sdl2_ttf
```

Install on Linux

Run the following command (depending on your package manager, of course):

```
sudo apt-get install libsdl2-ttf-dev
```

Other system/package manager

You can download the library at `https://www.libsdl.org/projects/SDL_ttf/`.

Follow the instructions and install it on your system, then just run the projects. If no errors appear, then it means you installed it correctly.

Time to start the real thing!

Loading font

Before going any further, we actually need a font. I chose **Lucida console**, but pick the one you prefer, it doesn't really matter. Once downloaded, put it in the `assets` folder as well. Now, time to actually load the font:

```
let font = ttf_context.load_font("assets/lucida.ttf", 128).expect("
    Couldn't load the font");
```

Note that if you want to apply a style to your font (such as bold, italic, strikethrough, or underline), that's the object on which you need to apply it. Here is an example:

```
font.set_style(sdl2::ttf::STYLE_BOLD);
```

Now, two steps are remaining to be able to actually display text:

1. Render the text.
2. Create a texture from it.

Let's write a function in order to do so:

```
fn create_texture_from_text<'a>(texture_creator: &'a
    TextureCreator<WindowContext>,
    font: &sdl2::ttf::Font,
    text: &str,
    r: u8, g: u8, b: u8,
    ) -> Option<Texture<'a>> {
      if let Ok(surface) = font.render(text)
        .blended(Color::RGB(r, g, b)) {
        texture_creator.create_texture_from_surface(&surface).ok()
      } else {
          None
      }
    }
```

Looks a lot like `create_texture_rect`, right?

Why not test it? Let's call the function and paste the texture onto the screen to see:

```
let rendered_text = create_texture_from_text(&texture_creator,
    &font, "test", 255, 255, 255).expect("Cannot render text");
canvas.copy(&rendered_text, None, Some(Rect::new(width as i32 -
    40, 0, 40, 30)))
.expect("Couldn't copy text");
```

And it looks like this:

Figure 4.3

For the texture rectangle, I use the following rule: one character is a block of 10 x 30 pixels. So in this example, since `test` has 4 letters, we need a block of 40 x 30 pixels. Let's write a function to make this easier:

```
fn get_rect_from_text(text: &str, x: i32, y: i32) -> Option<Rect> {
    Some(Rect::new(x, y, text.len() as u32 * 20, 30))
}
```

Ok, so now is the time to render the game information and write a new function to do it:

```
fn display_game_information<'a>(tetris: &Tetris,
    canvas: &mut Canvas<Window>,
    texture_creator: &'a TextureCreator<WindowContext>,
    font: &sdl2::ttf::Font,
    start_x_point: i32) {
    let score_text = format!("Score: {}", tetris.score);
    let lines_sent_text = format!("Lines sent: {}", tetris.nb_lines);
    let level_text = format!("Level: {}", tetris.current_level);

    let score = create_texture_from_text(&texture_creator, &font,
        &score_text, 255, 255, 255)
        .expect("Cannot render text");
    let lines_sent = create_texture_from_text(&texture_creator, &font,
        &lines_sent_text, 255, 255, 255)
        .expect("Cannot render text");
    let level = create_texture_from_text(&texture_creator, &font,
        &level_text, 255, 255, 255)
        .expect("Cannot render text");
    canvas.copy(&score, None, get_rect_from_text(&score_text,
        start_x_point, 90))
            .expect("Couldn't copy text");
    canvas.copy(&lines_sent, None, get_rect_from_text(&score_text,
        start_x_point, 125))
            .expect("Couldn't copy text");
    canvas.copy(&level, None, get_rect_from_text(&score_text,
        start_x_point, 160))
            .expect("Couldn't copy text");
}
```

And then we call it, as follows:

```
display_game_information(&tetris, &mut canvas, &texture_creator, &font,
    width as i32 - grid_x - 10);
```

And now it looks like this:

Figure 4.4

Wonderful, we have the game information in real time! Isn't it awesome? What? It's ugly and overlaps the game? Let's move the game then! Instead of centering it, we'll give it a fixed x position (which will make our formula way simpler).

First, let's update our `grid_x` variable:

```
let grid_x = 20;
```

Then, let's update so `canvas.copy` calls:

```
canvas.copy(&border,
        None,
        Rect::new(10,
                (height - TETRIS_HEIGHT as u32 * 16) as i32 / 2 - 10,
                TETRIS_HEIGHT as u32 * 10 + 20, TETRIS_HEIGHT as u32
```

```
* 16 + 20))
    .expect("Couldn't copy texture into window");
  canvas.copy(&grid,
    None,
    Rect::new(20,
    (height - TETRIS_HEIGHT as u32 * 16) as i32 / 2,
     TETRIS_HEIGHT as u32 * 10, TETRIS_HEIGHT as u32 * 16))
    .expect("Couldn't copy texture into window");
```

And that's it. You now have a nice Tetris playing:

Figure 4.5

We could improve the display a bit by adding a border around the text, or even display a preview of the next piece, or even add a *ghost*, but I think that, from this point, you can add them easily.

That's it for this Tetris, have fun while playing with the `sdl2`!

Summary

We now have a fully working Tetris. In the last three chapters, we saw how to use the `sdl2` crate, how to add dependencies to Rust projects, how to handle I/O (with files), and how modules were working.

Even if we stop here for this Tetris project, you can continue this project (and it'd be even a good idea to improve yourself in `sdl2`!). A few ideas of missing things you could add:

- Change the background depending on the current level
- Asking the players, once the game is over, if they want to start a new game
- Adding the next tetrimino preview
- Adding a ghost (to see where the tetrimino will fall)
- And so much more. Just have fun while adding new features!

As you can see, a lot of things are possible. Have fun!

5
Creating a Music Player

In previous chapters you created an awesome game, so now let's move on to another exciting topic—desktop applications. We'll use the Rust bindings of the GTK+ library in order to code an MP3 music player. We'll have the opportunity to learn about threads to code the music player itself in the next chapter. But, in this chapter, we'll focus on the graphical interface, how to manage the layout of the interface, and how to manage user events.

We will cover the following topics in this chapter:

- Windows
- Widgets
- Events
- Closures
- Event loops
- Containers

Installing the prerequisite

Since GTK+ is a C library, we'll need to install it first. The Rust bindings use GTK+ version 3, so make sure you do not install the old version 2.

Installing GTK+ on Linux

On Linux, GTK+ can be installed through the package manager of your distribution.

On Ubuntu (or other Debian derivatives):

```
sudo apt-get install libgtk-3-dev
```

Installing GTK+ on Mac

On OSX, you just need to run the following command:

```
brew install gtk+3 gnome-icon-theme
```

Installing GTK+ on Windows

On Windows, you'll need to first download and install MSYS2, which provides a Unix-like environment on Windows. After it is installed, issue the following command in a MSYS2 shell:

```
pacman -S mingw-w64-x86_64-gtk3
```

Creating your first window

Now we're ready to start using GTK+ from Rust. Let's create a new project for our music player:

```
cargo new rusic --bin
```

Add the dependency on the gio and gtk crates in your Cargo.toml file:

```
gio = "^0.3.0"
gtk = "^0.3.0"
```

Replace the content of the `src/main.rs` file with this:

```
extern crate gio;
extern crate gtk;

use std::env;

use gio::{ApplicationExt, ApplicationExtManual, ApplicationFlags};
use gtk::{
    Application,
    ApplicationWindow,
    WidgetExt,
    GtkWindowExt,
};

fn main() {
    let application = Application::new("com.github.rust-by-
      example", ApplicationFlags::empty())
        .expect("Application initialization failed");
    application.connect_startup(|application| {
        let window = ApplicationWindow::new(&application);
        window.set_title("Rusic");
        window.show();
    });
    application.connect_activate(|_| {});
    application.run(&env::args().collect::<Vec<_>>());
}
```

Then, run the application with `cargo run`. You should see a small and empty window:

Figure 5.1

If you saw this window, it means you have installed GTK+ correctly.

Let's explain this code in smaller chunks:

```
extern crate gio;
extern crate gtk;
```

As usual, when using an external crate, we need to declare it.

Then, we import the types and modules we'll use from the standard library, gio, and gtk:

```
use std::env;

use gio::{ApplicationExt, ApplicationExtManual, ApplicationFlags};
use gtk::{
    Application,
    ApplicationWindow,
    WidgetExt,
    GtkWindowExt,
};
```

After that, we start the main function:

```
fn main() {
    let application = Application::new("com.github.rust-by-
    example",
    ApplicationFlags::empty())
        .expect("Application initialization failed");
```

The first line of this function creates a new gio application. We provide an application ID that can be used to make sure the application is only run once. An Application makes it easier to manage applications and its windows.

Next, we create the window, set its title, and show it to the screen:

```
application.connect_startup(|application| {
    let window = ApplicationWindow::new(&application);
    window.set_title("Rusic");
    window.show();
});
application.connect_activate(|_| {});
```

After creating a new window, we set its title and show it.

Here, we're actually handling an event; the `startup` is a signal that is emitted when the application is registered- so, when it is ready to be used. As you can see in the documentation on GTK+ (`https://developer.gnome.org/gio/stable/GApplication.html#GApplication-startup`), signals are represented by strings. This signal is actually called `startup`, but the Rust method we used to connect this signal is `connect_startup`. So, we need to add `connect_` before the signal name and change the dashes to underscores.

Closure

The argument of this method is somewhat special:

```
|application| {
    let window = ApplicationWindow::new(&application);
    window.set_title("Rusic");
    window.show();
}
```

This is what we call a closure. A closure is a concise way of declaring a function that does not have a name and can capture the environment. Capturing the environment means that it can access the variables from outside the closure, something which is not possible to do with normal functions. The methods to connect a signal will run the function (in this case, a closure) passed as an argument. Here, create the window.

We could have decided to create a normal function, as the following code does:

```
fn startup_handler(application: &Application) {
    let window = ApplicationWindow::new(&application);
    window.set_title("Rusic");
    window.show();
}

// In the main function:

application.connect_startup(startup_handler);
```

But that is less convenient than using a closure. Besides the fact that you might need to import other crates and types, you need to specify the types of the parameters and the return type. Indeed, type inference is available for closures but not for functions. Also, the function must be declared elsewhere, so it can become less readable than using a closure.

The rest of the `main` function is:

```
application.run(&env::args().collect::<Vec<_>>());
}
```

This starts the `gtk` event loop. This is an infinite loop that processes the user events like a button click or a request to close a window. It also manages other things like timeouts and asynchronous, IO-like network requests.

Some event handlers require you to return a value, which is the case for the signal `delete_event` where we need to return `Inhibit(false)`.

Preventing the default behavior of an event

The `Inhibit` type is only a wrapper over the `bool` type. It is used to indicate whether we should stop propagating the event to the default handler or not. To see what this means, let's add an event handler for the window:

```
window.connect_delete_event(|_, _| {
    Inhibit(true)
});
```

If you run it, you'll note that we cannot close the window anymore. That's because we returned `Inhibit(true)` to indicate that we want to prevent the default behavior of the `delete_event` signal, which is to close the window.

Now let's try a slight variant of the previous code:

```
window.connect_delete_event(|_, _| {
    Inhibit(false)
});
```

In this case, we do not prevent the default handler from being run, so the window will be closed.

Creating a toolbar

We'll start our music player by adding a toolbar with the buttons needed for such software:

- Open a file
- Play
- Pause
- Stop
- Previous/next song
- Remove song from playlist

That'll be a good start for our first non-empty window.

First of all, we'll need some additional import statements:

```
use gtk::{
    ContainerExt,
    SeparatorToolItem,
    Toolbar,
    ToolButton,
};
```

Then, we'll declare a constant because we'll use this value elsewhere:

```
const PLAY_STOCK: &str = "gtk-media-play";
```

We'll explain what this is very soon.

We'll now create a toolbar and add it to the window:

```
fn main() {
    // Same code to initialize gtk, create the window.
    application.connect_startup(|application| {
        // ...

        let toolbar = Toolbar::new();
        window.add(&toolbar);
```

Note: Don't call `window.show()` yet, as we'll use another method ahead.

This code is pretty straightforward. The only thing to note is that the `gtk-rs` API requires a reference to values in most cases; in this case, we send a reference to the toolbar as a parameter to the `add()` method.

You'll see this `add()` method called literally everywhere. It allows you to add a widget to another. A widget is a component (visual or not) of a user interface. It can be a button, a menu, a separator, but it can also be an invisible component such as a box allowing you to place the widgets horizontally. We'll talk about containers like `gtk::Box` and how to lay out our widgets later in this chapter.

Let's add a button to this toolbar:

```
let open_button = ToolButton::new_from_stock("gtk-open");
toolbar.add(&open_button);
```

This creates a toolbar button and adds it to the toolbar.

Stock item

Instead of using the usual `new()` constructor, we decided to use the `new_from_stock()` one here. This takes a string as an argument. This string is an identifier for the item that represents a built-in menu or toolbar item, such as `Open` or `Save`. These items have an icon and a label that is translated according to the user locale. By using stock items, you can quickly create a beautiful application that will look the same as other applications built with GTK+.

Let's show this window containing the toolbar:

```
        window.show_all();
    });
```

This goes right at the end of the startup event handler. Here, we use `show_all()` instead of only `show()` because we have more widgets to show. Instead of using `show_all()`, we could call `show()` on every single widget, but this can become cumbersome; that's why `show_all()` exists.

If you run this application, you'll see the following window with an open button:

Figure 5.2

Let's add the open buttons we'll need:

```
toolbar.add(&SeparatorToolItem::new());

let previous_button = ToolButton::new_from_stock("gtk-media-previous");
toolbar.add(&previous_button);

let play_button = ToolButton::new_from_stock(PLAY_STOCK);
toolbar.add(&play_button);

let stop_button = ToolButton::new_from_stock("gtk-media-stop");
toolbar.add(&stop_button);
```

```
let next_button = ToolButton::new_from_stock("gtk-media-next");
toolbar.add(&next_button);

toolbar.add(&SeparatorToolItem::new());

let remove_button = ToolButton::new_from_stock("gtk-remove");
toolbar.add(&remove_button);

toolbar.add(&SeparatorToolItem::new());

let quit_button = ToolButton::new_from_stock("gtk-quit");
toolbar.add(&quit_button);
```

This code should go right before the call to `window.show_all()`. `SeparatorToolItem`, which was added several times to separate the buttons logically so that buttons for similar actions are grouped together.

Now we have an application that is starting to look like a music player, as follows:

Figure 5.3

Improving the organization of the application

The `main` function is starting to get bigger, so we'll refactor our code a little to make it easier to update in the upcoming sections and chapters.

First, we'll create a new module called `toolbar`. As a reminder, here's how to do so:

1. Create a new file: `src/toolbar.rs`.
2. Add a statement, `mod toolbar;`, at the top of the file `main.rs`.

This new module `toolbar` will start with the import statement and the `const` declaration:

```
use gtk::{
    ContainerExt,
    SeparatorToolItem,
    Toolbar,
    ToolButton,
};

const PLAY_STOCK: &str = "gtk-media-play";
```

We'll then create a new structure holding all the widgets that compose the toolbar:

```
pub struct MusicToolbar {
    open_button: ToolButton,
    next_button: ToolButton,
    play_button: ToolButton,
    previous_button: ToolButton,
    quit_button: ToolButton,
    remove_button: ToolButton,
    stop_button: ToolButton,
    toolbar: Toolbar,
}
```

We use the `pub` keyword here because we want to be able to use this type from other modules.

Then, we'll create a constructor for this `struct` that will create all the buttons, like we did earlier:

```
impl MusicToolbar {
    pub fn new() -> Self {
        let toolbar = Toolbar::new();

        let open_button = ToolButton::new_from_stock("gtk-open");
        toolbar.add(&open_button);

        // ...

        let quit_button = ToolButton::new_from_stock("gtk-quit");
        toolbar.add(&quit_button);

        MusicToolbar {
            open_button,
            next_button,
            play_button,
            previous_button,
```

```
                    quit_button,
                    remove_button,
                    stop_button,
                    toolbar
                }
            }
        }
```

The only difference with the previous code is that we now return a `struct`
`MusicToolbar`. We'll also add a method in this `impl` to be able to access the
`gtk::Toolbar` widget from the outside:

```
        pub fn toolbar(&self) -> &Toolbar {
            &self.toolbar
        }
```

That's all for now for this `toolbar` module. Let's go back to the `main` module. First, we
need to import our new `MusicToolbar` type:

```
        use toolbar::MusicToolbar;
```

Next, we'll create a structure like we did for our toolbar:

```
        struct App {
            toolbar: MusicToolbar,
            window: ApplicationWindow,
        }
```

And we will also create a constructor for it:

```
        impl App {
            fn new(application: Application) -> Self {
                let window = ApplicationWindow::new(&application);
                window.set_title("Rusic");

                let toolbar = MusicToolbar::new();
                window.add(toolbar.toolbar());

                window.show_all();

                let app = App {
                    toolbar,
                    window,
                };

                app.connect_events();
```

```
                app
        }
    }
```

Here, we created the window as we did before and then created our own `MusicToolbar` structure. We add the wrapped toolbar widget by sending the result of the `toolbar()` method (which returns the `gtk` widget) to the `add()` method.

After that, we used a little trick that enabled us to call a method on the `struct` yet to be created; we first assign the `struct` to a variable, then call the method and return the variable. This method is defined next, within the same `impl` block:

```
fn connect_events(&self) {
}
```

We'll fill in this method in the next chapter.

Adding tool button events

We'll continue by adding event handlers to some of the buttons.

First of all, we'll need new `use` statements:

```
use gtk::{
    ToolButtonExt,
    WidgetExt,
};

use App;
```

We import `ToolButtonExt`, which provides methods to be called on `ToolButton` and `App` from the `main` module, because we'll add a new method to this type:

```
impl App {
    pub fn connect_toolbar_events(&self) {
        let window = self.window.clone();
        self.toolbar.quit_button.connect_clicked(move |_| {
            window.destroy();
        });
    }
}
```

In Rust, it's perfectly valid to declare a method in a module different to where the type was created. Here, we say that clicking the quit button will destroy the window, which will effectively exit the application.

Let's add another event that will toggle the play button image with the pause image:

```
let play_button = self.toolbar.play_button.clone();
self.toolbar.play_button.connect_clicked(move |_| {
    if play_button.get_stock_id() == Some(PLAY_STOCK.to_string()) {
        play_button.set_stock_id(PAUSE_STOCK);
    } else {
        play_button.set_stock_id(PLAY_STOCK);
    }
});
```

This code requires a new constant to be added next to `PLAY_STOCK`:

```
const PAUSE_STOCK: &str = "gtk-media-pause";
```

Let's first look at the body of the closure before looking at the peculiarities of this code. Here, we use a condition to check whether the button is showing the play image—if it is, we switch to the pause stock item. Otherwise, we switch back to the play icon.

But why do we need to clone the button and use this `move` keyword before the closure? Let's try the normal way, that is, how you would do that in most programming languages:

```
self.toolbar.play_button.connect_clicked(|_| {
    if self.toolbar.play_button.get_stock_id() ==
Some(PLAY_STOCK.to_string()) {
        self.toolbar.play_button.set_stock_id(PAUSE_STOCK);
    } else {
        self.toolbar.play_button.set_stock_id(PLAY_STOCK);
    }
});
```

If we do that, we get the following compilation error:

```
error[E0477]: the type `[closure@src/toolbar.rs:79:50: 85:10 self:&&App]`
does not fulfill the required lifetime
  --> src/toolbar.rs:79:34
   |
79 |            self.toolbar.play_button.connect_clicked(|_| {
   |                                     ^^^^^^^^^^^^^^^
   |
   = note: type must satisfy the static lifetime

error[E0495]: cannot infer an appropriate lifetime for capture of `self` by
```

```
closure due to conflicting requirements
  --> src/toolbar.rs:79:50
   |
79 |              self.toolbar.play_button.connect_clicked(|_| {
   |              _____^
80 | |                  if self.toolbar.play_button.get_stock_id() ==
Some(PLAY_STOCK.to_string()) {
81 | |                      self.toolbar.play_button.set_stock_id(PAUSE_STOCK);
82 | |                  } else {
83 | |                      self.toolbar.play_button.set_stock_id(PLAY_STOCK);
84 | |                  }
85 | |              });
   | |_____^
```

And it continues even further to explain why the lifetime cannot be inferred.

Let's look at the signature of the connect_clicked() method to understand what's going on:

```
fn connect_clicked<F: Fn(&Self) + 'static>(&self, f: F) -> u64
```

The Fn(&Self) part means the function requires something that looks like a function that takes a parameter that is a reference to Self (ToolButton in this case). The 'static part is a lifetime annotation.

Lifetime

Lifetime is one of the Rust features that the compiler uses to ensure memory safety. The lifetime specifies the minimum duration an object must live to be used safely. Let's try to do something that is allowed in certain programming languages, but is actually an error to do so:

```
fn get_element_inc(elements: &[i32], index: usize) -> &i32 {
    let element = elements[index] + 1;
    &element
}
```

Here, we try to return a reference from a stack-allocated value. The problem is that this value will be deallocated when the function returns and the caller will try to access this deallocated value. In other programming languages, this code will compile fine and produce (hopefully) a segmentation fault at runtime. But Rust is a safe programming language and refuses to compile such code:

```
error[E0597]: `element` does not live long enough
 --> src/main.rs:3:6
  |
3 |      &element
  |       ^^^^^^^ does not live long enough
4 | }
  | - borrowed value only lives until here
```

The compile noticed that the value `element` will be deallocated at the end of the function; that's what the sentence on the last line means. This is right, because the lifetime of `element` starts from its declaration until the end of the scope where it is declared; here, the scope is the function. Here's an illustration of the lifetime of `element`:

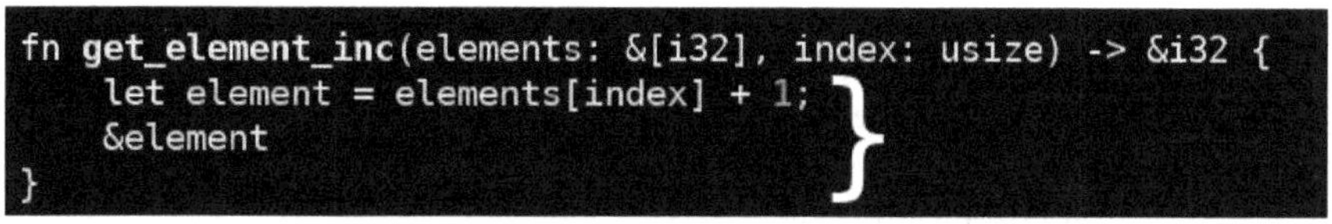

Figure 5.4

But how does the compiler know what the required lifetime is for the returned value? To answer this question, let's add the lifetime annotations that were added by the compiler:

```
fn get_element_inc<'a>(elements: &'a [i32], index: usize) -> &'a
i32 {
    let element = elements[index] + 1;
    &element
}
```

As you can see, the syntax for lifetimes is the same as the one used for labels—`'label`. When we want to specify the lifetimes, we need to declare the lifetime names between angle brackets, in a similar way to how we declare generic types. In this case, we specified that the lifetime of the returned value must be the same as the one from the parameter `elements`.

Let's annotate the code again with lifetimes:

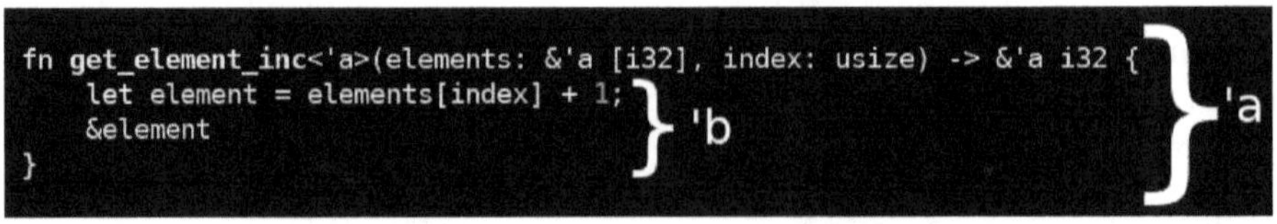

Figure 5.5

Here, we clearly see that the lifetime of the returned value is smaller than the required one; that's why the compiler rejected our code.

In this case, there are two ways to fix this code (without changing the signature). One way to get a value that satisfies the lifetime 'a is to get a reference to a value of the same lifetime; the parameter `elements` also has the lifetime 'a , so we can write the following code:

```
fn get_element<'a>(elements: &'a [i32], index: usize) -> &'a i32 {
    &elements[index]
}
```

Another way is to return a reference to a value of lifetime 'static. This special lifetime is equal to the duration of the program, that is, the value must live until the end of the program. One way to get such a lifetime is to use a literal:

```
fn get_element<'a>(elements: &'a [i32], index: usize) -> &'a i32 {
    &42
}
```

The lifetime 'static satisfies the constraint 'a because 'static lives longer than the latter.

In both of these examples, the lifetime annotations were not required. We didn't have to specify the lifetime in the first place, thanks to a feature called lifetime elision; the compiler can infer what the required lifetimes are in most cases by following these simple rules:

- A different lifetime parameter is assigned to each parameter

- If there's only one parameter that needs a lifetime, that lifetime is assigned to every lifetime in the return value (as for our `get_element` function)
- If there are multiple parameters that need a lifetime, but one of them is for `&self`, the lifetime for `self` is assigned to every lifetime in the return value

Let's go back to the method signature:

```
fn connect_clicked<F: Fn(&Self) + 'static>(&self, f: F) -> u64
```

Here, we notice that the parameter `f` has the `'static` lifetime. We now know that this means that this parameter must live until the end of the program. That's why we cannot use the *normal* version of the closure: because the lifetime of `self` is not `'static`, meaning the `app` will get deallocated when the `main` function ends. To make this work, we cloned the `play_button` variable:

```
let play_button = self.toolbar.play_button.clone();
```

Now we can use this new variable in the closure.

 Note: Take note that cloning a GTK+ widget is really cheap; only a pointer is cloned.

However, trying to do the following will still result in a compilation error:

```
let play_button = self.toolbar.play_button.clone();
self.toolbar.play_button.connect_clicked(|_| {
    if play_button.get_stock_id() == Some(PLAY_STOCK.to_string()) {
        play_button.set_stock_id(PAUSE_STOCK);
    } else {
        play_button.set_stock_id(PLAY_STOCK);
    }
});
```

Here's the error:

```
error[E0373]: closure may outlive the current function, but it borrows
`play_button`, which is owned by the current function
  --> src/toolbar.rs:80:50
   |
80 |          self.toolbar.play_button.connect_clicked(|_| {
   |                                                    ^^^ may outlive
borrowed value `play_button`
81 |             if play_button.get_stock_id() ==
Some(PLAY_STOCK.to_string()) {
```

```
    |
    |                      ----------- `play_button` is borrowed here
    |
    help: to force the closure to take ownership of `play_button` (and any
    other referenced variables), use the `move` keyword
    |
 80 |              self.toolbar.play_button.connect_clicked(move |_| {
    |                                                       ^^^^^^^^
```

The problem with this code is that the closure can (and will) be called after the function returns, but the variable button is declared in the method `connect_toolbar_events()` and will be deallocated when it returns. Again, Rust prevents us from having a segmentation fault by checking if we correctly use references. The compiler talks about ownership; let's look at what that is.

Ownership

In Rust, there's no garbage collector to deallocate the memory when it's not needed anymore. Also, there's no need for the programmer to specify where the memory should be deallocated. But how can this work? The compiler is able to determine when to deallocate the memory thanks to the concept of ownership; only one variable can own a value. By this simple rule, the matter of when to deallocate the value is simple: when the owner goes out of scope, the value is deallocated.

Let's see an example of how deallocation is related to scope:

```
let mut vec = vec!["string".to_string()];
if !vec.is_empty() {
    let element = vec.remove(0);
    // element is deallocated at the end of this scope.
}
```

Here, we remove an element from the vector in a new scope—the block for the condition. The variable `element` will own the value that was removed from the vector (we also say that the value was moved from the vector to the variable `element`). Since it owns the value, the variable is not responsible for deallocating it when it goes out of scope. Thus, after the condition, the value `"string"` will be freed and cannot be accessed anymore.

Let's get back to our code:

```
self.toolbar.play_button.connect_clicked(move |_| {
    if play_button.get_stock_id() == Some(PLAY_STOCK.to_string()) {
        play_button.set_stock_id(PAUSE_STOCK);
    } else {
        play_button.set_stock_id(PLAY_STOCK);
    }
});
```

We added the keyword `move` to closure to indicate that the value must be moved into the closure. (That's actually what the compiler told us to do, if you remember the error message.) By doing so, we satisfy the borrow checker because the value is not borrowed anymore. This was causing a lifetime error, but has now been moved into the closure and will thus live as long as the closure itself.

Don't forget to add the call to this method in the method `App::new()`, right after the call to `connect_events()`:

```
app.connect_events();
app.connect_toolbar_events();
```

Containers

We'll now add other widgets to our window: an image to show the cover of the song that is currently being played and a cursor to see the progression of the music. However, it is not possible to add multiple widgets to a window. To do so, we need to use containers.

Containers are a way to manage how multiple widgets will be shown.

Types of containers

Here are simple non-visual containers:

- `gtk::Box`: disposes widgets either horizontally or vertically
- `gtk::Grid`: disposes widgets in rows and columns, like a table
- `gtk::Fixed`: displays widgets at a very specific position in pixels
- `gtk::Stack`: displays only one widget at a time

All of these widgets, except `gtk::Fixed`, automatically rearrange the widgets when the window is resized. That's why you should avoid using this one.

Here are some more fancy containers:

- `gtk::Notebook`: displays only one widget at a time, but the user can select which one to show by clicking on a tab
- `gtk::Paned`: displays two widgets, separated by a handle that the user can drag to adjust the division between the widgets

The Box container

We'll use a `gtk::Box` to arrange our widgets. First of all, remove the call to `Window::add()` that we added before:

```
window.add(toolbar.toolbar());
```

We remove this call because we'll instead add the toolbar to the box and the box to the window. Let's do that, but before we do, we'll add a couple of new imports:

```
use gtk::{
    Adjustment,
    Image,
    ImageExt,
    Scale,
    ScaleExt,
};
use gtk::Orientation::{Horizontal, Vertical};
```

Then, we create the box:

```
let vbox = gtk::Box::new(Vertical, 0);
window.add(&vbox);
```

(This code goes into the `App::new()` method.)

Here, we fully qualified `gtk::Box` because `Box` is a type from the standard library that is automatically imported. We specified that the orientation of the box is vertical and there's no spacing (0) between the children widgets of the container.

Now we're ready to add widgets to this box:

```
let toolbar = MusicToolbar::new();
vbox.add(toolbar.toolbar());

let cover = Image::new();
cover.set_from_file("cover.jpg");
vbox.add(&cover);
```

We first add our toolbar, then add an image and load a cover from a static file because we haven't yet written the code to extract the cover from an MP3 file.

Let's also add the cursor widget:

```
let adjustment = Adjustment::new(0.0, 0.0, 10.0, 0.0, 0.0, 0.0);
let scale = Scale::new(Horizontal, &adjustment);
scale.set_draw_value(false);
vbox.add(&scale);
```

The cursor widget is named `Scale`. This widget needs an `Adjustment`, which is an object that represents which values the cursor can take, and also contains the current value and the increment values. Again, since we don't know how to fetch the duration of a song from an MP3 file, we hardcode values for `Adjustment`. We also disable the feature to show the actual value of the cursor by calling `set_draw_value(false)`.

If you run the application, you'll see the following:

Figure 5.6

(We can almost hear the music when looking at it.)

To conclude this section, we'll add a few fields to the App structure so that it becomes:

```
struct App {
    adjustment: Adjustment,
    cover: Image,
    toolbar: MusicToolbar,
    window: ApplicationWindow,
}
```

The end of the App constructor is then updated to:

```
impl App {
    fn new(application: Application) -> Self {
        // ...

        window.show_all();

        let app = App {
            adjustment,
            cover,
            toolbar,
            window,
        };

        app.connect_events();
        app.connect_toolbar_events();

        app
    }
}
```

Adding a playlist

We're now ready to add the playlist widget to our music player.

We'll use new crates, so add the following to the main.rs file:

```
extern crate gdk_pixbuf;
extern crate id3;
```

The crate `gdk_pixbuf` will be used to show and manipulate the cover and the `id3` crate to get the metadata from MP3 files.

Also, add the following to `Cargo.toml`:

```
gdk-pixbuf = "^0.3.0"
id3 = "^0.2.0"
```

Next, we'll create a new module to contain this new widget:

```
mod playlist;
```

We'll start this module by adding a bunch of `use` statements:

```
use std::path::Path;

use gdk_pixbuf::{InterpType, Pixbuf, PixbufLoader};
use gtk::{
    CellLayoutExt,
    CellRendererPixbuf,
    CellRendererText,
    ListStore,
    ListStoreExt,
    ListStoreExtManual,
    StaticType,
    ToValue,
    TreeIter,
    TreeModelExt,
    TreeSelectionExt,
    TreeView,
    TreeViewColumn,
    TreeViewColumnExt,
    TreeViewExt,
    Type,
    WidgetExt,
};
use id3::Tag;
```

These will be followed by some constants:

```
const THUMBNAIL_COLUMN: u32 = 0;
const TITLE_COLUMN: u32 = 1;
const ARTIST_COLUMN: u32 = 2;
const ALBUM_COLUMN: u32 = 3;
const GENRE_COLUMN: u32 = 4;
const YEAR_COLUMN: u32 = 5;
const TRACK_COLUMN: u32 = 6;
const PATH_COLUMN: u32 = 7;
```

```
const PIXBUF_COLUMN: u32 = 8;

const IMAGE_SIZE: i32 = 256;
const THUMBNAIL_SIZE: i32 = 64;
```

The `*_COLUMN` constant represents the column we'll show in the playlist. The last one, `PIXBUF_COLUMN`, is a bit special: it will be a hidden column holding the cover of a bigger size so that we can show this image in the `cover` widget we created earlier.

Next, we'll create a new structure to hold the widget and its model:

```
pub struct Playlist {
    model: ListStore,
    treeview: TreeView,
}
```

The MVC pattern

For the list and tree widgets, GTK+ follows the MVC pattern. MVC stands for Model-View-Controller.

Now we can add a constructor for our playlist:

```
impl Playlist {
    pub fn new() -> Self {
        let model = ListStore::new(&[
            Pixbuf::static_type(),
            Type::String,
            Type::String,
            Type::String,
            Type::String,
            Type::String,
            Type::String,
            Type::String,
            Pixbuf::static_type(),
        ]);
        let treeview = TreeView::new_with_model(&model);
        treeview.set_hexpand(true);
        treeview.set_vexpand(true);

        Self::create_columns(&treeview);

        Playlist {
            model,
            treeview,
```

```
            }
          }
        }
```

The `gtk::ListStore` type is a model to represent the data as a list. Its constructor needs the types of the columns; in this case, most of the types are strings for the metadata of the MP3 files, such as the song title and author name. The first `Pixbuf` is for the thumbnail image and the last one is for the bigger image only shown for the music currently playing.

Next, we create a `TreeView`, which will actually be a view for a list since we initialize it with our list model. We then modify the widget so that it expands both vertically and horizontally, meaning that the widget will use as much space as possible. Finally, just before we return the `struct Playlist`, we call the `create_columns()` method, which will create the columns to be shown in this view. Let's see this new method:

```
fn create_columns(treeview: &TreeView) {
    Self::add_pixbuf_column(treeview, THUMBNAIL_COLUMN as i32,
     Visible);
    Self::add_text_column(treeview, "Title", TITLE_COLUMN as i32);
    Self::add_text_column(treeview, "Artist", ARTIST_COLUMN as i32);
    Self::add_text_column(treeview, "Album", ALBUM_COLUMN as i32);
    Self::add_text_column(treeview, "Genre", GENRE_COLUMN as i32);
    Self::add_text_column(treeview, "Year", YEAR_COLUMN as i32);
    Self::add_text_column(treeview, "Track", TRACK_COLUMN as i32);
    Self::add_pixbuf_column(treeview, PIXBUF_COLUMN as i32, Invisible);
}
```

Here, we call two methods to create the different types of columns—we specify the header label and the column number of every column. As for the last parameter of the `add_pixbuf_column()` method, it indicates whether the column is visible or not. This parameter is of a custom type, so let's declare it:

```
use self::Visibility::*;

#[derive(PartialEq)]
enum Visibility {
    Invisible,
    Visible,
}
```

We also added a `use` statement to be able to directly use `Visible` instead of having to fully qualify it (`Visibility::Visible`).

Let's write the `add_text_column()` method:

```
fn add_text_column(treeview: &TreeView, title: &str, column: i32) {
    let view_column = TreeViewColumn::new();
    view_column.set_title(title);
    let cell = CellRendererText::new();
    view_column.set_expand(true);
    view_column.pack_start(&cell, true);
    view_column.add_attribute(&cell, "text", column);
    treeview.append_column(&view_column);
}
```

We start by creating the column itself and setting the label of the header by calling `set_title()`. Then, we create a `CellRenderer`, which indicates how the data from the model should be rendered in the view; here, we only want to show some text, so we chose `CellRendererText`, we set it to take up as much space as possible, and added the renderer to the column. Next comes a very important line:

```
view_column.add_attribute(&cell, "text", column);
```

This line specifies that the view will set the `text` attribute from the data that comes from the model at the specified column.

At the end, we add the column to the view.

Now we'll write a similar function for the `pixbuf`:

```
fn add_pixbuf_column(treeview: &TreeView, column: i32, visibility:
Visibility) {
    let view_column = TreeViewColumn::new();
    if visibility == Visible {
        let cell = CellRendererPixbuf::new();
        view_column.pack_start(&cell, true);
        view_column.add_attribute(&cell, "pixbuf", column);
    }
    treeview.append_column(&view_column);
}
```

Here, we create a new type of renderer (`CellRendererPixbuf`), which will show an image instead of text. This time, we set the `pixbuf` attribute because we want to show an image. The renderer is only created if the column is visible.

Now, all that's left is to write a function to get the actual widget to be able to add the widget in the `main` module:

```
pub fn view(&self) -> &TreeView {
    &self.treeview
}
```

Let's go back to the method `App::new()` and create the playlist:

```
let playlist = Playlist::new();
vbox.add(playlist.view());
```

(Add this code right before creating the `Image`.)

We'll also add a `playlist` attribute in the structure:

```
struct App {
    adjustment: Adjustment,
    cover: Image,
    playlist: Playlist,
    toolbar: MusicToolbar,
    window: Window,
}
```

Also, don't forget to edit the creation of the structure to include the following new field:

```
let app = App {
    adjustment,
    cover,
    playlist,
    toolbar,
    window,
};
```

We're now ready to launch our application again to see an empty playlist:

Figure 5.7

Opening MP3 files

Let's finish this chapter by adding the ability to open MP3 files and show their metadata in the playlist widget we just created.

First of all, we'll remove this line:

```
cover.set_from_file("cover.jpg");
```

This is because the image will be set from the data of the MP3 files we play.

We'll use a new crate, so add this line in the [dependencies] section of your Cargo.toml:

```
gtk-sys = "^0.5.0"
```

Also, add the following line to your main.rs:

```
extern crate gtk_sys;
```

The *-sys crates of the gtk-rs ecosystem are low-level crates, the ones that directly bind to the GTK+ C library. Since they're very low-level and require the use of unsafe code, wrappers have been made; these are crates without the -sys suffix, such as gtk and gdk.

Reference-counting pointer

We'll also change some code before we continue. Since we'll want to share our Playlist widget with different parts of our code, including some event handlers, we need a way of sharing a reference that will last long enough (remember the issue we had with the lifetime). One easy way of doing so is to use a reference-counting pointer type—Rc. So, in our App structure, let's change the playlist field to use an Rc:

```
struct App {
    adjustment: Adjustment,
    cover: Image,
    playlist: Rc<Playlist>,
    toolbar: MusicToolbar,
    window: Window,
}
```

This requires a new import at the top of the main module:

```
use std::rc::Rc;
```

Also, the creation of the playlist needs to be updated:

```
let playlist = Rc::new(Playlist::new());
```

We now wrap the Paylist inside an Rc. We can still use the playlist like before, as long as we're calling immutable methods, that is, methods that take &self but not &mut self. So, the next line is still valid:

```
vbox.add(playlist.view());
```

Before we create the method to add an MP3 file to the playlist, we'll need another method to set the pixbuf values in the model from the MP3 metadata. In the impl Playlist, add the following method:

```
const INTERP_HYPER: InterpType = 3;

fn set_pixbuf(&self, row: &TreeIter, tag: &Tag) {
    if let Some(picture) = tag.pictures().next() {
        let pixbuf_loader = PixbufLoader::new();
        pixbuf_loader.set_size(IMAGE_SIZE, IMAGE_SIZE);
        pixbuf_loader.loader_write(&picture.data).unwrap();
        if let Some(pixbuf) = pixbuf_loader.get_pixbuf() {
            let thumbnail = pixbuf.scale_simple(THUMBNAIL_SIZE,
            THUMBNAIL_SIZE, INTERP_HYPER).unwrap();
            self.model.set_value(row, THUMBNAIL_COLUMN,
            &thumbnail.to_value());
```

```
                    self.model.set_value(row, PIXBUF_COLUMN,
                        &pixbuf.to_value());
                }
                pixbuf_loader.close().unwrap();
            }
        }
```

The type `Tag` represents the metadata of an MP3 file. We get the first picture contained in the file and we load it. If the loading was successful, we resize it to get a thumbnail and then we set the values in the model.

ID3— MP3 metadata

We're now ready to get all the relevant metadata from the MP3 files and add them to the playlist. Let's start the `Playlist::add()` method by fetching the metadata:

```
pub fn add(&self, path: &Path) {
    let filename =
     path.file_stem().unwrap_or_default().to_str().unwrap_or_default();

    let row = self.model.append();

    if let Ok(tag) = Tag::read_from_path(path) {
        let title = tag.title().unwrap_or(filename);
        let artist = tag.artist().unwrap_or("(no artist)");
        let album = tag.album().unwrap_or("(no album)");
        let genre = tag.genre().unwrap_or("(no genre)");
        let year = tag.year().map(|year|
        year.to_string()).unwrap_or("(no
        year)".to_string());
        let track = tag.track().map(|track|
        track.to_string()).unwrap_or("??".to_string());
        let total_tracks = tag.total_tracks().map(|total_tracks|
        total_tracks.to_string()).unwrap_or("??".to_string());
        let track_value = format!("{} / {}", track, total_tracks);
```

We first get the filename without the extension and convert it to a string; we'll show this if there's no song title in the file. Then, we read the metadata from the file and assign a default value such as `"(no artist)"` in case a value is missing by calling `unwrap_or()`, which gets the value from `Option` if or returns the argument if the value is `None`.

Now let's see the rest of the method:

```
                self.set_pixbuf(&row, &tag);

                self.model.set_value(&row, TITLE_COLUMN, &title.to_value());
                self.model.set_value(&row, ARTIST_COLUMN, &artist.to_value());
                self.model.set_value(&row, ALBUM_COLUMN, &album.to_value());
                self.model.set_value(&row, GENRE_COLUMN, &genre.to_value());
                self.model.set_value(&row, YEAR_COLUMN, &year.to_value());
                self.model.set_value(&row, TRACK_COLUMN,
                    &track_value.to_value());
            }
            else {
                self.model.set_value(&row, TITLE_COLUMN, &filename.to_value());
            }

            let path = path.to_str().unwrap_or_default();
            self.model.set_value(&row, PATH_COLUMN, &path.to_value());
        }
```

Here, we create a new row in the model and call the `set_pixbuf()` we created just before. After that, we set the value in the new row. One special value is the path, which will be useful later when we want to play the selected song from the playlist; we'll only need to fetch the path and then play it.

Opening files with a file dialog

There's another function we'll need before we can handle the click event of the open button. We need a function that'll show a file dialog to allow the user to select a file:

```
            use std::path::PathBuf;

            use gtk::{FileChooserAction, FileChooserDialog, FileFilter};

            fn show_open_dialog(parent: &ApplicationWindow) -> Option<PathBuf>
            {
                let mut file = None;
                let dialog = FileChooserDialog::new(Some("Select an MP3 audio
                  file"),
                    Some(parent), FileChooserAction::Open);
                let filter = FileFilter::new();
                filter.add_mime_type("audio/mp3");
                filter.set_name("MP3 audio file");
                dialog.add_filter(&filter);
                dialog.add_button("Cancel", RESPONSE_CANCEL);
```

```
            dialog.add_button("Accept", RESPONSE_ACCEPT);
            let result = dialog.run();
            if result == RESPONSE_ACCEPT {
                file = dialog.get_filename();
            }
            dialog.destroy();
            file
    }
```

This function starts by creating a new file dialog of the type open. Afterwards, it adds a filter to this dialog so that it only shows MP3 files. Then, we add two buttons using some constants that we'll define later. At the moment, we can show the dialog by calling run(); this function blocks until the dialog is closed and returns which button was clicked. After that, we check whether the accept button was clicked to save the filename that was selected by the user and we return that filename.

Here are the constants needed by the previous function:

```
        use gtk_sys::{GTK_RESPONSE_ACCEPT, GTK_RESPONSE_CANCEL};

        const RESPONSE_ACCEPT: i32 = GTK_RESPONSE_ACCEPT as i32;
        const RESPONSE_CANCEL: i32 = GTK_RESPONSE_CANCEL as i32;
```

We're now ready to handle the click event of the open button. Add the following in the method App::connect_toolbar_events():

```
        let parent = self.window.clone();
        let playlist = self.playlist.clone();
        self.toolbar.open_button.connect_clicked(move |_| {
            let file = show_open_dialog(&parent);
            if let Some(file) = file {
                playlist.add(&file);
            }
        });
```

In the event handler, we call the function we just defined and, if a file was selected, we call the add() method of the playlist.

You can now try the application and open an MP3 file. Here's what you'll see:

Figure 5.8

Let's add two more features before we end this chapter. The first one is to remove a song from the playlist.

Deleting a song

We need to add a method to the `Playlist` struct to remove the selected item:

```
pub fn remove_selection(&self) {
    let selection = self.treeview.get_selection();
    if let Some((_, iter)) = selection.get_selected() {
        self.model.remove(&iter);
    }
}
```

This first starts by getting the selection and, if there was one, we remove it from the model. We can now add an event handler for the remove button in the `App::connect_toolbar_events()` method:

```
let playlist = self.playlist.clone();
self.toolbar.remove_button.connect_clicked(move |_| {
    playlist.remove_selection();
});
```

There's nothing new in this code; we simply clone the reference-counted playlist and call a method on it when the button is clicked.

Displaying the cover when playing a song

The other feature to add is to show a bigger cover when we click the play button. We'll start by adding a function to get the image from the selection in the playlist:

```
pub fn pixbuf(&self) -> Option<Pixbuf> {
    let selection = self.treeview.get_selection();
    if let Some((_, iter)) = selection.get_selected() {
        let value = self.model.get_value(&iter, PIXBUF_COLUMN as i32);
        return value.get::<Pixbuf>();
    }
    None
}
```

This method to be added to the `Playlist` structure starts by getting the selection; if there's one, it simply gets the `pixbuf` from the model and returns it. Otherwise, it returns `None`.

We can now write a function that will fetch the cover from the playlist and show the image:

```
use gtk::Image;

use playlist::Playlist;

fn set_cover(cover: &Image, playlist: &Playlist) {
    cover.set_from_pixbuf(playlist.pixbuf().as_ref());
    cover.show();
}
```

Add this function in the `toolbar` module. And, finally, we can call this function from the click event handler of the play button:

```
let playlist = self.playlist.clone();
let cover = self.cover.clone();
self.toolbar.play_button.connect_clicked(move |_| {
    if play_button.get_stock_id() == Some(PLAY_STOCK.to_string()) {
        play_button.set_stock_id(PAUSE_STOCK);
        set_cover(&cover, &playlist);
    } else {
        play_button.set_stock_id(PLAY_STOCK);
    }
});
```

Here's the result after adding a song and clicking play:

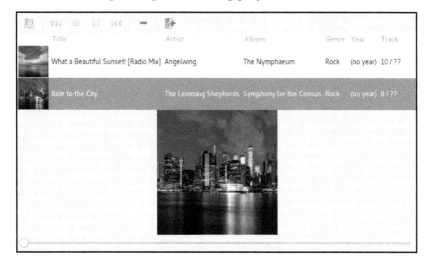

Figure 5.9

Summary

This chapter started by showing you how to install GTK+ on your machine. You then learned how to use `gtk-rs` to create windows, to manage user events like mouse click, to add different types of widgets to your window, to arrange your widgets with containers, and to show beautiful icons with stock items. You also saw how to use complex GTK+ widgets that use the MVC pattern.

You also gained more knowledge of Rust in the areas of closures, lifetimes, and ownerships, which are key concepts in this language.

Finally, you learned how to extract the metadata of an MP3 file by getting the ID3 tags.

In the next chapter, we'll improve the music player so that it can actually play a song.

6
Implementing the Engine of the Music Player

In the previous chapter, we implemented the user interface of the music player, but it is unable to play any music. We'll tackle that challenge in this chapter. We'll create the engine of the music player so that it can play MP3 files. To do this, we'll need to use threads so that playing a song does not freeze the interface, so it will be a good opportunity to learn about concurrency in Rust.

We will cover the following topics in this chapter:

- MP3 decoder
- Threads
- Mutex and Mutex guards
- Send/Sync traits
- RAII
- Thread safety
- Interior mutability

Installing the dependencies

For this chapter, we'll need two libraries: `pulseaudio` and `libmad`.

The former will be used to play the music, while the latter is for decoding MP3 files.

Installing dependencies on Linux

On Linux, these dependencies can be installed through the package manager of your distribution.

On Ubuntu (or other Debian derivatives):

```
sudo apt-get install libmad0-dev libpulse-dev
```

Installing dependencies on Mac

On OSX, the required dependencies can be installed through the system package manager, as follows:

```
brew install libmad pulseaudio
```

Installing dependencies on Windows

On Windows, run the following command in a MSYS2 shell:

```
pacman -S mingw-w64-libmad
```

Think, click the link to download the zip file from this page: `https://www.freedesktop.org/wiki/Software/PulseAudio/Ports/Windows/Support/` (When the book was written, the link for the current version was `http://bosmans.ch/pulseaudio/pulseaudio-1.1.zip`). Then, follow the same instructions as the ones from `Chapter 2`, *Starting with SDL*, to use the library from Rust.

Decoding MP3 files

We'll start this chapter by learning how to decode an MP3 file to a format suitable to be played by the operating system using the `simplemad` crate, a binding for `libmad`.

Adding dependencies

Let's add the following to `Cargo.toml`:

```
crossbeam = "^0.3.0"
pulse-simple = "^1.0.0"
simplemad = "^0.8.1"
```

We also added the `pulse-simple` and `crossbeam` crates because we'll need them later. The former will be used to play the songs with `pulseaudio` and the latter will be used to implement the event loop of the music player engine.

We also need to add the following statements in `main.rs`:

```
extern crate crossbeam;
extern crate pulse_simple;
extern crate simplemad;

mod mp3;
```

In addition to the `extern crate` statements, we have a `mod` statement since we'll create a new module for the MP3 decoder.

Implementing an MP3 decoder

We're now ready to create this new module. Create a new `mp3.rs` file with the following content:

```
use std::io::{Read, Seek, SeekFrom};
use std::time::Duration;

use simplemad;
```

We start this module with some import statements as usual. The important one is simplemad, which will be used to decode the frames of an MP3 file:

```
pub struct Mp3Decoder<R> where R: Read {
    reader: simplemad::Decoder<R>,
    current_frame: simplemad::Frame,
    current_frame_channel: usize,
    current_frame_sample_pos: usize,
    current_time: u64,
}
```

We saw in Chapter 1, *Basics of Rust,* that we can add trait bounds to generic parameters in a function. We can also add them to the generic parameters of a type. Here we see an alternative syntax using a where clause. The previous structure declaration is the same as the following:

```
pub struct Mp3Decoder<R: Read> {
    // ...
}
```

The where clause is useful when we have a lot a generic parameters.

This structure contains information about the current frame and time as well as the decoder itself, which comes from the simplemad crate. This Decoder also requires a generic parameter that implements the Read trait, so we just use our own R parameter since we specified that it must implement this trait.

Before we move on to the constructor of this type, we'll implement a couple of utility functions. Let's start with a function that converts Duration to a number of milliseconds (this function will go in the main.rs file since we'll use it in another module):

```
fn to_millis(duration: Duration) -> u64 {
    duration.as_secs() * 1000 + duration.subsec_nanos() as u64 /
1_000_000
}
```

Here, we simply multiply the number of seconds by 1,000 and divide the number of nanoseconds by 1,000,000. This function requires you to add an import statement for Duration:

```
use std::time::Duration;
```

Next, we'll write a function to check whether a stream of data is an MP3 file:

```
fn is_mp3<R>(mut data: R) -> bool where R: Read + Seek {
    let stream_pos = data.seek(SeekFrom::Current(0)).unwrap();
    let is_mp3 = simplemad::Decoder::decode(data.by_ref()).is_ok();
    data.seek(SeekFrom::Start(stream_pos)).unwrap();
    is_mp3
}
```

To do so, we try to decode the stream and if the result is `Ok`, then the data is an MP3 file. We then go back to the beginning of the file before returning whether it is an MP3 file or not.

The next function we'll need is one to decode the next frame of an MP3 file:

```
fn next_frame<R: Read>(decoder: &mut simplemad::Decoder<R>) ->
simplemad::Frame {
    decoder.filter_map(|f| f.ok()).next()
        .unwrap_or_else(|| {
            simplemad::Frame {
                bit_rate: 0,
                layer: Default::default(),
                mode: Default::default(),
                sample_rate: 44100,
                samples: vec![Vec::new()],
                position: Duration::from_secs(0),
                duration: Duration::from_secs(0),
            }
        })
}
```

Here, we simply get the next frame from the decoder and flatten the `Option<Result<Frame>>` to `Option<Frame>` by calling `and_then(Result::ok)`. If there's no frame, we return a default frame.

Now, let's implement the constructor of our MP3 decoder:

```
impl<R> Mp3Decoder<R> where R: Read + Seek {
    pub fn new(mut data: R) -> Result<Mp3Decoder<R>, R> {
        if !is_mp3(data.by_ref()) {
            return Err(data);
        }

        let mut reader = simplemad::Decoder::decode(data).unwrap();

        let current_frame = next_frame(&mut reader);
        let current_time = to_millis(current_frame.duration);
```

```
Ok(Mp3Decoder {
    reader,
    current_frame,
    current_frame_channel: 0,
    current_frame_sample_pos: 0,
    current_time,
})
    }
}
```

You need to add an import statement at the top of this file to be able to use the to_millis function, which is in the main module:

```
use to_millis;
```

Since the use statements are relative to the root of the crate, we only need to write the function name because this function is at the crate's root.

The constructor first checks whether the stream contains MP3 data, if not, we return an error. Otherwise, we create a Decoder from the simplemad crate. Then, we read the first frame and get its time in milliseconds.

Next, we write two methods to get the current time and the rate of the MP3 file:

```
pub fn current_time(&self) -> u64 {
    self.current_time
}

pub fn samples_rate(&self) -> u32 {
    self.current_frame.sample_rate
}
```

These methods are to be added in the impl Mp3Decoder block. The last method to be added to this structure is a method to compute the duration of a song:

```
pub fn compute_duration(mut data: R) -> Option<Duration> {
    if !is_mp3(data.by_ref()) {
        return None;
    }

    let decoder = simplemad::Decoder::decode_headers(data).unwrap();
    Some(decoder.filter_map(|frame| {
        match frame {
            Ok(frame) => Some(frame.duration),
            Err(_) => None,
        }
    })
})
```

```
        .sum())
    }
```

Here we create an associated function: it first checks whether it is MP3 data. Here, instead of using `Decoder::decode()`, we use `Decoder::decode_headers()` because we only need the frame duration and it is faster to only decode the headers. The `decoder` is an iterator and we call `filter_map()` on it. As you saw in `Chapter 2`, *Starting with SDL*, `filter_map()` transforms and filters the elements of an iterator. Transforming a value is done by returning `Some(new_value)`, while filtering out a value is done by returning `None`. After that, we call `sum()` on the resulting iterator to get the sum of all the durations.

Getting the frame samples

The only remaining feature needed for our MP3 decoder is to be able to iterate over the samples. We'll first write a function to get the next sample:

```
fn next_sample<R: Read>(decoder: &mut Mp3Decoder<R>) -> Option<i16>
{
    if decoder.current_frame.samples[0].len() == 0 {
        return None;
    }

    // getting the sample and converting it from fixed step to i16
    let sample =
decoder.current_frame.samples[decoder.current_frame_channel]
        [decoder.current_frame_sample_pos];
    let sample = sample.to_i32() + (1 << (28 - 16));
    let sample = if sample >= 0x10000000 { 0x10000000 - 1 } else if
sample <=
        -0x10000000 { -0x10000000 } else { sample };
    let sample = sample >> (28 + 1 - 16);
    let sample = sample as i16;

    decoder.current_frame_channel += 1;

    if decoder.current_frame_channel <
decoder.current_frame.samples.len() {
        return Some(sample);
    }

    decoder.current_frame_channel = 0;
    decoder.current_frame_sample_pos += 1;

    if decoder.current_frame_sample_pos <
```

```
        decoder.current_frame.samples[0].len() {
            return Some(sample);
        }

        decoder.current_frame = next_frame(&mut decoder.reader);
        decoder.current_frame_channel = 0;
        decoder.current_frame_sample_pos = 0;
        decoder.current_time +=
    to_millis(decoder.current_frame.duration);

        return Some(sample);
    }
```

This function is doing some bit shifting to get the sample and then fetch the next frame. We're now ready to implement an iterator that will use this function:

```
    impl<R> Iterator for Mp3Decoder<R> where R: Read {
        type Item = i16;

        fn next(&mut self) -> Option<i16> {
            next_sample(self)
        }

        fn size_hint(&self) -> (usize, Option<usize>) {
            (self.current_frame.samples[0].len(), None)
        }
    }
```

As you can see, we can implement our own iterator by implementing the `Iterator` trait. The only required method is `next()`. By implementing this simple method, we get a whole bunch of features because this trait has a lot of default methods. The `type Item` is also required. We implement the `size_hint()` method, even though it is an optional one.

Playing music

With the MP3 decoder done, we're now ready to play some music. We'll create a new module, called player, which we will add at the top of `main.rs`:

```
    mod player;
```

We'll start this module by creating a new `player.rs` file with the following import statements:

```
use std::fs::File;
use std::io::BufReader;
use std::path::{Path, PathBuf};
use std::sync::{Arc, Condvar, Mutex};
use std::thread;

use crossbeam::sync::SegQueue;
use pulse_simple::Playback;

use mp3::Mp3Decoder;
use self::Action::*;
```

We'll also create some constants:

```
const BUFFER_SIZE: usize = 1000;
const DEFAULT_RATE: u32 = 44100;
```

The buffer size is the number of samples we'll decode and play to avoid having slowdowns when playing the song and also to avoid using 100% of the CPU by constantly reading and decoding the data at the same time as playing. The default rate will be used when we cannot find one in the MP3 file.

Event loop

To simplify the development of our playing engine, we'll use the concept of an event loop. Some actions will be sent to the thread playing the music through this event loop. For instance, we will be able to emit a `Load("file.mp3")` event, the thread will decode this MP3 file, and start playing it. Another example of an event is `Stop`, which will stop playing and unload the data.

Let's create an enumeration for the possible actions:

```
enum Action {
    Load(PathBuf),
    Stop,
}
```

We're now ready to create the structure of the event loop:

```
#[derive(Clone)]
struct EventLoop {
    queue: Arc<SegQueue<Action>>,
    playing: Arc<Mutex<bool>>,
}
```

There's a lot of unknown stuff in this structure, so let's break it down.

Atomic reference counting

First of all, we use the `Arc` type. It is similar to the `Rc` type that we used in the previous chapter, in that it is a type providing reference counting. The difference between these two types is that `Arc` uses atomic operations to increment its counter. By being atomic, it is safe to be used by multiple threads while `Rc` cannot be safely used across threads (and the compiler prevents us from trying to do so). The standard library provides these two types so that you can choose the cost you want to pay. If you don't need to share a reference-counted value with multiple threads, choose `Rc` as it is more efficient than `Arc`. If you try to send an `Rc` to another thread, the compiler will trigger an error:

```
error[E0277]: the trait bound `std::rc::Rc<i32>: std::marker::Send` is not
satisfied in `[closure@src/main.rs:6:19: 8:6 rc:std::rc::Rc<i32>]`
  --> src/main.rs:6:5
   |
6  |     thread::spawn(move || {
   |     ^^^^^^^^^^^^^ `std::rc::Rc<i32>` cannot be sent between threads
safely
   |
   = help: within `[closure@src/main.rs:6:19: 8:6 rc:std::rc::Rc<i32>]`, the
trait `std::marker::Send` is not implemented for `std::rc::Rc<i32>`
   = note: required because it appears within the type
`[closure@src/main.rs:6:19: 8:6 rc:std::rc::Rc<i32>]`
   = note: required by `std::thread::spawn`
```

In this case, you'll need to switch to an `Arc`. This error will make more sense when we see what the `Send` trait is.

Mutual exclusion

In the `playing` field, the `Arc` contains a `Mutex`. A mutex provides mutual exclusion, meaning that it allows us to lock its inner value (in this case, a `bool`) preventing other threads from manipulating the same value at the same time. It prevents data races, which is a cause of undefined behavior, by preventing concurrent reads and writes on a value.

Send trait

But how can the compiler prevent us from doing data races? This is thanks to the `Send` and `Sync` marker traits. A type that implements the `Send` trait is safe to be sent to another thread. As you may have guessed, `Rc` does not implement `Send`. Since it does not use atomic operations to increment its counter, if two threads were to increment it at the same time, that would be a data race.

Sync trait

Let's discuss the second of these marker traits: `Sync`. A type that implements the `Sync` trait is safe to be shared with multiple threads. An example of a `Sync` type is `Mutex`. It is safe because the only way to get a value from `Mutex` is to lock it, which is mutually exclusive (another thread cannot access the same value at the same time).

Lock-free data structures

The only remaining type to explain is `SegQueue`, from the `crossbeam` crate. This type is a lock-free queue, meaning that it can be used concurrently by multiple threads without a lock. The implementation of lock-free data structures is beyond the scope of this book, but it suffices to say that it uses atomic operations behind the scenes so that we don't need to use a `Mutex` to mutate this value in mutable threads at the same time. We still need to wrap this queue in an `Arc` to be able to share it with multiple threads.

We're using a lock-free data structure because we'll be constantly checking whether there's a new element in this queue while possibly adding new elements to this queue from another thread. If we were to use `Mutex<VecDeque<Action>>`, it would be less efficient because calling `lock()` on `Mutex` waits if the lock is held by another thread.

Let's get back to our event loop. Let's add a constructor for `EventLoop`:

```
impl EventLoop {
    fn new() -> Self {
        EventLoop {
            queue: Arc::new(SegQueue::new()),
            playing: Arc::new(Mutex::new(false)),
        }
    }
}
```

This constructor simply creates the queue and the Boolean wrapped in a `Mutex`.

Before we use it, we'll create a `State` structure that will contain various data shared between the GUI thread and the music player thread, put this code in the `main` module:

```
struct State {
    stopped: bool,
}
```

Also, add a `state` field in the `App` structure:

```
struct App {
    adjustment: Adjustment,
    cover: Image,
    playlist: Rc<Playlist>,
    state: Arc<Mutex<State>>,
    toolbar: MusicToolbar,
    window: Window,
}
```

This requires a new import statement:

```
use std::sync::{Arc, Mutex};
```

Since this value will be shared with another thread, we need to wrap it in `Arc<Mutex>`. Then, in the constructor, create this value and assign it to this new field, while also sending it to the `Playlist` constructor:

```
impl App {
    fn new() -> Self {
        // ...

        let state = Arc::new(Mutex::new(State {
            stopped: true,
        }));
```

```
        let playlist = Rc::new(Playlist::new(state.clone()));

        // ...

        let app = App {
            adjustment,
            cover,
            playlist,
            state,
            toolbar,
            window,
        };

        // ...
    }
}
```

Let's update the `Playlist` constructor:

```
impl Playlist {
    pub(crate) fn new(state: Arc<Mutex<State>>) -> Self {
        let model = ListStore::new(&[
            Pixbuf::static_type(),
            Type::String,
            Type::String,
            Type::String,
            Type::String,
            Type::String,
            Type::String,
            Type::String,
            Pixbuf::static_type(),
        ]);
        let treeview = TreeView::new_with_model(&model);
        treeview.set_hexpand(true);
        treeview.set_vexpand(true);

        Self::create_columns(&treeview);

        Playlist {
            model,
            player: Player::new(state.clone()),
            treeview,
        }
    }
}
```

The structure requires a new field, so let's add it:

```
pub struct Playlist {
    model: ListStore,
    player: Player,
    treeview: TreeView,
}
```

This also needs new import statements:

```
use std::sync::{Arc, Mutex};

use State;
use player::Player;
```

We use the `pub(crate)` syntax to silent an error. Since we're using a private type (`State`) in a public method, the compiler throws an error. This syntax means that the function is public to the other modules of the crate, but other crates cannot access it. Here, we only send the `state` to the `Player` constructor, which we will implement right away.

Playing music

We'll create a new `Player` structure to wrap the event loop. The player will be usable from the main thread to control the music. Here's the structure itself:

```
pub struct Player {
    app_state: Arc<Mutex<super::State>>,
    event_loop: EventLoop,
}
```

And here's the start of its constructor:

```
impl Player {
    pub(crate) fn new(app_state: Arc<Mutex<super::State>>) -> Self
{
        let event_loop = EventLoop::new();

        {
            let app_state = app_state.clone();
            let event_loop = event_loop.clone();
            thread::spawn(move || {
                // ...
            });
        }
```

```
                Player {
                    app_state,
                    event_loop,
                }
            }
        }
```

We start by creating a new event loop. Then, we start a new thread. We used a new scope to avoid having to rename the variables that will be sent to the thread because these variables are used in the initialization of the structure at the end of the constructor. Again, we need to use a `move` closure because we're sending a copy of the event loop and the application state to the thread.

Let's see the first part of the thread's closure:

```
thread::spawn(move || {
    let mut buffer = [[0; 2]; BUFFER_SIZE];
    let mut playback = Playback::new("MP3", "MP3 Playback", None,
    DEFAULT_RATE);
    let mut source = None;
    loop {
        if let Some(action) = event_loop.queue.try_pop() {
            match action {
                Load(path) => {
                    let file = File::open(path).unwrap();
                    source =
Some(Mp3Decoder::new(BufReader::new(file)).unwrap());
                    let rate = source.as_ref().map(|source|
source.samples_rate()).unwrap_or(DEFAULT_RATE);
                    playback = Playback::new("MP3", "MP3 Playback",
                     None, rate);
                    app_state.lock().unwrap().stopped = false;
                },
                Stop => {},
            }
        }
        // ...
    }
});
```

We start by creating a buffer to contain the samples to be played. Then we'll create a `Playback`, which is an object that will allow us to play music on the hardware. We'll also create a `source` variable that will contain an `Mp3Decoder`. We then start an infinite loop and try to get the first element in the queue: if there's an element in the queue, `Some(action)` is returned. That's why we used `if let` to pattern match against the result of this method call. We then match against the action to see which action it is: if it is a `Load` action, we open the file with the specified path and create an `Mp3Decoder` with a buffered reader of this file. We then try to get the sample rate of the song and create a new `Playback` with this rate. We'll handle the `Stop` action later.

Finally, we see our first use of `Mutex`:

```
app_state.lock().unwrap().stopped = false;
```

Let's rewrite it in another way to see what's going on:

```
let mut guard = app_state.lock().unwrap();
guard.stopped = false;
```

We first call `lock()`, which returns a `Result<MutexGuard<T>, PoisonError<MutexGuard<T>>>`.

Mutex guard

A mutex guard is a scoped lock: this means that the mutex will be automatically unlocked when going out of scope. It is a nice way to ensure that users will use a `Mutex` and won't forget to unlock it.

RAII

But how does it work behind the scene? Rust uses the idiom of **Resource Acquisition Is Initialization(RAII)** for short. With this idiom, a resource is allocated in the constructor and released in its destructor. In Rust, destructors are implemented by the `Drop` trait. So, to get back to mutex guards, the mutex is unlocked when the destructor of `MutexGuard` is called, so, as in the previous example, when the `guard` variable goes out of scope.

Let's get back to our infinite loop:

```
loop {
    if let Some(action) = event_loop.queue.try_pop() {
        // ...
    } else if *event_loop.playing.lock().unwrap() {
        let mut written = false;
        if let Some(ref mut source) = source {
            let size = iter_to_buffer(source, &mut buffer);
            if size > 0 {
                playback.write(&buffer[..size]);
                written = true;
            }
        }

        if !written {
            app_state.lock().unwrap().stopped = true;
            *event_loop.playing.lock().unwrap() = false;
            source = None;
        }
    }
}
```

Here, we check whether the playing value is true (again using the `lock().unwrap()` trick). We must use a `*` to access the value of a `MutexGuard` because it implements `Deref`. That means we don't have direct access to the underlying value. But since it implements the `Deref` trait, we can access it by dereferencing the guard (with a `*`). We didn't need this trick before because we accessed a field and Rust automatically dereferences fields.

We then create a `written` variable that will be `true` if the player was able to play a sample. If it was unable to play one, this means the song came to an end. In this case, we set the `stopped` value to `true` and `playing` to `false`.

To play the samples, we call `iter_to_buffer`, which will take the value from the decoder (which is an `Iterator`) and write them to the buffer. Afterward, it will write the buffer to the `playback` in order to play the samples on your sound card.

Let's look at this `iter_to_buffer` function:

```
fn iter_to_buffer<I: Iterator<Item=i16>>(iter: &mut I, buffer: &mut
[[i16; 2]; BUFFER_SIZE]) -> usize {
    let mut iter = iter.take(BUFFER_SIZE);
    let mut index = 0;
    while let Some(sample1) = iter.next() {
        if let Some(sample2) = iter.next() {
            buffer[index][0] = sample1;
```

```
                buffer[index][1] = sample2;
            }
            index += 1;
        }
        index
    }
```

We start by taking `BUFFER_SIZE` elements from the iterator and add them to the buffer two at a time (for two channels). We then return the number of elements written to the buffer.

Using the music player

We're now ready to use our music engine. Let's add a couple of new methods to `Playlist`.

Let's start with a method to get the path of the selection:

```
fn selected_path(&self) -> Option<String> {
    let selection = self.treeview.get_selection();
    if let Some((_, iter)) = selection.get_selected() {
        let value = self.model.get_value(&iter, PATH_COLUMN as i32);
        return value.get::<String>();
    }
    None
}
```

We start by getting the selection, then we get the iterator for the selection. From the iterator, we can get the value at the specified column to get the path. We can now add a method to load the selected song:

```
pub fn play(&self) -> bool {
    if let Some(path) = self.selected_path() {
        self.player.load(&path);
        true
    } else {
        false
    }
}
```

If there's a selected song, we load it into the music engine. We return true if a song was loaded.

We'll now use this method in the event handler of the play button:

```
impl App {
    pub fn connect_toolbar_events(&self) {
        // ...

        let playlist = self.playlist.clone();
        let play_image = self.toolbar.play_image.clone();
        let cover = self.cover.clone();
        let state = self.state.clone();
        self.toolbar.play_button.connect_clicked(move |_| {
            if state.lock().unwrap().stopped {
                if playlist.play() {
                    set_image_icon(&play_image, PAUSE_ICON);
                    set_cover(&cover, &playlist);
                }
            } else {
                set_image_icon(&play_image, PLAY_ICON);
            }
        });

        // ...
    }
}
```

We create a copy of the `playlist` variable because it is moved into the closure. In the latter, we then call the `play()` method we created just before. We only change the image of the button and show the cover if a song starts to play.

You can now try the music player: open an MP3 file, click play, and you should hear the song. Let's continue to develop the software since many features are missing.

Pausing and resuming the song

We'll start by adding a field indicating whether the player is in pause or not. This field will be changed by methods such as `play` or `resume`. However, remember that our `Playlist` is wrapped in an `Rc`, so that we can use it in different places, namely in the event handlers. Also, remember that Rust forbids mutation when there are mutable references to a value. How can we update this field while still using a reference-counted pointer? One way is to use interior mutability.

Interior mutability

Interior mutability is a concept granting mutable an inner value of a type with an immutable reference. Is this safe to do? Yes, totally, because we need to respect certain constraints. One way to have interior mutability is to wrap our `Cell` type. The constraint of this type is that if we want to get the value from the `Cell` from an immutable reference, the wrapped type must implement the `Copy` trait. We'll see the other commonly-used type for interior mutability later in this chapter. For now, let's add our field to the `Player` type:

```
use std::cell::Cell;

pub struct Player {
    app_state: Arc<Mutex<super::State>>,
    event_loop: EventLoop,
    paused: Cell<bool>,
}
```

Let's update the construction of the structure:

```
impl Player {
    pub(crate) fn new(app_state: Arc<Mutex<super::State>>) -> Self
    {
        // ...

        Player {
            app_state,
            event_loop,
            paused: Cell::new(false),
        }
    }
}
```

We can now add a method to check whether the music is paused or not:

```
pub fn is_paused(&self) -> bool {
    self.paused.get()
}
```

Here, we need to call `Cell::get()` to get a copy of the inner value. We can now add methods to play and resume the song:

```
pub fn pause(&self) {
    self.paused.set(true);
    self.app_state.lock().unwrap().stopped = true;
    self.set_playing(false);
}

pub fn resume(&self) {
    self.paused.set(false);
    self.app_state.lock().unwrap().stopped = false;
    self.set_playing(true);
}
```

Here we see that we need to call `Cell::set()` to update the value of the `Cell`. We can do that even though we only have an immutable reference and, once again, it is completely safe to do so. Then, we update the `stopped` field of the application state because the click handler for the play button will use it to decide whether we want to play or resume the music. We also call `set_playing()` to indicate to the player thread whether it needs to continue playing the song or not. This method is defined as such:

```
fn set_playing(&self, playing: bool) {
    *self.event_loop.playing.lock().unwrap() = playing;
    let (ref lock, ref condition_variable) =
  *self.event_loop.condition_variable;
    let mut started = lock.lock().unwrap();
    *started = playing;
    if playing {
        condition_variable.notify_one();
    }
}
```

It sets the `playing` variable and then notifies the player thread to wake it up if `playing` is `true`.

We'll now add a `pause()` method to our `Playlist` type that will call the `pause()` method we've just created when the user clicks pause:

```
pub fn pause(&self) {
    self.player.pause();
}
```

To use it, we'll update the click handler of the play button:

```
self.toolbar.play_button.connect_clicked(move |_| {
    if state.lock().unwrap().stopped {
        if playlist.play() {
            set_image_icon(&play_image, PAUSE_ICON);
            set_cover(&cover, &playlist);
        }
    } else {
        playlist.pause();
        set_image_icon(&play_image, PLAY_ICON);
    }
});
```

We added the call to pause in the `else` block.

We now want to update the `play()` method. Now that we can pause the song, there are two new cases to consider for this method:

- If the song is playing, we want to pause it.
- If the song is paused, we either want to resume the song if the same one is selected or start a new song if another one is selected.

That's why we need a new field in our `Playlist` structure:

```
pub struct Playlist {
    current_song: RefCell<Option<String>>,
    model: ListStore,
    player: Player,
    treeview: TreeView,
}
```

We added a field that will contain the path of the currently playing song. Here we wrap the `Option<String>` into a `RefCell`, which is another way to have interior mutability. We cannot use a `Cell` because the `String` type does not implement the `Copy` trait. So, what is the difference between `Cell` and `RefCell`? The `RefCell` type will check the borrowing rules at runtime: if two borrows happen at the same time, it will panic. We have to be careful when using `RefCell`: it is better to have compile-time borrowing checks if possible. But when using `gtk-rs`, we sometimes need to share a mutable state with the event handler and the best way to do that is to use `RefCell`.

In the next chapter, we'll learn how to use a library that abstracts the state management so that you won't need to use RefCell and you won't get any panic at runtime. This requires a new import statement:

```
use std::cell::RefCell;
```

We need to update the constructor to initialize this value:

```
impl Playlist {
    pub(crate) fn new(state: Arc<Mutex<State>>) -> Self {
        // ...

        Playlist {
            current_song: RefCell::new(None),
            model,
            player: Player::new(state.clone()),
            treeview,
        }
    }
}
```

There's one more method to add in Playlist before we move on to update the play() method:

```
pub fn path(&self) -> Option<String> {
    self.current_song.borrow().clone()
}
```

This method returns a copy of the current song path. Since the field is a RefCell, we need to call borrow() in order to get access to the inner value. This method returns the equivalent of an immutable reference. We'll soon see how to have a mutable reference. As with Mutex, the borrow is lexical and the borrow will end at the end of the function. We're now ready to update the play() method:

```
pub fn play(&self) -> bool {
    if let Some(path) = self.selected_path() {
        if self.player.is_paused() && Some(&path) ==
         self.path().as_ref() {
            self.player.resume();
        } else {
            self.player.load(&path);
            *self.current_song.borrow_mut() = Some(path.into());
        }
        true
    } else {
        false
```

```
        }
    }
```

We call `resume()` if the song was paused and if the selected path is the same as the currently playing song path. If this condition is `false`, we load the specified path and save this path in our field. To do so, we call `borrow_mut()` to get a mutable reference. Once again, we need to prefix the expression with `*` so that `DerefMut::deref_mut()` gets called. Run the project and you'll see that you can pause and resume the song.

Let's now add a way to stop the song. We'll start by adding a method to the `Player`, as usual:

```
pub fn stop(&self) {
    self.paused.set(false);
    self.app_state.lock().unwrap().stopped = true;
    self.emit(Stop);
    self.set_playing(false);
}
```

We first set the `paused` field to `false` so that the playlist won't try to resume the song the next time the play button is clicked. We then set the `stopped` field to `true`, this will cause the next click of this button to play the song instead of trying to pause it. We then emit the `Stop` action to the event loop and indicate to the engine thread that it should not play music anymore.

The `emit` method is very simple:

```
fn emit(&self, action: Action) {
    self.event_loop.queue.push(action);
}
```

It simply pushes the `action` in the queue of the event loop.

Let's now handle this `Stop` event:

```
Stop => {
    source = None;
},
```

We only reset the source to `None` because we won't need it anymore.

Then, we're ready to add a `stop()` method to the `Playlist`:

```
pub fn stop(&self) {
    *self.current_song.borrow_mut() = None;
    self.player.stop();
}
```

We first reset the `current_song` field to `None` in such a way that the next call to `play()` won't attempt to resume the song. We then call the `stop()` method we created earlier.

We're now ready to use this new method by creating a new event handler for the stop button, add this code to the `connect_toolbar_events()` method:

```
let playlist = self.playlist.clone();
let play_image = self.toolbar.play_image.clone();
let cover = self.cover.clone();
self.toolbar.stop_button.connect_clicked(move |_| {
    playlist.stop();
    cover.hide();
    set_image_icon(&play_image, PLAY_ICON);
});
```

So, when we click stop, we call the `Playlist::stop()` method in order to stop playing the music. We also hide the cover and set back the play button to show the play icon. You can now try again in the music player to see this new feature in action.

Now let's add the actions for the two remaining buttons: previous and next.

We first need to create a new method in the `Playlist`:

```
pub fn next(&self) -> bool {
    let selection = self.treeview.get_selection();
    let next_iter =
        if let Some((_, iter)) = selection.get_selected() {
            if !self.model.iter_next(&iter) {
                return false;
            }
            Some(iter)
        }
        else {
            self.model.get_iter_first()
        };
    if let Some(ref iter) = next_iter {
        selection.select_iter(iter);
        self.play();
```

```
        }
        next_iter.is_some()
    }
```

We start by getting the selection. Then we check whether an item is selected: in this case, we try to get the item after the selection. Otherwise, we get the first item on the list. Then, if we were able to get an item, we select it and start playing the song. We return whether we changed the selection or not.

The `previous()` method is similar:

```
pub fn previous(&self) -> bool {
    let selection = self.treeview.get_selection();
    let previous_iter =
        if let Some((_, iter)) = selection.get_selected() {
            if !self.model.iter_previous(&iter) {
                return false;
            }
            Some(iter)
        }
        else {
            self.model.iter_nth_child(None, max(0,
             self.model.iter_n_children(None)
             - 1))
        };
    if let Some(ref iter) = previous_iter {
        selection.select_iter(iter);
        self.play();
    }
    previous_iter.is_some()
}
```

However, there's no `get_iter_last()` method, so we get the last element with `iter_nth_child()`.

This requires a new import statement to be added at the top of the file:

```
use std::cmp::max;
```

With these new methods, we're ready to handle the click events for the buttons. Let's start with the next button:

```
let playlist = self.playlist.clone();
let play_image = self.toolbar.play_image.clone();
let cover = self.cover.clone();
self.toolbar.next_button.connect_clicked(move |_| {
    if playlist.next() {
        set_image_icon(&play_image, PAUSE_ICON);
        set_cover(&cover, &playlist);
    }
});
```

We simply call the `next()` method we just created and if a new song was selected, we update the icon of the play button and show the new cover. The previous button handler is exactly the same except that we call `previous()` instead:

```
let playlist = self.playlist.clone();
let play_image = self.toolbar.play_image.clone();
let cover = self.cover.clone();
self.toolbar.previous_button.connect_clicked(move |_| {
    if playlist.previous() {
        set_image_icon(&play_image, PAUSE_ICON);
        set_cover(&cover, &playlist);
    }
});
```

Showing the progression of the song

It would be nice to see the cursor moving when the song plays. Let's tackle this challenge right now.

We'll start by adding a method to our `Player` to get the duration of a song:

```
use std::time::Duration;

pub fn compute_duration<P: AsRef<Path>>(path: P) ->
 Option<Duration> {
    let file = File::open(path).unwrap();
    Mp3Decoder::compute_duration(BufReader::new(file))
}
```

We simply call the `compute_duration()` method we created earlier. Next, we'll modify the `Playlist` to call this function. But before we do so, we'll modify the `State` type from the `main` module to include additional information:

```
use std::collections::HashMap;

struct State {
    current_time: u64,
    durations: HashMap<String, u64>,
    stopped: bool,
}
```

We added a `current_time` field, which will contain how much time elapsed since the song started playing. We also store the duration of the songs in a `HashMap` so that we only compute it once for each path. We now need to update the initialization of the `State` in the `App` constructor:

```
let current_time = 0;
let durations = HashMap::new();
let state = Arc::new(Mutex::new(State {
    current_time,
    durations,
    stopped: true,
}));
```

Let's go back to the `Playlist`. It will now contain the `State` in its structure:

```
pub struct Playlist {
    current_song: RefCell<Option<String>>,
    model: ListStore,
    player: Player,
    state: Arc<Mutex<State>>,
    treeview: TreeView,
}
```

This should be reflected in its constructor:

```
Playlist {
    current_song: RefCell::new(None),
    model,
    player: Player::new(state.clone()),
    state,
    treeview,
}
```

Here, the `state` field was added. We'll now add a method that will compute the duration in another thread:

```
use std::thread;
use to_millis;

fn compute_duration(&self, path: &Path) {
    let state = self.state.clone();
    let path = path.to_string_lossy().to_string();
    thread::spawn(move || {
        if let Some(duration) = Player::compute_duration(&path)
        {
            let mut state = state.lock().unwrap();
            state.durations.insert(path, to_millis(duration));
        }
    });
}
```

In the thread's closure, we compute the duration and when it's done, we lock the state to insert the duration in the `HashMap`. We compute the duration in another thread because it can take time and we don't want to block the user interface during this computation. We now call this method in `Playlist::add()`:

```
pub fn add(&self, path: &Path) {
    self.compute_duration(path);

    // ...
}
```

We'll update the `Adjustment` so that its upper value is `0.0` in the beginning:

```
let adjustment = Adjustment::new(0.0, 0.0, 0.0, 0.0, 0.0, 0.0);
```

This is to avoid seeing the cursor moving too quickly when the duration is not yet computed.

Finally, we'll add the code to update the UI in the `App::connect_events()` method:

```
use gtk::{AdjustmentExt, Continue};
use toolbar::{set_image_icon, PAUSE_ICON, PLAY_ICON};

fn connect_events(&self) {
    let playlist = self.playlist.clone();
    let adjustment = self.adjustment.clone();
    let state = self.state.clone();
    let play_image = self.toolbar.play_image.clone();
    gtk::timeout_add(100, move || {
        let state = state.lock().unwrap();
        if let Some(path) = playlist.path() {
            if let Some(&duration) = state.durations.get(&path)
            {
                adjustment.set_upper(duration as f64);
            }
        }
        if state.stopped {
            set_image_icon(&play_image, PLAY_ICON);
        } else {
            set_image_icon(&play_image, PAUSE_ICON);
        }
        adjustment.set_value(state.current_time as f64);
        Continue(true)
    });
}
```

The `gtk::timeout_add()` method will be run every 100 milliseconds as long as its closure returns `Continue(false)`. This closure starts by checking whether the duration is in the HashMap, and sets the upper value of the cursor as this duration. If the value is not in the HashMap, it means it wasn't computed yet. After that, we check whether the `stopped` field is true, that means the song ended and the engine thread is no longer playing it. In this case, we want to show the play icon. If the song is still playing, we show the pause icon. Finally, we set the current value of the cursor from the `current_time` field.

The cursor will now move automatically as the song plays. Here's how the player looks now:

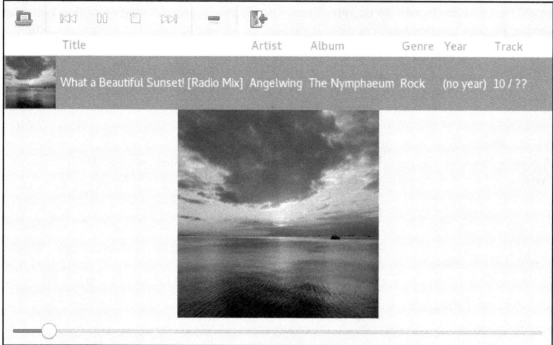

Figure 6.1

Improving CPU usage

One issue you may have noticed is that when no song is playing, the software will use 100% of the CPU. This is because of the infinite loop in the music engine thread. It will do nothing except loop when the song is paused or when there's no song to play. Let's now fix this issue.

Condition variable

What we want to do is to make the thread sleep when it has nothing to do. We also want to be able to wake the thread up from the main thread. This is exactly what condition variables are for. So, let's add one to our engine. We'll start by adding a `condition_variable` field to the `EventLoop`:

```
struct EventLoop {
    condition_variable: Arc<(Mutex<bool>, Condvar)>,
    queue: Arc<SegQueue<Action>>,
    playing: Arc<Mutex<bool>>,
}
```

A condition variable is usually used together with a Boolean value (wrapped in a `Mutex`). We need to rewrite the constructor of `EventLoop` to initialize this new field:

```
impl EventLoop {
    fn new() -> Self {
        EventLoop {
            condition_variable: Arc::new((Mutex::new(false),
Condvar::new())),
            queue: Arc::new(SegQueue::new()),
            playing: Arc::new(Mutex::new(false)),
        }
    }
}
```

Next, we need to block the thread when it has nothing to do. Here's the start of the new code of the thread in `Player::new()`:

```
{
    let app_state = app_state.clone();
    let event_loop = event_loop.clone();
    let condition_variable = event_loop.condition_variable.clone();
    thread::spawn(move || {
        let block = || {
            let (ref lock, ref condition_variable) =
              *condition_variable;
            let mut started = lock.lock().unwrap();
            *started = false;
            while !*started {
                started =
                  condition_variable.wait(started).unwrap();
            }
        };
```

We create a copy of the condition variable and we move this copy into the thread. Then, in the beginning of the closure, we lock the Boolean value associated with the condition variable to set it to `false`. Afterward, we loop: while this value is `false`, we block the current thread. We created a closure instead of a normal function because normal functions cannot capture values. The following code is the same as before:

```
let mut buffer = [[0; 2]; BUFFER_SIZE];
let mut playback = Playback::new("MP3", "MP3 Playback", None,
 DEFAULT_RATE);
let mut source = None;
loop {
    if let Some(action) = event_loop.queue.try_pop() {
        match action {
            Load(path) => {
                let file = File::open(path).unwrap();
                source =
 Some(Mp3Decoder::new(BufReader::new(file)).unwrap());
                let rate = source.as_ref().map(|source|
                 source.samples_rate()).unwrap_or(DEFAULT_RATE);
                playback = Playback::new("MP3", "MP3 Playback",
                 None, rate);
                app_state.lock().unwrap().stopped = false;
            },
            Stop => {
                source = None;
            },
        }
    } else if *event_loop.playing.lock().unwrap() {
        let mut written = false;
        if let Some(ref mut source) = source {
            let size = iter_to_buffer(source, &mut buffer);
            if size > 0 {
                app_state.lock().unwrap().current_time =
                 source.current_time();
                playback.write(&buffer[..size]);
                written = true;
            }
        }
```

But the rest of the closure is a bit different:

```
            if !written {
                app_state.lock().unwrap().stopped = true;
                *event_loop.playing.lock().unwrap() = false;
                source = None;
                block();
            }
        } else {
            block();
        }
    }
});
}
```

If the player was unable to play song (that is, the song came into an end), we call the closure to block the thread. We also block the thread if the player is paused. With the condition variable, the software stopped using 100% CPU.

Showing the song's current time

Currently, we only display the progression of the song. The user has no way to know the duration and for how many seconds the song has been playing. Let's fix that by adding labels that will show the current time and the duration.

We'll need two new import statements in the `main` module:

```
use gtk::{Label, LabelExt};
```

We'll also add two `label` in our `App` structure:

```
struct App {
    adjustment: Adjustment,
    cover: Image,
    current_time_label: Label,
    duration_label: Label,
    playlist: Rc<Playlist>,
    state: Arc<Mutex<State>>,
    toolbar: MusicToolbar,
    window: Window,
}
```

One `label` for the current time and the other for the duration. Since we want to show the different `label` on the right of the cursor, we'll create a horizontal box, this code should be added in `App::new()`:

```
let hbox = gtk::Box::new(Horizontal, 10);
vbox.add(&hbox);

let adjustment = Adjustment::new(0.0, 0.0, 10.0, 0.0, 0.0, 0.0);
let scale = Scale::new(Horizontal, &adjustment);
scale.set_draw_value(false);
scale.set_hexpand(true);
hbox.add(&scale);
```

The `Scale` widget is now added to `hbox` instead of `vbox`. And we call `set_hexpand()` so that the widget takes as much horizontal space as possible.

We're now ready to create our `label`'s:

```
let current_time_label = Label::new(None);
hbox.add(&current_time_label);

let slash_label = Label::new("/");
hbox.add(&slash_label);

let duration_label = Label::new(None);
duration_label.set_margin_right(10);
hbox.add(&duration_label);
```

We create three `label`; the third one being a separator. We set a right margin to the last `label` so that it is not too close to the border of the window. Further, in the `App` constructor, we need to update the initialization of the structure:

```
let app = App {
    adjustment,
    cover,
    current_time_label,
    duration_label,
    playlist,
    state,
    toolbar,
    window,
};
```

We added the two `label`.

We'll create a function to convert a number of milliseconds to a `String` of the `minute:second` format:

```
fn millis_to_minutes(millis: u64) -> String {
    let mut seconds = millis / 1_000;
    let minutes = seconds / 60;
    seconds %= 60;
    format!("{}:{:02}", minutes, seconds)
}
```

In this function, we first convert the milliseconds to seconds by dividing by one thousand. We then get the number of minutes by dividing the seconds by 60. Afterward, we compute the number of seconds that are not included in the minutes with the modulo operation. Finally, we format the minutes and seconds as a `String`. As you can see, we used a special `{:02}` formatter. The 2 means that we want to print the number as two characters, even if the number is less than 0. The 0 after the colon indicates that we want to prepend 0 instead of spaces.

With this new function, we can rewrite the timer to update (in the method `App::connect_events()`) the `label`'s:

```
let current_time_label = self.current_time_label.clone();
let duration_label = self.duration_label.clone();
let playlist = self.playlist.clone();
let adjustment = self.adjustment.clone();
let state = self.state.clone();
let play_image = self.toolbar.play_image.clone();
gtk::timeout_add(100, move || {
    let state = state.lock().unwrap();
    if let Some(path) = playlist.path() {
        if let Some(&duration) = state.durations.get(&path) {
            adjustment.set_upper(duration as f64);
            duration_label.set_text(&millis_to_minutes(duration));
        }
    }
    if state.stopped {
        set_image_icon(&play_image, PLAY_ICON);
    } else {
        set_image_icon(&play_image, PAUSE_ICON);
current_time_label.set_text(&millis_to_minutes(state.current_time))
;
    }
    adjustment.set_value(state.current_time as f64);
    Continue(true)
});
```

Here are the changes from the previous version. When we get the duration, we update the duration `label`. And when the song is not stopped (that is, when it is playing), we update the current time `label`.

We need to change the stop button handler so that it resets the text of these `label`'s.

Finally, we can update the handler:

```
let current_time_label = self.current_time_label.clone();
let duration_label = self.duration_label.clone();
let playlist = self.playlist.clone();
let play_image = self.toolbar.play_image.clone();
let cover = self.cover.clone();
self.toolbar.stop_button.connect_clicked(move |_| {
    current_time_label.set_text("");
    duration_label.set_text("");
    playlist.stop();
    cover.hide();
    set_image_icon(&play_image, PLAY_ICON);
});
```

We clone the widgets to move them into the closure and set the text of the `label`'s to the empty string.

Here's the result you should see when running the application:

Figure 6.2

Loading and saving the playlist

We have the ability to create a playlist in our music player, but we cannot save a playlist to a file in order to be able to load one later. Let's add this feature to our project.

We'll save the playlist in the m3u file format and to handle this format, we'll use the m3u crate. So let's add it to our Cargo.toml file:

```
m3u = "^1.0.0"
```

Add this line to the main module:

```
extern crate m3u;
```

Saving a playlist

We'll start by adding a button to save the playlist. First, we add a field in the MusicToolbar structure for the button:

```
pub struct MusicToolbar {
    open_button: ToolButton,
    next_button: ToolButton,
    play_button: ToolButton,
    pub play_image: Image,
    previous_button: ToolButton,
    quit_button: ToolButton,
    remove_button: ToolButton,
    save_button: ToolButton,
    stop_button: ToolButton,
    toolbar: Toolbar,
}
```

And in the constructor, we'll create this button:

```
impl MusicToolbar {
    pub fn new() -> Self {
        let toolbar = Toolbar::new();

        let (open_button, _) = new_tool_button("document-open");
        toolbar.add(&open_button);

        let (save_button, _) = new_tool_button("document-save");
        toolbar.add(&save_button);

        toolbar.add(&SeparatorToolItem::new());
```

```
        // ...

        let toolbar = MusicToolbar {
            open_button,
            next_button,
            play_button,
            play_image,
            previous_button,
            quit_button,
            remove_button,
            save_button,
            stop_button,
            toolbar
        };

        toolbar
    }
}
```

Next, we'll add a save method in the Playlist structure:

```
use std::fs::File;

use m3u;

    pub fn save(&self, path: &Path) {
        let mut file = File::create(path).unwrap();
        let mut writer = m3u::Writer::new(&mut file);

        let mut write_iter = |iter: &TreeIter| {
            let value = self.model.get_value(&iter, PATH_COLUMN as
                i32);
            let path = value.get::<String>().unwrap();
            writer.write_entry(&m3u::path_entry(path)).unwrap();
        };

        if let Some(iter) = self.model.get_iter_first() {
            write_iter(&iter);
            while self.model.iter_next(&iter) {
                write_iter(&iter);
            }
        }
    }
```

Here, we first create a m3u::Writer with a File that we've created. This writer will be used to write the entry to the file. We create a closure that gets the path from an iterator of our TreeView and writes this path to the file. We chose to create a closure to avoid repeating the code, as we'll need this code twice. After that, we get the first iterator and write its contents before looping until there's no more row in the view.

We're now ready to call this code. First, we'll create a function in the module toolbar to show a save file dialog. It is similar to the show_open_dialog() function we wrote in the previous chapter:

```
fn show_save_dialog(parent: &ApplicationWindow) -> Option<PathBuf>
{
    let mut file = None;
    let dialog = FileChooserDialog::new(Some("Choose a destination
     M3U playlist
    file"), Some(parent), FileChooserAct    ion::Save);
    let filter = FileFilter::new();
    filter.add_mime_type("audio/x-mpegurl");
    filter.set_name("M3U playlist file");
    dialog.set_do_overwrite_confirmation(true);
    dialog.add_filter(&filter);
    dialog.add_button("Cancel", RESPONSE_CANCEL);
    dialog.add_button("Save", RESPONSE_ACCEPT);
    let result = dialog.run();
    if result == RESPONSE_ACCEPT {
        file = dialog.get_filename();
    }
    dialog.destroy();
    file
}
```

Here, we use the FileChooserAction::Save type instead of FileChooserAction::Open. We use a different filter and mime type. We also call set_do_overwrite_confirmation() which is very important. It will ask for a confirmation if the user asks to overwrite a file. The rest of the function is exactly the same as the one to open a file, except that the label of the button is now Save.

We can now use this function in the event handler of the save button:

```
let parent = self.window.clone();
let playlist = self.playlist.clone();
self.toolbar.save_button.connect_clicked(move |_| {
    let file = show_save_dialog(&parent);
    if let Some(file) = file {
        playlist.save(&file);
    }
});
```

We simply call the function `show_save_dialog()` and give the resulting file to the `Playlist::save()` method. You can now try to save a playlist in the application:

Figure 6.3

Loading a playlist

We can save playlists, but still cannot load them. Let's start by adding a `load()` method to `Playlist`:

```
pub fn load(&self, path: &Path) {
    let mut reader = m3u::Reader::open(path).unwrap();
    for entry in reader.entries() {
        if let Ok(m3u::Entry::Path(path)) = entry {
            self.add(&path);
        }
    }
}
```

Here, we create a `m3u::Reader` with the specified path. We loop over the entry and if we were able to retrieve a `m3u::Entry::Path`, we add it to the playlist widget.

We'll now modify the open dialog to allow selecting M3U files:

```
fn show_open_dialog(parent: &ApplicationWindow) -> Option<PathBuf>
{
    let mut file = None;
    let dialog = FileChooserDialog::new(Some("Select an MP3 audio
file"),
    Some(parent), FileChooserAction::Open);

    let mp3_filter = FileFilter::new();
    mp3_filter.add_mime_type("audio/mp3");
    mp3_filter.set_name("MP3 audio file");
    dialog.add_filter(&mp3_filter);

    let m3u_filter = FileFilter::new();
    m3u_filter.add_mime_type("audio/x-mpegurl");
    m3u_filter.set_name("M3U playlist file");
    dialog.add_filter(&m3u_filter);

    dialog.add_button("Cancel", RESPONSE_CANCEL);
    dialog.add_button("Accept", RESPONSE_ACCEPT);
    let result = dialog.run();
    if result == RESPONSE_ACCEPT {
        file = dialog.get_filename();
    }
    dialog.destroy();
    file
}
```

We'll now change the open button event handler to select which action to do depending on the file type:

```
impl App {
    pub fn connect_toolbar_events(&self) {
        let parent = self.window.clone();
        let playlist = self.playlist.clone();
        self.toolbar.open_button.connect_clicked(move |_| {
            let file = show_open_dialog(&parent);
            if let Some(file) = file {
                if let Some(ext) = file.extension() {
                    match ext.to_str().unwrap() {
                        "mp3" => playlist.add(&file),
                        "m3u" => playlist.load(&file),
                        extension => {
                            let dialog =
                              MessageDialog::new(Some(&parent),
                              DialogFlags::empty(), MessageType::Error,
```

```
                                ButtonsType::Ok, &format!("Cannot open
                                    file with
                                    extension .{}", extension));
                        dialog.run();
                        dialog.destroy();
                    },
                }
            }
        }
    });

    // ...
    }
}
```

This requires a couple of new import statements:

```
use gtk::{
    ButtonsType,
    DialogFlags,
    MessageDialog,
    MessageType,
};
```

This new event handler now checks the file extension, if it is mp3, it will call the
Playlist::add() method as we were doing earlier. If it is m3u, we call our new
Playlist::load() method. Otherwise, we show an error message to the user:

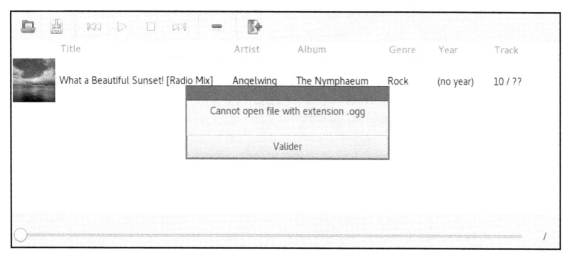

Figure 6.4

You can now try to load a playlist in our music player, don't forget to change the filter in order to see M3U files in the dialog.

Using gstreamer for playback

Implementing an engine to play music was a good exercise to learn about threading. However, for a real program, you could simply use gstreamer for the music playback. So, let's see how to use this library in our music player.

Remove the following dependencies in your Cargo.toml:

```
crossbeam = "^0.3.0"
pulse-simple = "^1.0.0"
simplemad = "^0.8.1"
```

And remove their corresponding extern crate statements. We can also remove the mp3 and player modules as we'll use gstreamer instead. Now, we can add our dependencies for gstreamer:

```
gstreamer = "^0.9.1"
gstreamer-player = "^0.9.0"
```

And add their corresponding extern crate statements:

```
extern crate gstreamer as gst;
extern crate gstreamer_player as gst_player;
```

At the beginning of the main function, we need to initialize gstreamer:

```
gst::init().expect("gstreamer initialization failed");
```

We no longer need our State structure, so we remove it and the state field in the App structure. And now, we can update our playlist module. First, let's add a few use statements:

```
use gst::{ClockTime, ElementExt};
use gst_player;
use gtk::Cast;
```

We remove the `state` field and update the `player` one in the `Playlist` structure:

```
pub struct Playlist {
    current_song: RefCell<Option<String>>,
    model: ListStore,
    player: gst_player::Player,
    treeview: TreeView,
}
```

The `Playlist` constructor does not need the `state` anymore:

```
impl Playlist {
    pub(crate) fn new() -> Self {
        let model = ListStore::new(&[
            Pixbuf::static_type(),
            Type::String,
            Type::String,
            Type::String,
            Type::String,
            Type::String,
            Type::String,
            Type::String,
            Pixbuf::static_type(),
        ]);
        let treeview = TreeView::new_with_model(&model);
        treeview.set_hexpand(true);
        treeview.set_vexpand(true);

        Self::create_columns(&treeview);

        let dispatcher =
gst_player::PlayerGMainContextSignalDispatcher::new(None);
        let player = gst_player::Player::new(None,
        Some(&dispatcher.upcast::
        <gst_player::PlayerSignalDispatcher>
        ())));

        Playlist {
            current_song: RefCell::new(None),
            model,
            player,
            treeview,
        }
    }
}
```

Here, we create the `Player` from the `gstreamer` crate. We need to remove the `compute_duration()` method and all its uses because we'll use `gstreamer` to get the song's duration:

```
pub fn get_duration(&self) -> ClockTime {
    self.player.get_duration()
}

pub fn get_current_time(&self) -> ClockTime {
    self.player.get_position()
}

pub fn is_playing(&self) -> bool {
    self.player.get_pipeline()
        .map(|element| element.get_state(gst::CLOCK_TIME_NONE).1 ==
        gst::State::Playing)
        .unwrap_or(false)
}
```

Here, we create a few methods that will be useful to show the time and when the song is playing. Finally, we can update the `play()` method to use `gstreamer` instead:

```
pub fn play(&self) -> bool {
    if self.selected_path() == self.player.get_uri() {
        self.player.play();
        return false;
    }
    if let Some(path) = self.selected_path() {
        let uri = format!("file://{}", path);
        self.player.set_uri(&uri);
        self.player.play();
        true
    } else {
        false
    }
}
```

Let's go back to the `main` module to update the creation of the playlist:

```
let playlist = Rc::new(Playlist::new());
```

One more thing to update is the code to show the current time:

```
gtk::timeout_add(100, move || {
    let duration = playlist.get_duration();
    adjustment.set_upper(duration.nanoseconds().unwrap_or(0) as
    f64);
    duration_label.set_text(&format!("{:.0}", duration));

    let current_time = playlist.get_current_time();
    if !playlist.is_playing() {
        set_image_icon(&play_image, PLAY_ICON);
    } else {
        set_image_icon(&play_image, PAUSE_ICON);
        current_time_label.set_text(&format!("{:.0}",
          current_time));
    }
    adjustment.set_value(current_time.nanoseconds().unwrap_or(0) as
f64);
    Continue(true)
});
```

We now use the methods we created a bit earlier and some from `gstreamer`.

Finally, we update the `toolbar` module. First, the `play_button` event handler:

```
self.toolbar.play_button.connect_clicked(move |_| {
    if !playlist.is_playing() {
        if playlist.play() {
            set_image_icon(&play_image, PAUSE_ICON);
            set_cover(&cover, &playlist);
        }
    } else {
        playlist.pause();
        set_image_icon(&play_image, PLAY_ICON);
    }
});
```

We now use the `is_playing()` method instead of the `state`. Let's also remove the `FileFilter` from the `show_open_dialog()` function because `gstreamer` supports more formats than just MP3. And to be able to open them, we need to update the `open_button` event handler:

```
self.toolbar.open_button.connect_clicked(move |_| {
    let file = show_open_dialog(&parent);
    if let Some(file) = file {
        if let Some(ext) = file.extension() {
            match ext.to_str().unwrap() {
```

```
            "mp3" | "ogg" => playlist.add(&file),
            "m3u" => playlist.load(&file),
            extension => {
                let dialog = MessageDialog::new(Some(&parent),
                  DialogFlags::empty(), MessageType::Error,
                  ButtonsType::Ok, &format!("Cannot open file
                    with extension . {}", extension));
                dialog.run();
                dialog.destroy();
            },
        }
    }
  }
});
```

Here, we only added the `ogg` format, but you can also add other formats.

Summary

This chapter started by showing you how to decode MP3 data with the `simplemad` crate. You then learned how to write a music engine, this showed you how to use threads and different threading objects such as `Mutex`, lock-free data structures, and condition variables. You also learned how Rust can ensure thread safety. You also saw how to mutable the fields of a value when you have an immutable reference with interior mutability. During the whole chapter, we added the missing features to the music player such as play, pause, previous, and next song.

In the next chapter, we'll improve the modularity of the music player by rewriting it with the `relm` crate.

7
Music Player in a More Rusty Way with Relm

In the previous chapter, we finished our music player. It is completely fine, but using `gtk-rs` directly in Rust can be error-prone. That's why we'll rewrite our music player using `relm`, an idiomatic GUI library for Rust. `Relm` is based on `gtk-rs`, so the application will look the same at the end. However, the code will be cleaner and more declarative.

We will cover the following topics in this chapter:

- Relm
- Relm widgets
- Model-view-controller
- Declarative view
- Message passing

Reasons to use relm instead of gtk-rs directly

As you have seen in the previous chapters, we used concepts that were not really obvious, and doing certain things that would normally be easy to do aren't that easy when using GTK+ with Rust. These are some of the many reasons to use `relm`.

State mutation

It might not be clear from the previous chapter, but we indirectly used Rc<RefCell<T>> to do state mutation. Indeed, our `Playlist` type contains a RefCell<Option<String>> and we wrapped our `Playlist` inside a reference-counted pointer. This was to be able to mutate the state in reaction to events, for instance playing the song when clicking the play button:

```
let playlist = self.playlist.clone();
let play_image = self.toolbar.play_image.clone();
let cover = self.cover.clone();
let state = self.state.clone();
self.toolbar.play_button.connect_clicked(move |_| {
    if state.lock().unwrap().stopped {
        if playlist.play() {
            set_image_icon(&play_image, PAUSE_ICON);
            set_cover(&cover, &playlist);
        }
    } else {
        playlist.pause();
        set_image_icon(&play_image, PLAY_ICON);
    }
});
```

Having to use all these calls to `clone()` is cumbersome and using the RefCell<T> type can lead to issues that are hard to debug in complex applications. The issue with this type is that the borrow checking happens at runtime. For instance, the following application:

```
use std::cell::RefCell;
use std::collections::HashMap;

fn main() {
    let cell = RefCell::new(HashMap::new());
    cell.borrow_mut().insert("one", 1);
    let borrowed_cell = cell.borrow();
    if let Some(key) = borrowed_cell.get("one") {
```

```
        cell.borrow_mut().insert("two", 2);
    }
}
```

Will panic:

```
thread 'main' panicked at 'already borrowed: BorrowMutError',
/checkout/src/libcore/result.rs:906:4
```

Even though it is obvious why it panics in this example (we called `borrow_mut()` when the borrow was still alive in `borrowed_cell`), in more complex applications, it will be harder to understand why the panic happens, especially if we wrap the `RefCell<T>` in an `Rc` and clone it everywhere. This brings us to the second issue with this type: using `Rc<T>` encourages us to clone our data and share it too much which increases the coupling between our modules.

The `relm` crate takes a different approach: widgets owns their data and the different widgets communicate between them using message passing.

Asynchronous user interface

Another common issue when creating user interfaces is that we might want to perform an action that might take time (such as a network request) without freezing the UI. By being based on `tokio`, an asynchronous I/O framework for Rust, `relm` allows you to easily program graphical user interfaces that can perform network requests without freezing the interface itself.

Creating custom widgets

In object-oriented languages, it is very easy to create new widgets and use them like built-in widgets. In this paradigm, you only need to create a new class that inherits from a widget and that's it.

In `Chapter 5`, *Creating a Music Player*, we created custom widgets, such as `Playlist` and `MusicToolbar`, but we needed to create a function to get the real GTK+ widget:

```
pub fn view(&self) -> &TreeView {
    &self.treeview
}
```

An alternative would have been to implement the `Deref` trait:

```
use std::ops::Deref;

impl Deref for Playlist {
    type Target = TreeView;

    fn deref(&self) -> &TreeView {
        &self.treeview
    }
}
```

That implementation would allow us to add the widget to its `parent` like this:

```
parent.add(&*playlist);
```

(Note the leading `*` in front of `playlist` which is the call to `deref()`.)

Instead of adding it in the following way:

```
parent.add(playlist.view());
```

But it is still different than when using normal `gtk` widgets.

`Relm` solves all of these issues. Let's start using this crate.

Creating a window with relm

First of all, we'll use the nightly version of the Rust compiler.

 While using this nightly version is not strictly necessary to use `relm`, it provides a syntax that is a bit nicer using a feature that is only available on this version.

That will be a good opportunity to learn how to install a different version of the compiler. Nightly is the unstable version of Rust; it's a version that is compiled almost every day. Some unstable features of Rust are only available on nightly. But, don't worry, we'll also see how to use `relm` on the stable version of Rust.

Installing Rust nightly

With `rustup`, the tool we installed in Chapter 1, *Basics of Rust*, it is very easy to install nightly:

```
rustup default nightly
```

Running this command will install the nightly version of the tools (`cargo`, `rustc`, and so on). Also, it will switch the corresponding commands to use the nightly version.

If you want to go back to the stable version, issue the following command:

```
rustup default stable
```

The nightly version is updated very frequently, so you might want to update it every week or more often. To do so, you need to run this command:

```
rustup update
```

This will also update the stable version if a new version was released (one stable version is released every 6 weeks).

Now that we are using Rust nightly, we're ready to create a `new` project:

```
cargo new rusic-relm --bin
```

Add the following dependencies in the `Cargo.toml` file:

```
[dependencies]
gtk = "^0.3.0"
gtk-sys = "^0.5.0"
relm = "^0.11.0"
relm-attributes = "^0.11.0"
relm-derive = "^0.11.0"
```

We still need `gtk` because `relm` is based on it. Let's add the corresponding `extern crate` statements:

```
#![feature(proc_macro)]

extern crate gtk;
extern crate gtk_sys;
#[macro_use]
extern crate relm;
extern crate relm_attributes;
#[macro_use]
extern crate relm_derive;
```

`relm` provides some macros, that's why we needed to add `#[macro_use]`. We'll start slowly by creating a simple window with `relm`.

Widget

This crate is centered around the concept of widgets, which are different than the `gtk` widgets. In `relm`, a widget is composed of a view, a model, and a method to update the model in reaction to events. The concept of widget is implemented by a trait in `relm`: the `Widget` trait.

Model

We'll start with an empty model and we'll populate it later in this chapter:

```
pub struct Model {
}
```

As you can see, a model can be a simple structure. It could also be `()` if your widget don't need a model. Actually, it can be any type you want.

Besides the model, a widget needs to know the initial value of its model. To specify what it is, we need to implement the `model()` method of the `Widget` trait:

```
#[widget]
impl Widget for App {
    fn model() -> Model {
        Model {
        }
    }

    // ...
}
```

Here, we use the `#[widget]` attribute provided by the `relm_attributes` crate. Attributes are currently an unstable feature of the language, that's why we use nightly. We'll see in the section about the declarative view why this attribute is needed. So, let's go back to our `model()` model, we only return `Model {}` for now as our model does not contain any data. Other methods are needed for this trait, so this implementation is incomplete for now.

Messages

`Relm` widgets communicate by sending messages to other widgets, but also to themselves. For instance, when the `delete_event` signal is emitted, we can emit the `Quit` message to our widget and take appropriate action when we receive this message. A message is modeled as an `enum` using the custom derive `Msg` that is specific to `relm`:

```
#[derive(Msg)]
pub enum Msg {
    Quit,
}
```

This custom derive is provided by the `relm_derive` crate.

View

Views are created in a declarative way in `relm` as a part of the `Widget` trait:

```
use gtk::{
    GtkWindowExt,
    Inhibit,
    WidgetExt,
};
use relm::Widget;
use relm_attributes::widget;

use self::Msg::*;

#[widget]
impl Widget for App {
    // ...

    view! {
        gtk::Window {
            title: "Rusic",
            delete_event(_, _) => (Quit, Inhibit(false)),
        }
    }
}
```

We first imported some stuff from the `gtk` crate. Then we imported the `Widget` trait from `relm` and the `widget` attribute. Later, we imported the variant of our `enum Msg` because we use it in this code. To declare the view, we use the `view!` macro. This macro is very particular, it is not a macro that is declared as `macro_rules!`, as we saw in Chapter 1, *Basics of Rust*. Instead, it is parsed by the procedural macro implementing the `#[widget]` attribute in order to provide a syntax that is not allowed in Rust.

To declare our view, we first specify the name of the `gtk::Window` widget.

 We cannot import `gtk::Window` to be able to use only `Window` in the declaration of the view.

After that, we use curly brackets and inside them, we specify the properties and events handled by the widget.

Properties

Here, we declare that the `title` property is `"Rusic"`. So we transformed the `set_title()` call from `gtk` to the `title` property, only the part after `set_` is needed. Actually, `relm` will convert the property (`title: "Rusic"`) to the `set_title("Rusic")` call, as we'll see later.

Events

The syntax of the event handler is a bit special:

```
delete_event(_, _) => (Quit, Inhibit(false)),
```

First, we only need to write `delete_event(_, _) =>` instead of `connect_delete_event(move |_, _| { })`. If we needed the arguments of the signal, we could have written the name of an identifier instead of using underscores (_). On the right side of the fat arrow (=>), we specify two things between parentheses and separated by a comma. First, there's `Quit`, which is the message that will be sent to the current widget when the event is emitted. And second is the value to return to the `gtk` callback. Here, we return `Inhibit(false)` to specify that we don't want to prevent the default event handler from running.

Code generation

The code generated by the attribute is a normal Rust method that looks like:

```
fn view(relm: &Relm<Self>, model: Self::Model) -> Self {
    // This method does not actually exist, but relm directly create
a window using the functions from the sys crates.
    let window = gtk::Window::new();
    window.set_title("Rusic");

    window.show();

    connect!(relm, window, connect_delete_event(_, _), return
      (Some(Quit), Inhibit(false)));

    Win {
        model,
        window: window,
    }
}
```

Update function

The only remaining required method of the `Widget` trait is `update()`. In this method, we'll manage the `Quit` message:

```
#[widget]
impl Widget for App {
    fn update(&mut self, event: Msg) {
        match event {
            Quit => gtk::main_quit(),
        }
    }

    // ...
}
```

Here, we specify that when we receive the `Quit` message, we call `gtk::main_quit()`, which is a function similar to `Application::quit()` that we used in `Chapter 5`, *Creating a Music Player*.

It should be noted that the `#[widget]` attribute will also generate the `App` structure that will contain the widgets and the model.

We can finally show this window by calling its `run()` method in the `main` function:

```
fn main() {
    App::run(()).unwrap();
}
```

Later, we'll see why we need to specify `()` as a parameter to `run()`.

Adding child widgets

We saw the basics of how to create a widget with relm. Now, let's continue the creation of our user interface. We'll start by adding the toolbar. Besides specifying properties and signals in the `view!` macro, we can also nest widgets in order to add a child to a container. So, to add `gtk::Box` as a child of our window, we simply need to nest the former inside the latter:

```
view! {
    gtk::Window {
        title: "Rusic",
        delete_event(_, _) => (Quit, Inhibit(false)),
        gtk::Box {
        },
    }
}
```

And to add a toolbar to the `gtk::Box`, we create a new level of nesting:

```
view! {
    gtk::Window {
        title: "Rusic",
        delete_event(_, _) => (Quit, Inhibit(false)),
        gtk::Box {
            orientation: Vertical,
            #[name="toolbar"]
            gtk::Toolbar {
            },
        },
    }
}
```

Here, we can see that there's an attribute: the `#[name]` attribute gives a name to a widget which will allow us to access this widget by the specified identifier, as we'll see later. We'll encounter other attributes in the rest of this chapter.

We'll add an attribute to our model to keep the image to be shown on the play/pause button:

```
use gtk::Image;

pub const PAUSE_ICON: &str = "gtk-media-pause";
pub const PLAY_ICON: &str = "gtk-media-play";

pub struct Model {
    play_image: Image,
}
```

We also added the constants for the name of the images representing the state of the button. We need to update the model() method to specify this new field:

```
fn model() -> Model {
    Model {
        play_image: new_icon(PLAY_ICON),
    }
}
```

This uses the following function to create an image:

```
fn new_icon(icon: &str) -> Image {
    Image::new_from_file(format!("assets/{}.png", icon))
}
```

Let's add the items to the toolbar:

```
use gtk::{
    OrientableExt,
    ToolButtonExt,
};
use gtk::Orientation::Vertical;

view! {
    gtk::Window {
        title: "Rusic",
        delete_event(_, _) => (Quit, Inhibit(false)),
        gtk::Box {
            orientation: Vertical,
            #[name="toolbar"]
            gtk::Toolbar {
                gtk::ToolButton {
                    icon_widget: &new_icon("document-open"),
                    clicked => Open,
                },
                gtk::ToolButton {
```

```
                    icon_widget: &new_icon("document-save"),
                    clicked => Save,
                },
                gtk::SeparatorToolItem {
                },
                gtk::ToolButton {
                    icon_widget: &new_icon("gtk-media-previous"),
                },
                gtk::ToolButton {
                    icon_widget: &self.model.play_image,
                    clicked => PlayPause,
                },
                gtk::ToolButton {
                    icon_widget: &new_icon("gtk-media-stop"),
                    clicked => Stop,
                },
                gtk::ToolButton {
                    icon_widget: &new_icon("gtk-media-next"),
                },
                gtk::SeparatorToolItem {
                },
                gtk::ToolButton {
                    icon_widget: &new_icon("remove"),
                },
                gtk::SeparatorToolItem {
                },
                gtk::ToolButton {
                    icon_widget: &new_icon("gtk-quit"),
                    clicked => Quit,
                },
            },
        },
    }
}
```

Here, there's no new syntax shown. Take note that we can specify function calls as well as model attributes in the value of a property. We needed to put a & before new_icon() because the code is translated as such:

```
tool_button.set_icon_widget(&new_icon("gtk-quit"));
```

And this set_icon_widget() method requires something that can be converted into an Option<&P> where P is a widget. It requires a reference, so we give it a reference.

One-way data binding

Setting a property from a model attribute is very frequent in relm and it actually creates a one-way bond between the model attribute and the property. This means that when the attribute is updated, the widget property will be updated as well. There are some restrictions to this feature though:

- Only an assignment to a model attribute will update the property.
- This assignment *must* be inside an implementation decorated with the `#[widget]` attribute.

These restrictions come from the fact that `relm` only analyzes the source code decorated by this attribute. And it only considers assignment to be an update of the model data.

This might require changing some code. For instance, the following code will not trigger a property update:

```
self.model.string.push_str("string");
```

You can rewrite it this way in order for `relm` to consider it an update:

```
self.model.string += "string";
```

As you can see, `relm` recognizes not only the = assignment, but also the assignments using an operator such as +=.

We used many new messages in the previous code, so let's update our enumeration accordingly:

```
#[derive(Msg)]
pub enum Msg {
    Open,
    PlayPause,
    Quit,
    Save,
    Stop,
}
```

We also need to change the `update()` method to consider these new messages:

```
fn update(&mut self, event: Msg) {
    match event {
        Open => (),
        PlayPause => (),
        Quit => gtk::main_quit(),
        Save => (),
        Stop => (),
    }
}
```

For now, since we only code the interface, we do nothing when we receive these messages.

Post-initialization of the view

If you run the application, you'll see that the images are not shown on the toolbar buttons. This is because of the way `relm` works. When it generates the code, it calls the `show()` method on every widget, instead of `show_all()`. So, the toolbar and the tool buttons will be shown, but not the images, as they are only attributes of the buttons, they are not created using the widget syntax. To solve this issue, we'll call `show_all()` on the toolbar in the `init_view()` method:

```
#[widget]
impl Widget for App {
    fn init_view(&mut self) {
        self.toolbar.show_all();
    }

    // ...
}
```

That's why we gave a name to the toolbar widget earlier: we needed to call a method on this widget here. The `init_view()` method is called after the `view` is created. This is useful to execute some code to customize the view when it's not possible to do so using the `view!` syntax. If you run the application again, you'll see that the buttons now have an image.

Let's now add the cover image widget and the cursor widget. For the image, we'll need to add a new crate to `Cargo.toml`:

```
[dependencies]
gdk-pixbuf = "^0.3.0"
```

Let's also add the corresponding `extern crate` statement:

```
extern crate gdk_pixbuf;
```

We also need new import statements:

```
use gdk_pixbuf::Pixbuf;
use gtk::{
    Adjustment,
    BoxExt,
    ImageExt,
    LabelExt,
    ScaleExt,
};
use gtk::Orientation::Horizontal;
```

Let's add a couple of new fields to our `Model`:

```
pub struct Model {
    adjustment: Adjustment,
    cover_pixbuf: Option<Pixbuf>,
    cover_visible: bool,
    current_duration: u64,
    current_time: u64,
    play_image: Image,
}
```

Most of the new fields existed in the application we developed in the two previous chapters. The `cover_visible` attribute is new, though. We'll use it to know whether we should show the image of the cover. Don't forget to update the initialization of the model:

```
fn model() -> Model {
    Model {
        adjustment: Adjustment::new(0.0, 0.0, 0.0, 0.0, 0.0, 0.0),
        cover_pixbuf: None,
        cover_visible: false,
        current_duration: 0,
        current_time: 0,
        play_image: new_icon(PLAY_ICON),
    }
}
```

We can now add the `Image` after the `Toolbar` widget:

```
gtk::Image {
    from_pixbuf: self.model.cover_pixbuf.as_ref(),
    visible: self.model.cover_visible,
},
```

Here, we call `as_ref()` on the `cover_pixbuf` attribute, because, once again, the method (`set_from_pixbuf()`) requires something that can be converted into a `Option<&Pixbuf>`. We also specify that the `visible` property of the image is bound to the `cover_visible` model attribute. This means that we'll be able to hide the image by setting this attribute to `false`.

We'll then add the cursor, which will give us the following view:

```
view! {
    gtk::Window {
        title: "Rusic",
        delete_event(_, _) => (Quit, Inhibit(false)),
        gtk::Box {
            orientation: Vertical,
            #[name="toolbar"]
            gtk::Toolbar {
                // ...
            },
            gtk::Image {
                from_pixbuf: self.model.cover_pixbuf.as_ref(),
                visible: self.model.cover_visible,
            },
            gtk::Box {
                orientation: Horizontal,
                spacing: 10,
                gtk::Scale(Horizontal, &self.model.adjustment) {
                    draw_value: false,
                    hexpand: true,
                },
                gtk::Label {
                    text:
&millis_to_minutes(self.model.current_time),
                },
                gtk::Label {
                    text: "/",
                },
                gtk::Label {
                    margin_right: 10,
                    text:
&millis_to_minutes(self.model.current_duration),
```

```
                },
              },
            },
          }
        }
```

This require the following method, which we saw in the previous chapter:

```
fn millis_to_minutes(millis: u64) -> String {
    let mut seconds = millis / 1_000;
    let minutes = seconds / 60;
    seconds %= 60;
    format!("{}:{:02}", minutes, seconds)
}
```

We used another way to create a widget:

```
gtk::Scale(Horizontal, &self.model.adjustment) {
    draw_value: false,
    hexpand: true,
}
```

This syntax will call the constructor of the widget, like so:

```
gtk::Scale::new(Horizontal, &self.model.adjustment);
```

We could also have used the traditional syntax to create a widget:

```
use gtk::RangeExt;

gtk::Scale {
    adjustment: &self.model.adjustment,
    orientation: Horizontal,
    draw_value: false,
    hexpand: true,
}
```

These are just two ways to do the same thing.

Dialogs

For the open and save dialog, we'll use the same functions as in the previous chapter:

```
use std::path::PathBuf;

use gtk::{FileChooserAction, FileChooserDialog, FileFilter};
use gtk_sys::{GTK_RESPONSE_ACCEPT, GTK_RESPONSE_CANCEL};

const RESPONSE_ACCEPT: i32 = GTK_RESPONSE_ACCEPT as i32;
const RESPONSE_CANCEL: i32 = GTK_RESPONSE_CANCEL as i32;

fn show_open_dialog(parent: &Window) -> Option<PathBuf> {
    let mut file = None;
    let dialog = FileChooserDialog::new(Some("Select an MP3 audio
file"),
        Some(parent), FileChooserAction::Open);

    let mp3_filter = FileFilter::new();
    mp3_filter.add_mime_type("audio/mp3");
    mp3_filter.set_name("MP3 audio file");
    dialog.add_filter(&mp3_filter);

    let m3u_filter = FileFilter::new();
    m3u_filter.add_mime_type("audio/x-mpegurl");
    m3u_filter.set_name("M3U playlist file");
    dialog.add_filter(&m3u_filter);

    dialog.add_button("Cancel", RESPONSE_CANCEL);
    dialog.add_button("Accept", RESPONSE_ACCEPT);
    let result = dialog.run();
    if result == RESPONSE_ACCEPT {
        file = dialog.get_filename();
    }
    dialog.destroy();
    file
}

fn show_save_dialog(parent: &Window) -> Option<PathBuf> {
    let mut file = None;
    let dialog = FileChooserDialog::new(Some("Choose a destination
M3U playlist
    file"), Some(parent), FileChooserAction::Save);
    let filter = FileFilter::new();
    filter.add_mime_type("audio/x-mpegurl");
    filter.set_name("M3U playlist file");
    dialog.set_do_overwrite_confirmation(true);
```

```
    dialog.add_filter(&filter);
    dialog.add_button("Cancel", RESPONSE_CANCEL);
    dialog.add_button("Save", RESPONSE_ACCEPT);
    let result = dialog.run();
    if result == RESPONSE_ACCEPT {
        file = dialog.get_filename();
    }
    dialog.destroy();
    file
}
```

But this time, we'll put the code for the open action in a method on the App widget:

```
use gtk::{ButtonsType, DialogFlags, MessageDialog, MessageType};

impl App {
    fn open(&self) {
        let file = show_open_dialog(&self.window);
        if let Some(file) = file {
            let ext = file.extension().map(|ext|
             ext.to_str().unwrap().to_string());
            if let Some(ext) = ext {
                match ext.as_str() {
                    "mp3" => (),
                    "m3u" => (),
                    extension => {
                        let dialog =
                        MessageDialog::new(Some(&self.window),
                        DialogFlags::empty(), MessageType::Error,
                        ButtonsType::Ok, &format!("Cannot open file
                         with extension . {}", extension));
                        dialog.run();
                        dialog.destroy();
                    },
                }
            }
        }
    }
}
```

We can then call these functions in the `update()` method:

```
fn update(&mut self, event: Msg) {
    match event {
        Open => self.open(),
        PlayPause => (),
        Quit => gtk::main_quit(),
        Save => show_save_dialog(&self.window),
        Stop => (),
    }
}
```

Let's manage some of the other actions.

Other methods

This will require two new methods in the `impl Widget`:

```
#[widget]
impl Widget for App {
    // ...

    fn set_current_time(&mut self, time: u64) {
        self.model.current_time = time;
        self.model.adjustment.set_value(time as f64);
    }

    fn set_play_icon(&self, icon: &str) {
self.model.play_image.set_from_file(format!("assets/{}.png",
icon));
    }
}
```

But these methods have nothing to do with a `Widget`, so why are we allowed to add `custom` methods in a trait implementation? Well, the `#[widget]` attribute will take these methods and move them to a separate `impl App` where they belong. But why do we want to do this instead of placing them ourselves? That's because `relm` analyzes the assignments to the model attributes in the methods in the implementation decorated by the `#[widget]` attribute. As we saw earlier, an assignment to a model field will automatically update the view. If we placed these methods in a separate `impl App`, `relm` would have been unable to analyze these methods and generate the code to automatically update the view.

This is a frequent mistake, if your view is not updating when you're assigning to a model attribute, it's probably because your assignment is not within an implementation decorated by the `#[widget]` attribute.

We also need a new attribute for our model:

```
pub struct Model {
    adjustment: Adjustment,
    cover_pixbuf: Option<Pixbuf>,
    cover_visible: bool,
    current_duration: u64,
    current_time: u64,
    play_image: Image,
    stopped: bool,
}
```

We added a `stopped` attribute that we also need to add in the model initialization:

```
fn model() -> Model {
    Model {
        adjustment: Adjustment::new(0.0, 0.0, 0.0, 0.0, 0.0, 0.0),
        cover_pixbuf: None,
        cover_visible: false,
        current_duration: 0,
        current_time: 0,
        play_image: new_icon(PLAY_ICON),
        stopped: true,
    }
}
```

We can now change the `update()` method to use these new methods:

```
fn update(&mut self, event: Msg) {
    match event {
        Open => self.open(),
        PlayPause => {
            if !self.model.stopped {
                self.set_play_icon(PLAY_ICON);
            }
        },
        Quit => gtk::main_quit(),
        Save => show_save_dialog(&self.window),
        Stop => {
            self.set_current_time(0);
            self.model.current_duration = 0;
            self.model.cover_visible = false;
            self.set_play_icon(PLAY_ICON);
```

```
            },
        }
    }
```

The `update()` method receives `self` by a mutable reference, which allows us to update the model attributes.

Playlist

We're now ready to create a new widget: the playlist. We'll need the following new dependencies:

```
[dependencies]
id3 = "^0.2.0"
m3u = "^1.0.0"
```

Add their corresponding `extern crate` statements:

```
extern crate id3;
extern crate m3u;
```

Let's create a new module for our `playlist`:

```
mod playlist;
```

In the `src/playlist.rs` file, we start by creating our model:

```
use gtk::ListStore;

pub struct Model {
    current_song: Option<String>,
    model: ListStore,
    relm: Relm<Playlist>,
}
```

The `Relm` type comes from the `relm` crate:

```
use relm::Relm;
```

It is useful to send messages to a widget. We'll learn more about that in the section about widget communication. Let's add the model initialization function:

```
use gdk_pixbuf::Pixbuf;
use gtk::{StaticType, Type};

#[widget]
impl Widget for Playlist {
    fn model(relm: &Relm<Self>, _: ()) -> Model {
        Model {
            current_song: None,
            model: ListStore::new(&[
                Pixbuf::static_type(),
                Type::String,
                Type::String,
                Type::String,
                Type::String,
                Type::String,
                Type::String,
                Type::String,
                Pixbuf::static_type(),
            ]),
            relm: relm.clone(),
        }
    }
}
```

Here, we notice that we use a different signature for the `model()` method. How is this possible? The method of the trait cannot change, right? It is another convenience brought by the `#[widget]` crate. In many cases, we don't need these parameters, so they are automatically added if they are needed. The first parameter is `relm` and we save a copy of it in the model. The second parameter is the model initialization parameter. The `ListStore` is the same as in Chapter 5, *Creating a Music Player*, we only save it in our model because we'll need it later.

Model parameter

Let's talk more about this second parameter. It could be used to send data to the widget when we create it. Remember when we called `run()`:

```
App::run(()).unwrap();
```

Here, we specified `()` as the model parameter because we don't need one. But we could have used a different value, such as `42`, and this value would have been received in the second parameter of the `model()` method.

We're now ready to create the view:

```
use gtk;
use gtk::{TreeViewExt, WidgetExt};
use relm::Widget;
use relm_attributes::widget;

#[widget]
impl Widget for Playlist {
    // ...

    view! {
        #[name="treeview"]
        gtk::TreeView {
            hexpand: true,
            model: &self.model.model,
            vexpand: true,
        }
    }
}
```

It is really simple: we give it a name and set both the `hexpand` and `vexpand` properties to `true` and we bind the `model` property with our `ListStore`.

Let's create an empty `update()` method for now:

```
#[widget]
impl Widget for Playlist {
    // ...

    fn update(&mut self, event: Msg) {
    }
}
```

We'll see the `Msg` type later. We'll now add the columns exactly like we did it in Chapter 5, *Creating a Music Player*. Let's copy the following enumeration and constants:

```
use self::Visibility::*;

#[derive(PartialEq)]
enum Visibility {
    Invisible,
    Visible,
```

```
    }

    const THUMBNAIL_COLUMN: u32 = 0;
    const TITLE_COLUMN: u32 = 1;
    const ARTIST_COLUMN: u32 = 2;
    const ALBUM_COLUMN: u32 = 3;
    const GENRE_COLUMN: u32 = 4;
    const YEAR_COLUMN: u32 = 5;
    const TRACK_COLUMN: u32 = 6;
    const PATH_COLUMN: u32 = 7;
    const PIXBUF_COLUMN: u32 = 8;
```

And let's add new methods to the `Paylist`:

```
    impl Playlist {
        fn add_pixbuf_column(&self, column: i32, visibility:
    Visibility) {
            let view_column = TreeViewColumn::new();
            if visibility == Visible {
                let cell = CellRendererPixbuf::new();
                view_column.pack_start(&cell, true);
                view_column.add_attribute(&cell, "pixbuf", column);
            }
            self.treeview.append_column(&view_column);

        }

        fn add_text_column(&self, title: &str, column: i32) {
            let view_column = TreeViewColumn::new();
            view_column.set_title(title);
            let cell = CellRendererText::new();
            view_column.set_expand(true);
            view_column.pack_start(&cell, true);
            view_column.add_attribute(&cell, "text", column);
            self.treeview.append_column(&view_column);
        }

        fn create_columns(&self) {
            self.add_pixbuf_column(THUMBNAIL_COLUMN as i32, Visible);
            self.add_text_column("Title", TITLE_COLUMN as i32);
            self.add_text_column("Artist", ARTIST_COLUMN as i32);
            self.add_text_column("Album", ALBUM_COLUMN as i32);
            self.add_text_column("Genre", GENRE_COLUMN as i32);
            self.add_text_column("Year", YEAR_COLUMN as i32);
            self.add_text_column("Track", TRACK_COLUMN as i32);
            self.add_pixbuf_column(PIXBUF_COLUMN as i32, Invisible);
        }
    }
```

The difference from these functions in Chapter 5, *Creating a Music Player* is that here, we have direct access to the treeview as an attribute. This requires new import statements:

```
use gtk::{
    CellLayoutExt,
    CellRendererPixbuf,
    CellRendererText,
    TreeViewColumn,
    TreeViewColumnExt,
    TreeViewExt,
};
```

We'll now call the create_columns() method in the init_view() method:

```
#[widget]
impl Widget for Playlist {
    fn init_view(&mut self) {
        self.create_columns();
    }

    // ...
}
```

Let's start interacting with the playlist. We'll create a method to add a song to the playlist:

```
use std::path::Path;

use gtk::{ListStoreExt, ListStoreExtManual, ToValue};
use id3::Tag;

impl Playlist {
    fn add(&self, path: &Path) {
        let filename =
path.file_stem().unwrap_or_default().to_str().unwrap_or_default();

        let row = self.model.model.append();

        if let Ok(tag) = Tag::read_from_path(path) {
            let title = tag.title().unwrap_or(filename);
            let artist = tag.artist().unwrap_or("(no artist)");
            let album = tag.album().unwrap_or("(no album)");
            let genre = tag.genre().unwrap_or("(no genre)");
            let year = tag.year().map(|year|
            year.to_string()).unwrap_or("(no year)".to_string());
            let track = tag.track().map(|track|
             track.to_string()).unwrap_or("??".to_string());
            let total_tracks =
             tag.total_tracks().map(|total_tracks|
```

```
                total_tracks.to_string()).unwrap_or("??".to_string());
            let track_value = format!("{} / {}", track,
             total_tracks);

            self.set_pixbuf(&row, &tag);

            self.model.model.set_value(&row, TITLE_COLUMN,
             &title.to_value());
            self.model.model.set_value(&row, ARTIST_COLUMN,
             &artist.to_value());
            self.model.model.set_value(&row, ALBUM_COLUMN,
             &album.to_value());
            self.model.model.set_value(&row, GENRE_COLUMN,
             &genre.to_value());
            self.model.model.set_value(&row, YEAR_COLUMN,
             &year.to_value());
            self.model.model.set_value(&row, TRACK_COLUMN,
             &track_value.to_value());
        }
        else {
            self.model.model.set_value(&row, TITLE_COLUMN,
             &filename.to_value());
        }

        let path = path.to_str().unwrap_or_default();
        self.model.model.set_value(&row, PATH_COLUMN,
         &path.to_value());
    }
}
```

This calls the set_pixbuf() method, so let's define it:

```
use gdk_pixbuf::{InterpType, PixbufLoader};
use gtk::TreeIter;

const INTERP_HYPER: InterpType = 3;

const IMAGE_SIZE: i32 = 256;
const THUMBNAIL_SIZE: i32 = 64;

fn set_pixbuf(&self, row: &TreeIter, tag: &Tag) {
    if let Some(picture) = tag.pictures().next() {
        let pixbuf_loader = PixbufLoader::new();
        pixbuf_loader.set_size(IMAGE_SIZE, IMAGE_SIZE);
        pixbuf_loader.loader_write(&picture.data).unwrap();
        if let Some(pixbuf) = pixbuf_loader.get_pixbuf() {
            let thumbnail = pixbuf.scale_simple(THUMBNAIL_SIZE,
             THUMBNAIL_SIZE, INTERP_HYPER).unwrap();
```

```
            self.model.model.set_value(row, THUMBNAIL_COLUMN,
                &thumbnail.to_value());
            self.model.model.set_value(row, PIXBUF_COLUMN,
                &pixbuf.to_value());
        }
        pixbuf_loader.close().unwrap();
    }
}
```

It is very similar to the one created in Chapter 5, *Creating a Music Player*. This method will be called when we receive the AddSong(path) message, so let's now create our message type:

```
use std::path::PathBuf;

use self::Msg::*;

#[derive(Msg)]
pub enum Msg {
    AddSong(PathBuf),
    LoadSong(PathBuf),
    NextSong,
    PauseSong,
    PlaySong,
    PreviousSong,
    RemoveSong,
    SaveSong(PathBuf),
    SongStarted(Option<Pixbuf>),
    StopSong,
}
```

And let's modify the update() method accordingly:

```
fn update(&mut self, event: Msg) {
    match event {
        AddSong(path) => self.add(&path),
        LoadSong(path) => (),
        NextSong => (),
        PauseSong => (),
        PlaySong => (),
        PreviousSong => (),
        RemoveSong => (),
        SaveSong(path) => (),
        SongStarted(_) => (),
        StopSong => (),
    }
}
```

Here, we call the method `add()` when we receive the `AddSong` message. But where is this message emitted? Well, it will be emitted by the `App` type, when the user requests to open a file. It is time we go back to the main module and use this new `relm` widget.

Adding a relm widget

First, we'll need these new import statements:

```
use playlist::Playlist;
use playlist::Msg::{
    AddSong,
    LoadSong,
    NextSong,
    PlaySong,
    PauseSong,
    PreviousSong,
    RemoveSong,
    SaveSong,
    SongStarted,
    StopSong,
};
```

And then, add the `Playlist` widget below the toolbar:

```
view! {
    #[name="window"]
    gtk::Window {
        title: "Rusic",
        gtk::Box {
            orientation: Vertical,
            #[name="toolbar"]
            gtk::Toolbar {
                // ...
            },
            #[name="playlist"]
            Playlist {
            },
            gtk::Image {
                from_pixbuf: self.model.cover_pixbuf.as_ref(),
                visible: self.model.cover_visible,
            },
            gtk::Box {
                // ...
            },
        },
```

```
            delete_event(_, _) => (Quit, Inhibit(false)),
        }
    }
```

There's something different with using `relm` widgets and `gtk` widgets. `Relm` widgets must not contain a module prefix, while `gtk` widget must contain one. This is why we imported `Playlist`, but now `gtk::Toolbar`, for instance. But why is it needed? Well, `relm` widgets are different than `gtk` widgets, so they are not created or added to another widget in the same way. Thus, `relm` can distinguish them this way: if there's a prefix, this is a built-in `gtk` widget, otherwise it is a custom `relm` widget. When I say `gtk` widgets, this even includes `gtk` widgets from other crates, such as `webkit2gtk::WebView`.

Communicating between widgets

We'll now communicate between the widgets to indicate we want to add a song to the playlist. But before we do so, we'll look in more detail at how a widget can communicate with itself.

Communicating with the same widget

We previously saw how to communicate with the same widget. To send a message to the same widget from an event handler in the view, we simply need to specify the message to be sent on the right side of =>, like in the following example:

```
gtk::ToolButton {
    icon_widget: &new_icon("gtk-quit"),
    clicked => Quit,
}
```

Here, the `Quit` message is sent to the same widget (that is, `App`) when the user clicks this tool button. But this is syntax sugar for a call to the `emit()` method on the stream of events of a `relm` widget.

Emit

So, let's see how to send a message to the same widget without using this syntax: this is useful in more complex cases, such as when we want to conditionally send a message. Let's go back to our `Playlist` and add a `play()` method:

```
impl Playlist {
    fn play(&mut self) {
        if let Some(path) = self.selected_path() {
            self.model.current_song = Some(path.into());
            self.model.relm.stream().emit(SongStarted(self.pixbuf()));
        }
    }
}
```

This line sends a message to the current widget:

```
self.model.relm.stream().emit(SongStarted(self.pixbuf()));
```

We first get the event stream from the `relm` widget and then call `emit()` on it with a message. This `play()` method requires two new methods:

```
use gtk::{
    TreeModelExt,
    TreeSelectionExt,
};

impl Playlist {
    fn pixbuf(&self) -> Option<Pixbuf> {
        let selection = self.treeview.get_selection();
        if let Some((_, iter)) = selection.get_selected() {
            let value = self.model.model.get_value(&iter,
                PIXBUF_COLUMN as i32);
            return value.get::<Pixbuf>();
        }
        None
    }

    fn selected_path(&self) -> Option<String> {
        let selection = self.treeview.get_selection();
        if let Some((_, iter)) = selection.get_selected() {
```

```
                    let value = self.model.model.get_value(&iter,
            PATH_COLUMN as i32);
                    return value.get::<String>();
            }
            None
        }
    }
```

These are very similar to the ones we wrote in the previous chapters. We can now call the play() method in the update() method:

```
fn update(&mut self, event: Msg) {
    match event {
        AddSong(path) => self.add(&path),
        LoadSong(path) => (),
        NextSong => (),
        PauseSong => (),
        PlaySong => self.play(),
        PreviousSong => (),
        RemoveSong => (),
        SaveSong(path) => (),
        // To be listened by App.
        SongStarted(_) => (),
        StopSong => (),
    }
}
```

I also added a comment before SongStarted to indicate that this message will not be handled by the Paylist widget, but by the App widget. Now, let's see how to communicate between different widgets.

With different widgets

Let's update the open() method to communicate with the playlist:

```
impl App {
    fn open(&self) {
        let file = show_open_dialog(&self.window);
        if let Some(file) = file {
            let ext = file.extension().map(|ext|
ext.to_str().unwrap().to_string());
            if let Some(ext) = ext {
                match ext.as_str() {
                    "mp3" => self.playlist.emit(AddSong(file)),
                    "m3u" => self.playlist.emit(LoadSong(file)),
```

```
        extension => {
            let dialog = MessageDialog::new(Some(&self.window),
            DialogFlags::empty(), MessageType::Error,
            ButtonsType::Ok, &format!("Cannot open file with
             extension . {}", extension));
            dialog.run();
            dialog.destroy();
        },
    }
}
}
}
}
```

So, we call the same `emit()` method to send a message to another widget:

```
self.playlist.emit(AddSong(file))
```

Here, we sent a message that is not yet handled by the `Playlist` (`LoadSong`), so let's fix that:

```
use m3u;

impl Playlist {
    fn load(&self, path: &Path) {
        let mut reader = m3u::Reader::open(path).unwrap();
        for entry in reader.entries() {
            if let Ok(m3u::Entry::Path(path)) = entry {
                self.add(&path);
            }
        }
    }
}
```

This method is called in the `update()` method:

```
fn update(&mut self, event: Msg) {
    match event {
        AddSong(path) => self.add(&path),
        LoadSong(path) => self.load(&path),
        NextSong => (),
        PauseSong => (),
        PlaySong => self.play(),
        PreviousSong => (),
        RemoveSong => (),
        SaveSong(path) => (),
        // To be listened by App.
        SongStarted(_) => (),
```

```
            StopSong => (),
    }
}
```

Handle messages from a relm widget

Let's now see how to handle the `SongStarted` message. To do so, we use a syntax similar to the one for handling `gtk` events. The message is on the left side of `=>` while the handler is on the right side of it:

```
#[widget]
impl Widget for App {
    // ...

    view! {
        // ...
        #[name="playlist"]
        Playlist {
            SongStarted(ref pixbuf) => Started(pixbuf.clone()),
        }
    }
}
```

We can see here that when we receive the `SongStarted` message from the playlist, we emit the `Started` message on the same widget (`App`). We needed to use `ref` and then `clone()` the value contained in the message here because we do not own the message. Indeed, multiple widgets can listen to the same message, the widget that emitted the message and its parent. Before we handle this new message, we'll add it to our `Msg` enumeration:

```
#[derive(Msg)]
pub enum Msg {
    Open,
    PlayPause,
    Quit,
    Save,
    Started(Option<Pixbuf>),
    Stop,
}
```

This variant takes an optional `pixbuf` because some MP3 files do not have a cover image inside them. And here's how we handle this message:

```
fn update(&mut self, event: Msg) {
    match event {
        // ...
        Started(pixbuf) => {
            self.set_play_icon(PAUSE_ICON);
            self.model.cover_visible = true;
            self.model.cover_pixbuf = pixbuf;
        },
    }
}
```

When the song starts playing, we show the pause icon and the cover.

Syntax sugar to send a message to another relm widget

Sending a message to another widget with `emit()` is a bit verbose, so `relm` provides syntactic sugar for this case. Let's send a message to the playlist when the user clicks the remove button:

```
gtk::ToolButton {
    icon_widget: &new_icon("remove"),
    clicked => playlist@RemoveSong,
}
```

Here, we used the @ syntax to specify that the message will be sent to another widget. The part before the @ is the receiver widget, while the part after this character is the message. So, this code means that whenever the user clicks the remove button, send the `RemoveSong` message to the `playlist` widget.

Let's handle this message in the `Paylist::update()` method:

```
#[widget]
impl Widget for Playlist {
    fn update(&mut self, event: Msg) {
        match event {
            AddSong(path) => self.add(&path),
            LoadSong(path) => self.load(&path),
            NextSong => (),
            PauseSong => (),
            PlaySong => self.play(),
            PreviousSong => (),
            RemoveSong => self.remove_selection(),
```

```
                    SaveSong(path) => (),
                    // To be listened by App.
                    SongStarted(_) => (),
                    StopSong => (),
                }
            }


        // ...
    }
```

This calls the `remove_selection()` method, as shown here:

```
fn remove_selection(&self) {
    let selection = self.treeview.get_selection();
    if let Some((_, iter)) = selection.get_selected() {
        self.model.model.remove(&iter);
    }
}
```

This is the same method as the one from Chapter 5, *Creating a Music Player*. Now, let's send the remaining messages. The `PlaySong`, `PauseSong`, `SaveSong`, and `StopSong` messages are emitted in the `update()` method:

```
#[widget]
impl Widget for App {
    fn update(&mut self, event: Msg) {
        match event {
            PlayPause =>  {
                if self.model.stopped {
                    self.playlist.emit(PlaySong);
                } else {
                    self.playlist.emit(PauseSong);
                    self.set_play_icon(PLAY_ICON);
                }
            },
            Save => {
                let file = show_save_dialog(&self.window);
                if let Some(file) = file {
                    self.playlist.emit(SaveSong(file));
                }
            },
            Stop => {
                self.set_current_time(0);
                self.model.current_duration = 0;
                self.playlist.emit(StopSong);
                self.model.cover_visible = false;
                self.set_play_icon(PLAY_ICON);
```

```
            },
            // ...
        }
    }
}
```

The other messages are sent using the @ syntax in the view:

```
view! {
    #[name="window"]
    gtk::Window {
        title: "Rusic",
        gtk::Box {
            orientation: Vertical,
            #[name="toolbar"]
            gtk::Toolbar {
                // ...
                gtk::ToolButton {
                    icon_widget: &new_icon("gtk-media-previous"),
                    clicked => playlist@PreviousSong,
                },
                // ...
                gtk::ToolButton {
                    icon_widget: &new_icon("gtk-media-next"),
                    clicked => playlist@NextSong,
                },
            },
            // ...
        },
        delete_event(_, _) => (Quit, Inhibit(false)),
    }
}
```

We'll handle these messages in the `Paylist::update()` method:

```
fn update(&mut self, event: Msg) {
    match event {
        AddSong(path) => self.add(&path),
        LoadSong(path) => self.load(&path),
        NextSong => self.next(),
        PauseSong => (),
        PlaySong => self.play(),
        PreviousSong => self.previous(),
        RemoveSong => self.remove_selection(),
        SaveSong(path) => self.save(&path),
        // To be listened by App.
        SongStarted(_) => (),
        StopSong => self.stop(),
```

```
        }
    }
```

This requires some new methods:

```
fn next(&mut self) {
    let selection = self.treeview.get_selection();
    let next_iter =
        if let Some((_, iter)) = selection.get_selected() {
            if !self.model.model.iter_next(&iter) {
                return;
            }
            Some(iter)
        }
        else {
            self.model.model.get_iter_first()
        };
    if let Some(ref iter) = next_iter {
        selection.select_iter(iter);
        self.play();
    }
}

fn previous(&mut self) {
    let selection = self.treeview.get_selection();
    let previous_iter =
        if let Some((_, iter)) = selection.get_selected() {
            if !self.model.model.iter_previous(&iter) {
                return;
            }
            Some(iter)
        }
        else {
            self.model.model.iter_nth_child(None, max(0,
                self.model.model.iter_n_children(None) - 1))
        };
    if let Some(ref iter) = previous_iter {
        selection.select_iter(iter);
        self.play();
    }
}

use std::fs::File;

fn save(&self, path: &Path) {
    let mut file = File::create(path).unwrap();
    let mut writer = m3u::Writer::new(&mut file);
```

```
        let mut write_iter = |iter: &TreeIter| {
            let value = self.model.model.get_value(&iter, PATH_COLUMN
    as i32);
            let path = value.get::<String>().unwrap();
            writer.write_entry(&m3u::path_entry(path)).unwrap();
        };

        if let Some(iter) = self.model.model.get_iter_first() {
            write_iter(&iter);
            while self.model.model.iter_next(&iter) {
                write_iter(&iter);
            }
        }
    }
```

And function `stop`:

```
    fn stop(&mut self) {
        self.model.current_song = None;
    }
```

These methods are all similar to the ones we created in the previous chapters. You can run the application to see that we can open and remove songs, but we cannot play them yet. So let's fix this.

Playing music

First, add the `mp3` module:

```
    mod mp3;
```

Copy the `src/mp3.rs` file from the previous chapter.

We also need the following dependencies:

```
    [dependencies]
    crossbeam = "^0.3.0"
    futures = "^0.1.16"
    pulse-simple = "^1.0.0"
    simplemad = "^0.8.1"
```

And add these statements to the `main` module:

```
extern crate crossbeam;
extern crate futures;
extern crate pulse_simple;
extern crate simplemad;
```

We'll now add a `player` module:

```
mod player;
```

This new module will start with a bunch of import statements:

```
use std::cell::Cell;
use std::fs::File;
use std::io::BufReader;
use std::path::{Path, PathBuf};
use std::sync::{Arc, Condvar, Mutex};
use std::thread;
use std::time::Duration;

use crossbeam::sync::SegQueue;
use futures::{AsyncSink, Sink};
use futures::sync::mpsc::UnboundedSender;
use pulse_simple::Playback;

use mp3::Mp3Decoder;
use playlist::PlayerMsg::{
    self,
    PlayerPlay,
    PlayerStop,
    PlayerTime,
};
use self::Action::*;
```

We imported a new `PlayerMsg` type from the `playlist` module, so let's add it:

```
#[derive(Clone)]
pub enum PlayerMsg {
    PlayerPlay,
    PlayerStop,
    PlayerTime(u64),
}
```

We'll define some constants:

```
const BUFFER_SIZE: usize = 1000;
const DEFAULT_RATE: u32 = 44100;
```

And let's create the types that we'll need:

```
enum Action {
    Load(PathBuf),
    Stop,
}

#[derive(Clone)]
struct EventLoop {
    condition_variable: Arc<(Mutex<bool>, Condvar)>,
    queue: Arc<SegQueue<Action>>,
    playing: Arc<Mutex<bool>>,
}

pub struct Player {
    event_loop: EventLoop,
    paused: Cell<bool>,
    tx: UnboundedSender<PlayerMsg>,
}
```

The `Action` and `EventLoop` are the same as in the previous chapter, but the `Player` type is a bit different. Instead of having a field with the state of the application, it contains a sender that will be used to send messages to the playlist and ultimately to the application itself. So, instead of using a shared state and a timeout like we did in the previous chapter, we'll use message passing, which is more efficient.

We'll need a constructor for `EventLoop`:

```
impl EventLoop {
    fn new() -> Self {
        EventLoop {
            condition_variable: Arc::new((Mutex::new(false),
Condvar::new())),
            queue: Arc::new(SegQueue::new()),
            playing: Arc::new(Mutex::new(false)),
        }
    }
}
```

Let's create the constructor for `Player`:

```
impl Player {
    pub(crate) fn new(tx: UnboundedSender<PlayerMsg>) -> Self {
        let event_loop = EventLoop::new();

        {
            let mut tx = tx.clone();
            let event_loop = event_loop.clone();
            let condition_variable = event_loop.condition_variable.clone();
            thread::spawn(move || {
                let block = || {
                    let (ref lock, ref condition_variable) =
*condition_variable;
                    let mut started = lock.lock().unwrap();
                    *started = false;
                    while !*started {
                        started =
condition_variable.wait(started).unwrap();
                    }
                };

                let mut buffer = [[0; 2]; BUFFER_SIZE];
                let mut playback = Playback::new("MP3", "MP3 Playback",
None,
                DEFAULT_RATE);
                let mut source = None;
                loop {
                    if let Some(action) = event_loop.queue.try_pop() {
                        match action {
                            Load(path) => {
                                let file = File::open(path).unwrap();
                                source =
Some(Mp3Decoder::new(BufReader::new(file)).unwrap());
                                let rate = source.as_ref().map(|source|
```

```
source.samples_rate()).unwrap_or(DEFAULT_RATE);
                                playback = Playback::new("MP3", "MP3
Playback",
                            None, rate);
                            send(&mut tx, PlayerPlay);
                    },
                    Stop => {
                        source = None;
                    },
                }
            } else if *event_loop.playing.lock().unwrap() {
                let mut written = false;
                if let Some(ref mut source) = source {
                    let size = iter_to_buffer(source, &mut buffer);
                    if size > 0 {
                        send(&mut tx,
PlayerTime(source.current_time())));
                            playback.write(&buffer[..size]);
                            written = true;
                    }
                }

                if !written {
                    send(&mut tx, PlayerStop);
                    *event_loop.playing.lock().unwrap() = false;
                    source = None;
                    block();
                }
            } else {
                block();
            }
        }
    });
}

Player {
    event_loop,
    paused: Cell::new(false),
    tx,
}
    }
}
```

It is similar to the one we wrote in the previous chapter, but instead of using the shared state, we send messages back to the playlist. Here's an example of how we send these messages:

```
        send(&mut tx, PlayerTime(source.current_time()));
```

This sends the current time back to the UI so that it can display it. This requires the `send()` function to be defined:

```
fn send(tx: &mut UnboundedSender<PlayerMsg>, msg: PlayerMsg) {
    if let Ok(AsyncSink::Ready) = tx.start_send(msg) {
        tx.poll_complete().unwrap();
    } else {
        eprintln!("Unable to send message to sender");
    }
}
```

This code uses the `future` crate to send the message and it shows an error in case it fails. The `iter_to_buffer()` function is the same as the one from the previous chapter:

```
fn iter_to_buffer<I: Iterator<Item=i16>>(iter: &mut I, buffer: &mut
[[i16; 2]; BUFFER_SIZE]) -> usize {
    let mut iter = iter.take(BUFFER_SIZE);
    let mut index = 0;
    while let Some(sample1) = iter.next() {
        if let Some(sample2) = iter.next() {
            buffer[index][0] = sample1;
            buffer[index][1] = sample2;
        }
        index += 1;
    }
    index
}
```

We'll now add the methods to play and pause a song:

```
pub fn load<P: AsRef<Path>>(&self, path: P) {
    let pathbuf = path.as_ref().to_path_buf();
    self.emit(Load(pathbuf));
    self.set_playing(true);
}

pub fn pause(&mut self) {
    self.paused.set(true);
    self.send(PlayerStop);
    self.set_playing(false);
}

pub fn resume(&mut self) {
    self.paused.set(false);
    self.send(PlayerPlay);
    self.set_playing(true);
```

```
    }
```

They're very similar to the ones from the previous chapter, but we send a message instead of modifying a state. They require the following methods:

```
fn emit(&self, action: Action) {
    self.event_loop.queue.push(action);
}

fn send(&mut self, msg: PlayerMsg) {
    send(&mut self.tx, msg);
}

fn set_playing(&self, playing: bool) {
    *self.event_loop.playing.lock().unwrap() = playing;
    let (ref lock, ref condition_variable) =
*self.event_loop.condition_variable;
    let mut started = lock.lock().unwrap();
    *started = playing;
    if playing {
        condition_variable.notify_one();
    }
}
```

The `emit()` and `set_playing()` methods are the same as in the previous chapter. The `send()` method simply calls the `send()` function we defined earlier.

We'll also need these two methods:

```
pub fn is_paused(&self) -> bool {
    self.paused.get()
}

pub fn stop(&mut self) {
    self.paused.set(false);
    self.send(PlayerTime(0));
    self.send(PlayerStop);
    self.emit(Stop);
    self.set_playing(false);
}
```

The `is_paused()` method has not changed. And the `stop()` method is similar, but again, it sends messages instead of updating the application state directly. Let's go back to our `Paylist` to use this new player. The model will now contain the player itself:

```
use player::Player;

pub struct Model {
    current_song: Option<String>,
    player: Player,
    model: ListStore,
    relm: Relm<Playlist>,
}
```

The `Msg` type will contain a new variant called `PlayerMsgRecv` that will be emitted whenever the player sends a message:

```
#[derive(Msg)]
pub enum Msg {
    AddSong(PathBuf),
    LoadSong(PathBuf),
    NextSong,
    PauseSong,
    PlayerMsgRecv(PlayerMsg),
    PlaySong,
    PreviousSong,
    RemoveSong,
    SaveSong(PathBuf),
    SongStarted(Option<Pixbuf>),
    StopSong,
}
```

We're now ready to update the model initialization:

```
use futures::sync::mpsc;

fn model(relm: &Relm<Self>, _: ()) -> Model {
    let (tx, rx) = mpsc::unbounded();
    relm.connect_exec_ignore_err(rx, PlayerMsgRecv);
    Model {
        current_song: None,
        player: Player::new(tx),
        model: ListStore::new(&[
            Pixbuf::static_type(),
            Type::String,
            Type::String,
            Type::String,
            Type::String,
```

```
                Type::String,
                Type::String,
                Type::String,
                Pixbuf::static_type(),
            ]),
            relm: relm.clone(),
        }
    }
```

It now creates a sender and receiver pair from the mpsc type of the future crate. **MPSC** stands for **Multiple-Producers-Single-Consumer**. We now call the Relm::connect_exec_ignore_err() method, this method connects a Future or a Stream to a message. This means that whenever a value is produced in the Stream, a message will be emitted. The message needs to take a parameter of the same type as the value produced by the Stream. A Future represents a value that is possibly not yet available, but will be available in the future, unless an error happens. A Stream is similar, but can produce multiple values that will be available at different times in the future. Similar to the connect_exec_ignore_err() method, there's also the connect_exec() method, which takes another message variant as a parameter, this second message will be emitted when there's an error. Here, we simply ignore the errors.

In the update() method:

```
fn update(&mut self, event: Msg) {
    match event {
        // To be listened by App.
        PlayerMsgRecv(_) => (),
        // ...
    }
}
```

We have nothing to do with this message because it will be handled by the App widget. We'll now add a method to pause the player:

```
fn pause(&mut self) {
    self.model.player.pause();
}
```

Next we need to update the play() and stop() methods:

```
fn play(&mut self) {
    if let Some(path) = self.selected_path() {
        if self.model.player.is_paused() && Some(&path) ==
self.path().as_ref() {
            self.model.player.resume();
        } else {
```

```
                self.model.player.load(&path);
                self.model.current_song = Some(path.into());
        self.model.relm.stream().emit(SongStarted(self.pixbuf()));
                }
            }
        }

        fn stop(&mut self) {
            self.model.current_song = None;
            self.model.player.stop();
        }
```

The `stop()` method is the same, except that we can update the model directly, because we don't need to use the `RefCell` type anymore. The `play()` method will now load or resume the song depending on the state of the player.

The `play()` method requires a `path()` method:

```
        fn path(&self) -> Option<String> {
            self.model.current_song.clone()
        }
```

Let's go back to the `main` module to manage the messages sent by the player. First, we need a new variant for our `enum Msg`:

```
        #[derive(Msg)]
        pub enum Msg {
            MsgRecv(PlayerMsg),
            // ...
        }
```

We will handle this in the `update()` method:

```
        fn update(&mut self, event: Msg) {
            match event {
                MsgRecv(player_msg) => self.player_message(player_msg),
                // ...
            }
        }
```

This requires a new method to be added in `impl Widget for App`:

```
#[widget]
impl Widget for App {
    fn player_message(&mut self, player_msg: PlayerMsg) {
        match player_msg {
            PlayerPlay => {
                self.model.stopped = false;
                self.set_play_icon(PAUSE_ICON);
            },
            PlayerStop => {
                self.set_play_icon(PLAY_ICON);
                self.model.stopped = true;
            },
            PlayerTime(time) => self.set_current_time(time),
        }
    }
}
```

This is also a `custom` method, that is, a method that is not part of the `Widget` trait, but is analyzed by the `#[widget]` attribute. We put it there instead of a separate `impl App` because we updated the model. In this method, we either update the icon to display the play button or the current time.

Computing the song duration

The only remaining feature that needs to be implemented in order to be on par with the music player of the previous chapter is to compute and display the song duration. First, we will copy the `compute_duration()` method from the previous chapter and paste it in our `Player`:

```
pub fn compute_duration<P: AsRef<Path>>(path: P) ->
Option<Duration> {
    let file = File::open(path).unwrap();
    Mp3Decoder::compute_duration(BufReader::new(file))
}
```

We'll now call this method in the `Playlist`:

```
use std::thread;
use futures::sync::oneshot;

fn compute_duration(&self, path: &Path) {
    let path = path.to_path_buf();
    let (tx, rx) = oneshot::channel();
    thread::spawn(move || {
        if let Some(duration) = Player::compute_duration(&path) {
            tx.send((path, duration))
                .expect("Cannot send computed duration");
        }
    });
    self.model.relm.connect_exec_ignore_err(rx, |(path, duration)|
DurationComputed(path, duration));
}
```

Here, we use `oneshot` which is also a channel, similar to `mpsc`, but `oneshot` can only send a message once. The message sent is a tuple, so we convert it to our `Msg` type by using a new `DurationComputed` variant that we'll add to the type:

```
use std::time::Duration;

#[derive(Msg)]
pub enum Msg {
    AddSong(PathBuf),
    DurationComputed(PathBuf, Duration),
    SongDuration(u64),
    // ...
}
```

We've also added a `SongDuration` message that we'll use soon.

We need to call this method in `Playlist::add()`:

```
impl Playlist {
    fn add(&self, path: &Path) {
        self.compute_duration(path);
        // ...
    }
}
```

We then need to handle the new `DurationComputed` message in `Playlist::update()`:

```
use to_millis;

fn update(&mut self, event: Msg) {
    match event {
        DurationComputed(path, duration) => {
            let path = path.to_string_lossy().to_string();
            if self.model.current_song.as_ref() == Some(&path) {
self.model.relm.stream().emit(SongDuration(to_millis(duration)));
            }
            self.model.durations.insert(path, to_millis(duration));
        },
        // To be listened by App.
        SongDuration(_) => (),
        // ...
    }
}
```

Here, we insert the computed duration in the model. And if the song is the one currently being played, we send the `SongDuration` message so that the `App` widget can update itself.

This requires a new field for the durations in the model:

```
use std::collections::HashMap;

pub struct Model {
    current_song: Option<String>,
    durations: HashMap<String, u64>,
    player: Player,
    model: ListStore,
    relm: Relm<Playlist>,
}
```

Add the new model initialization:

```
fn model(relm: &Relm<Self>, _: ()) -> Model {
    // ...
    Model {
        durations: HashMap::new(),
        // ...
    }
}
```

This also requires the `to_millis()` function to be added in the `main` module, which is the same as in the previous chapter:

```
use std::time::Duration;

fn to_millis(duration: Duration) -> u64 {
    duration.as_secs() * 1000 + duration.subsec_nanos() as u64 /
1_000_000
}
```

Since the duration is only computed once, we also need to send it when we start playing the song, so let's update the `Playlist::play()` method:

```
fn play(&mut self) {
    if let Some(path) = self.selected_path() {
        if self.model.player.is_paused() && Some(&path) ==
self.path().as_ref() {
            self.model.player.resume();
        } else {
            self.model.player.load(&path);
            if let Some(&duration) =
self.model.durations.get(&path) {
self.model.relm.stream().emit(SongDuration(duration));
            }
            self.model.current_song = Some(path.into());
self.model.relm.stream().emit(SongStarted(self.pixbuf()));
        }
    }
}
```

We send the `SongDuration` message if we found it in the `HashMap` (it is possible that the song starts playing before the duration is computed).

Finally, we need to handle the following message in the `App` view:

```
view! {
    Playlist {
        PlayerMsgRecv(ref player_msg) =>
MsgRecv(player_msg.clone()),
        SongDuration(duration) => Duration(duration),
        SongStarted(ref pixbuf) => Started(pixbuf.clone()),
    }
    // ...
}
```

When we receive the `SongDuration` message from the playlist, we send the `Duration` message to `App`, so we need to add this variant to its `Msg` type:

```
#[derive(Msg)]
pub enum Msg {
    Duration(u64),
    // ...
}
```

We'll simply handle it in the `update()` method:

```
fn update(&mut self, event: Msg) {
    match event {
        Duration(duration) => {
            self.model.current_duration = duration;
            self.model.adjustment.set_upper(duration as f64);
        },
        // ...
    }
}
```

You can now run the application and see that it works exactly the same as the one from the previous chapter.

Using relm on stable Rust

In this whole chapter, we used Rust nightly to be able to use `custom` attributes, which are currently unstable. The `#[widget]` attribute provided by `relm` provides many advantages:

- Declarative view
- Data bindings
- Less typing

So it would be nice to be able to use a similar syntax on stable that provides the same advantages. And it is possible to do so, by using the `relm_widget!` macro. We'll rewrite the `App` widget to use this macro:

```
relm_widget! {
    impl Widget for App {
        fn init_view(&mut self) {
            self.toolbar.show_all();
        }
```

```
fn model() -> Model {
    Model {
        adjustment: Adjustment::new(0.0, 0.0, 0.0, 0.0,
0.0, 0.0),
        cover_pixbuf: None,
        cover_visible: false,
        current_duration: 0,
        current_time: 0,
        play_image: new_icon(PLAY_ICON),
        stopped: true,
    }
}

fn open(&self) {
    // ...
}

// ...

fn update(&mut self, event: Msg) {
    // ...
}

view! {
    #[name="window"]
    gtk::Window {
        title: "Rusic",
        // ...
    }
}
}
}
```

As you can see, we moved the external `open()` method inside the implementation decorated by the `relm_widget!` macro. This is due to a limitation of this macro, while it allows us to use the nice syntax provided by relm on stable Rust, we cannot access the fields of the model from outside the macro. The rest is exactly the same as the previous versions.

Relm widgets data binding

There are many other features available in relm and I wanted to show you the most important of them: the syntax that is provided to simulate property binding. As you may have noticed by now, there's no property in `relm` widgets, but you can use message passing to update the internal state of a `relm` widget. To make it more convenient, the `#[widget]` attribute also allows you to bind a model attribute to a message, this means that whenever the attribute is updated, the message will be emitted with this new value.

We'll add a toggle button to be able to switch between a simple and a detailed view for the playlist. The simple view will only show the cover and the title while the detailed view will show all the columns. First, let's add an attribute to the `App` model:

```
pub struct Model {
    detailed_view: bool,
    // ...
}

    fn model() -> Model {
        Model {
            detailed_view: false,
            // ...
        }
    }
```

This field specifies whether we're in the detailed view mode or not. We'll also need a message that will be emitted when we click the toggle button:

```
#[derive(Msg)]
pub enum Msg {
    ViewToggle,
    // ...
}
```

Then, we add the toggle button to the toolbar:

```
#[name="toggle_button"]
gtk::ToggleToolButton {
    label: "Detailed view",
    toggled => ViewToggle,
}
```

When we receive this message, we'll set the `model` attribute accordingly:

```
fn update(&mut self, event: Msg) {
    match event {
        ViewToggle => self.model.detailed_view =
self.toggle_button.get_active(),
        // ...
    }
}
```

Now, let's a message to the `Playlist`:

```
#[derive(Msg)]
pub enum Msg {
    DetailedView(bool),
    // ...
}
```

This is the message we'll use for the binding. Let's handle it:

```
fn update(&mut self, event: Msg) {
    match event {
        DetailedView(detailed) => self.set_detailed_view(detailed),
        // ...
    }
}

fn set_detailed_view(&self, detailed: bool) {
    for column in self.treeview.get_columns().iter().skip(2) {
        column.set_visible(detailed);
    }
}
```

The latter method toggles the visible of all columns except the first two. We can now create the binding in the `App` view:

```
use playlist::Msg::DetailedView;

view! {
    // ...
    #[name="playlist"]
    Playlist {
        // ...
        DetailedView: self.model.detailed_view,
    }
}
```

This code will send the `DetailedView` message with the specified attribute as the value whenever it changes.

Summary

In this chapter, we used `relm` to create a music player. We saw how simple it is to use rust nightly with `rustup`. We learned how to declaratively create views and use message passing to communicate between widgets. We also learned how to structure GUI applications by separating the model, the view, and the function to update the model in reaction to events. In the next chapter, we'll switch to another project: an FTP server.

8
Understanding FTP

This chapter is all about asynchronous programming in Rust. In order to show you how it works, we'll write an FTP server. However, to make it as easy as possible for you to understand, we'll break the subject down into the following topics:

- Presenting the FTP protocol
- Implementing a synchronous FTP server
- Presenting asynchronous programmation in Rust
- Asynchronously implementing the FTP server

These steps are all important in order to make you feel confident in Rust asynchronous programming.

Now, let's start by talking a bit about the FTP protocol!

File transfer protocol

The **file transfer protocol** (**FTP**) was created in 1971. Its final RFC is 959. If you're curious, you can read more about it at `https://tools.ietf.org/html/rfc959`.

Being an old protocol, a few commands don't have clear specifications, so some alternative specifications (that are more or less official) have been written in order to fill those blanks. We'll go back to them when writing the server.

Another important point to note is that FTP uses TCP connections.

Now that we've quickly introduced you to FTP, let's see how it works.

Introduction to FTP

A client connects to a server and then sends commands to the server. Each command receives an answer from the server with either a success or failure.

For example, the client will send the PWD command to the server:

```
=> PWD\r\n
<= 257 "/"\r\n
```

Here, the server answered 257 (which literally means *pathname created*) and then gave the current working directory the client is in (which is "/", in this case).

As you can see, every command ended with "". This is another standard in FTP—every command has to end with "". In case you don't know, "" stands for carriage return and "" stands for the backline.

Another thing to note—the answer from the server *always* contains a string before the "". Consider the following example:

```
=> NOOP\r\n
<= 250 Doing nothing\r\n
```

If the client's command doesn't require a precise output (except for the returned code), it's all up to the server. It's generally just a small sentence giving more information about what the server did (or what failed). On another server, the NOOP command could have given the following:

```
=> NOOP\r\n
<= 250 42 is life\r\n
```

Lastly, FTP works with two channels:

- The first channel is used to send small commands, such as updating a status
- The second channel is used to send a large amount of data, such as a file transfer or even listing a directory

A funny thing about this second channel is that it's up to the client to decide whether the server connects to the client or vice versa. But in almost every case, the client asks the server to connect to him for a second time, and the server picks a port and they're good to go.

We can now say that we're done with a quick introduction to FTP. If it still doesn't seem perfectly clear at this point, no need to worry: it'll become more obvious as we go through the implementation of the server.

So, let's start with a synchronous server implementation.

Implementing simple chunks of commands

Let's start slowly by first creating a very simple server that sends `"hello"` to a new client and then closes the connection:

```
use std::net::TcpListener;
use std::io::Write;

fn main() {
    let listener =
TcpListener::bind("0.0.0.0:1234").expect("Couldn't bind this
        address...");

        println!("Waiting for clients to connect...");
        for stream in listener.incoming() {
            Ok(stream) => {
                println!("New client!);
                if let Err(_) = stream.write(b"hello") {
                    println!("Failed to send hello... :'(");
                }
            }
            _ => {
                println!("A client tried to connect...")
            }
        }
    }
}
```

Pretty easy, right? As usual, let's explain what the code does:

```
let listener = TcpListener::bind("0.0.0.0:1234").expect("Couldn't
bind this address...");
```

For those who don't know much about the network, the preceding line of code is the most important for any server

It tries to *book* the port for your server only. If another software is using it, then the `bind` call will fail. The given string represents the address and port we want to *book*. The argument works as follows: `[IP]:[PORT]`. Here, we entered `0.0.0.0:1234`, which means that we want the port `1234` on the address `0.0.0.0`.

It might sound strange to allow a server to pick an IP address to use, but it's actually not the case. You can only choose between `localhost` (alias `127.0.0.1`) and `0.0.0.0`. The only difference between those two is that `0.0.0.0` allows other computers to connect to your own (if the port can be accessed from outside through the box provided by your internet access provider), whereas `127.0.0.1` can only be accessed from the computer it has been started on. But enough with network explanations—this isn't the point of this book, so let's move on!

The only other code that requires explanation is the following:

```
for stream in listener.incoming() {
```

The `incoming` method call allows us to iterate infinitely on newly received connections by returning an iterator. Then, the `for` loop just calls the `next` method of the iterator.

That's it for this small code sample. Now it's time to improve all this!

It'd be nice to handle every client separately and not close the connection as soon as we receive a new connection, wouldn't it? So, let's just update the previous code a bit:

```
use std::net::{TcpListener, TcpStream};
use std::thread;

fn handle_client(mut stream: TcpStream) {
    println!("new client connected!");
    // put client code handling here
}

fn main() {
    let listener =
TcpListener::bind("0.0.0.0:1234").expect("Couldn't bind this
    address...");

    println!("Waiting for clients to connect...");
    for stream in listener.incoming() {
        Ok(stream) => {
            thread::spawn(move || {
                handle_client(stream);
            });
        }
```

```
            _ => {
                println!("A client tried to connect...")
            }
        }
    }
```

Every time a new client connects to the server, we spawn a new thread and send the client's socket into it. This way, we can now handle every client on its own.

Now that we can get new clients connected, it's time to actually start implementing the FTP part of our server.

Starting with basics

Of course, since we need to read and write on sockets, having to do that again and again in every function wouldn't be very efficient. Therefore, we'll start by implementing functions to do that. For now, we won't handle errors *nicely* (yes, unwrap is evil).

Let's start with the write function:

```
use use std::net::TcpStream;
use std::io::Write;

fn send_cmd(stream: &mut TcpStream, code: ResultCode, message:
&str) {
    let msg = if message.is_empty() { CommandNotImplemented = 502,
        format!("{}\r\n", code as u32)
    } else {
        format!("{} {}\r\n", code as u32, message)
    };
    println!("<==== {}", msg);
    write!(stream, "{}", msg).unwrap()
}
```

OK, there's nothing fancy nor difficult to understand here. However, take a look at this:

- Every message ends with "" in FTP
- Every message has to be followed by a whitespace if you want to add parameters or information.

This also works in the exact same way when a client sends us a command.

What? Did I forget to provide you the `ResultCode` type? Indeed, you're absolutely right. Here it is:

```
#[derive(Debug, Clone, Copy)]
#[repr(u32)]
#[allow(dead_code)]
enum ResultCode {
    RestartMarkerReply = 110,
    ServiceReadInXXXMinutes = 120,
    DataConnectionAlreadyOpen = 125,
    FileStatusOk = 150,
    Ok = 200,
    CommandNotImplementedSuperfluousAtThisSite = 202,
    SystemStatus = 211,
    DirectoryStatus = 212,
    FileStatus = 213,
    HelpMessage = 214,
    SystemType = 215,
    ServiceReadyForNewUser = 220,
    ServiceClosingControlConnection = 221,
    DataConnectionOpen = 225,
    ClosingDataConnection = 226,
    EnteringPassiveMode = 227,
    UserLoggedIn = 230,
    RequestedFileActionOkay = 250,
    PATHNAMECreated = 257,
    UserNameOkayNeedPassword = 331,
    NeedAccountForLogin = 332,
    RequestedFileActionPendingFurtherInformation = 350,
    ServiceNotAvailable = 421,
    CantOpenDataConnection = 425,
    ConnectionClosed = 426,
    FileBusy = 450,
    LocalErrorInProcessing = 451,
    InsufficientStorageSpace = 452,
    UnknownCommand = 500,
    InvalidParameterOrArgument = 501,
    CommandNotImplemented = 502,
    BadSequenceOfCommands = 503,
    CommandNotImplementedForThatParameter = 504,
    NotLoggedIn = 530,
    NeedAccountForStoringFiles = 532,
    FileNotFound = 550,
    PageTypeUnknown = 551,
    ExceededStorageAllocation = 552,
    FileNameNotAllowed = 553,
}
```

Yep, not very beautiful... This is the exact representation of all FTP code types (errors, information, warnings, and so on). We can't do much better here; we have to rewrite all code so that we can understand it when we receive it and are able to give the correct code corresponding to the clients' commands.

Now, I suppose, you can guess what's coming next. The enum Command of course! This time, we'll fulfill it while we move forward on to the implementation of the commands:

```
use std::io;
use std::str;

#[derive(Clone, Copy, Debug)]
enum Command {
    Auth,
    Unknown(String),
}

impl AsRef<str> for Command {
    fn as_ref(&self) -> &str {
        match *self {
            Command::Auth => "AUTH",
            Command::Unknown(_) => "UNKN",
        }
    }
}

impl Command {
    pub fn new(input: Vec<u8>) -> io::Result<Self> {
        let mut iter = input.split(|&byte| byte == b' ');
        let mut command = iter.next().expect("command in
         input").to_vec();
        to_uppercase(&mut command);
        let data = iter.next();
        let command =
            match command.as_slice() {
              b"AUTH" => Command::Auth,
              s =>
Command::Unknown(str::from_utf8(s).unwrap_or("").to_owned()),
            };
        Ok(command)
    }
}
```

OK, let's get through this code:

```
enum Command {
    Auth,
    Unknown(String),
}
```

Every time we add a new command handling, we'll have to add a new variant to this enum. In case the command doesn't exist (or we haven't implemented it yet), Unknown will be returned with the command name. If the command is taking arguments, it'll be added just like we saw for Unknown. Let's take Cwd as an example:

```
enum Command {
    Auth,
    Cwd(PathBuf),
    Unknown(String),
}
```

As you can see, Cwd contains a PathBuf. Cwd stands for **change working directory** and takes the path of the directory that the client wants to go to.

Of course, you'd need to update as_ref by adding the following line to the match block:

```
Command::Cwd(_) => "CWD",
```

And you'd need to update the new method implementation by adding the following line into the match block:

```
b"CWD" => Command::Cwd(data.map(|bytes|
Path::new(str::from_utf8(bytes).unwrap()).to_path_buf()).unwrap()),
```

Now let's explain the AsRef trait implementation. It's very convenient when you want to write a generic function. Take a look at the following example:

```
fn foo<S: AsRef<str>>(f: S) {
    println!("{}", f.as_ref());
}
```

Thanks to this trait, as long as the type implements it, we can call as_ref on it. It's very useful in our case when sending messages to the client since we can just take a type implementing AsRef.

Now let's talk about the new method of the Command type:

```
pub fn new(input: Vec<u8>) -> io::Result<Self> {
    let mut iter = input.split(|&byte| byte == b' ');
```

```
    let mut command = iter.next().expect("command in
input").to_vec();
    to_uppercase(&mut command);
    let data = iter.next();
    let command =
        match command.as_slice() {
          b"AUTH" => Command::Auth,
          s =>
Command::Unknown(str::from_utf8(s).unwrap_or("").to_owned()),
        };
    Ok(command)
}
```

The point here is to convert the message received from the client. We need to do two things:

- Get the command
- Get the command's arguments (if any)

First, we create an iterator to split our vector, so we can separate the command from the arguments:

```
    let mut iter = input.split(|&byte| byte == b' ');
```

Then, we get the command:

```
    let mut command = iter.next().expect("command in input").to_vec();
```

At this point, command is a `Vec<u8>`. To then make the matching easier (because nothing in the RFC of the FTP talks about the fact that commands should be in uppercase or that `auth` is the same as `AUTH` or even `AuTh`), we call the `uppercase` function, which looks like this:

```
    fn to_uppercase(data: &mut [u8]) {
        for byte in data {
            if *byte >= 'a' as u8 && *byte <= 'z' as u8 {
                *byte -= 32;
            }
        }
    }
```

Next, we get the arguments by calling `next` on the iterator `iter`:

```
    let data = iter.next();
```

If there are no arguments, no problem! We'll just get `None`.

Finally, we match the commands:

```
match command.as_slice() {
    b"AUTH" => Command::Auth,
    s =>
Command::Unknown(str::from_utf8(s).unwrap_or("").to_owned()),
}
```

To do so, we convert our Vec<u8>> into a &[u8] (a slice of u8). To also convert a &str (such as AUTH) into a &[u8], we use the b operator (which is more like saying to the compiler, *Hey! Don't worry, just say it's a slice and not a &str!*) to allow the matching.

And we're good! We can now write the function to actually read the data from the client:

```
fn read_all_message(stream: &mut TcpStream) -> Vec<u8> {
    let buf = &mut [0; 1];
    let mut out = Vec::with_capacity(100);

    loop {
        match stream.read(buf) {
            Ok(received) if received > 0 => {
                if out.is_empty() && buf[0] == b' ' {
                    continue
                }
                out.push(buf[0]);
            }
            _ => return Vec::new(),
        }
        let len = out.len();
        if len > 1 && out[len - 2] == b'\r' && out[len - 1] ==
        b'\n' {
            out.pop();
            out.pop();
            return out;
        }
    }
}
```

Here, we read one byte at a time (and it's not a very efficient way to do so; we'll go back on this function later) and return when we get "". We have just added a little *security* by removing any whitespaces that would come before the command (so as long as we don't have any data in our vector, we won't add any whitespace).

If there is any error, we return an empty vector and stop the reading of the client input.

Like I said earlier, reading byte by byte isn't efficient, but is simpler to demonstrate how it works. So, for now, let's stick to this. This will be done completely differently once the asynchronous programming kicks in.

So, now that we can read and write FTP inputs it's time to actually start the implementation of the commands!

Let's start by creating a new structure:

```
#[allow(dead_code)]
struct Client {
    cwd: PathBuf,
    stream: TcpStream,
    name: Option<String>,
}
```

Here are some quick explanations for the preceding code:

- cwd stands for the current working directory
- stream is the client's socket
- name is the username you got from user authentication (which doesn't really matter, as we won't handle authentication in the first steps)

Now it's time to update the handle_client function:

```
fn handle_client(mut stream: TcpStream) {
    println!("new client connected!");
    send_cmd(&mut stream, ResultCode::ServiceReadyForNewUser,
"Welcome to this FTP
    server!");
    let client = Client::new(stream);
    loop {
        let data = read_all_message(&mut client.stream);
        if data.is_empty() {
            println!("client disconnected...");
            break;
        }
        client.handle_cmd(command::new(data));
    }
}
```

When a new client connects to the server, we send them a message to inform them that the server is ready. Then we create a new Client instance, listen on the client socket, and handle its commands. Simple, right?

Two things are missing from this code:

- The `Client::new` method
- The `Client::handle_cmd` method

Let's start with the first one:

```
impl Client {
    fn new(stream: TcpStream) -> Client {
        Client {
            cwd: PathBuf::from("/"),
            stream: stream,
            name: None,
        }
    }
}
```

Nothing fancy here; the current path is `"/"` (it corresponds to the root of the server, not to the root of the filesystem!). We have set the client's stream, and the name hasn't been defined yet.

Now let's see the `Client::handle_cmd` method (needless to say, it'll be the core of this FTP server):

```
fn handle_cmd(&mut self, cmd: Command) {
    println!("====> {:?}", cmd);
    match cmd {
        Command::Auth => send_cmd(&mut self.stream,
        ResultCode::CommandNotImplemented,
                                   "Not implemented"),
        Command::Unknown(s) => send_cmd(&mut self.stream,
         ResultCode::UnknownCommand,
                                         "Not implemented"),
    }
}
```

And that's it! Ok, so that's not really *it*. We still have a lot to add. But my point is, we now only have to add other commands here to make it all work.

Commands implementation

In the previous code, we only handled one command; any other command will receive an
`unknown command` answer from the server. Also, our `Auth` implementation says it's not
implemented. So, to sum this up, we handle one command that answers that it's not
implemented. Crazy, right? For the `Auth` command, we'll look at this later.

Now let's implement some commands *for real*. Let's start with a simple one: `Syst`. This is
supposed to return which system this FTP server is running on. For some reason, we won't
answer that, and we'll just send back an answer-nothing usable.

Implementing the SYST command

First, let's add a new entry into the `Command` enum (I won't do this every time, but the steps
will remain the same):

```
enum Command {
    Auth,
    Syst,
    Unknown(String),
}
```

Then, let's update the `as_ref` implementation:

```
impl AsRef<str> for Command {
    fn as_ref(&self) -> &str {
        match *self {
            Command::Auth => "AUTH",
            Command::Syst => "SYST",
            Command::Unknown(_) => "UNKN",
        }
    }
}
```

Finally, let's update the `Command::new` method:

```
impl Command {
    pub fn new(input: Vec<u8>) -> io::Result<Self> {
        let mut iter = input.split(|&byte| byte == b' ');
        let mut command = iter.next().expect("command in
         input").to_vec();
        to_uppercase(&mut command);
        let data = iter.next();
        let command =
            match command.as_slice() {
```

```
                b"AUTH" => Command::Auth,
                b"SYST" => Command::Syst,
                s =>
    Command::Unknown(str::from_utf8(s).unwrap_or("").to_owned()),
            };
        Ok(command)
    }
}
```

That's it! Like I said earlier, just remember those three steps every time you add a new command and everything should be fine.

Now let's implement the command:

```
fn handle_cmd(&mut self, cmd: Command) {
    println!("====> {:?}", cmd);
    match cmd {
        Command::Auth => send_cmd(&mut self.stream,
        ResultCode::CommandNotImplemented,
                        "Not implemented"),
        Command::Syst => send_cmd(&mut self.stream, ResultCode::Ok,
"I won't tell"),
        Command::Unknown(s) => send_cmd(&mut self.stream,
        ResultCode::UnknownCommand,
                            "Not implemented"),
    }
}
```

And that's it! We implemented a new command (which doesn't do much, but that isn't the point)!

Implementing the USER command

Since we have a `name` in our `Client` structure, it'd be nice to have some use for it, right? So, as the title says, let's implement the USER command. Since this command takes an argument, I'll go through the command implementation steps once again, so you'll have an example of a command taking a parameter.

First, let's update the `enum Command`:

```
enum Command {
    Auth,
    Syst,
    User(String),
    Unknown(String),
}
```

Then, we update the `as_ref` implementation:

```
impl AsRef<str> for Command {
    fn as_ref(&self) -> &str {
        match *self {
            Command::Auth => "AUTH",
            Command::Syst => "SYST",
            Command::User => "USER",
            Command::Unknown(_) => "UNKN",
        }
    }
}
```

Finally, we update the `Command::new` method:

```
impl Command {
    pub fn new(input: Vec<u8>) -> io::Result<Self> {
        let mut iter = input.split(|&byte| byte == b' ');
        let mut command = iter.next().expect("command in
input").to_vec();
        to_uppercase(&mut command);
        let data = iter.next();
        let command =
            match command.as_slice() {
                b"AUTH" => Command::Auth,
                b"SYST" => Command::Syst,
                b"USER" => Command::User(data.map(|bytes|
                String::from_utf8(bytes.to_vec()).expect("cannot
                 convert bytes to String")).unwrap_or_default()),
                s =>
Command::Unknown(str::from_utf8(s).unwrap_or("").to_owned()),
            };
        Ok(command)
    }
}
```

Phew, all done! Now we just need to implement the function (which is quite simple, I promise):

```
fn handle_cmd(&mut self, cmd: Command) {
    println!("====> {:?}", cmd);
    match cmd {
        Command::Auth => send_cmd(&mut self.stream,
         ResultCode::CommandNotImplemented,
                                  "Not implemented"),
        Command::Syst => send_cmd(&mut self.stream, ResultCode::Ok,
        "I won't tell"),
        Command::User(username) => {
```

```
                    if username.is_empty() {
                        send_cmd(&mut self.stream,
        ResultCode::InvalidParameterOrArgument,
                            "Invalid username")
                    } else {
                        self.name = username.to_owned();
                        send_cmd(&mut self.stream,
        ResultCode::UserLoggedIn,
                            &format!("Welcome {}!", username)),
                    }
                }
                Command::Unknown(s) => send_cmd(&mut self.stream,
                ResultCode::UnknownCommand,
                                    "Not implemented"),
            }
        }
```

Here's a little explanation just in case you need it; if we receive an empty username (or no username at all), we consider this as an invalid parameter and return `InvalidParameterOrArgument`. Otherwise, everything is fine and we return `UserLoggedIn`.

If you're wondering why we didn't return `ResultCode::Ok`, it's because the RFC states as such. Once again, every command, what it does, and what it should return is described there. If you feel lost, don't hesitate to read it again!

Implementing the NOOP command

This topic is quite a simple one. NOOP stands for no operation. It takes no argument and does nothing. Just because I'm a nice person, here's the code for the NOOP command in the `Client::handle_cmd` method:

```
        Command::NoOp => send_cmd(&mut self.stream, ResultCode::Ok, "Doing
        nothing..."),
```

Yes, I know, you're amazed by such wonderful code. But don't worry, you'll able to write something as good as this when you grow older!

It's now time to implement the next command!

Implementing the PWD command

This command is very simple as well. PWD stands for print working directory. Once again, it's not the one from your system but the one from your server (so again, "/" corresponds to the folder where you started the server).

The command doesn't take any argument, so there's no need to show you everything again. Let's just focus on the command handling:

```
Command::Pwd => {
    let msg = format!("{}", self.cwd.to_str().unwrap_or(""));
    if !msg.is_empty() {
        let message = format!("\"/{}\" ", msg);
        send_cmd(&mut self.stream, ResultCode::PATHNAMECreated,
        &format!("\"/{}\" ",
        msg))
    } else {
        send_cmd(&mut self.stream, ResultCode::FileNotFound, "No
        such file or directory")
    }
}
```

Nothing complicated; we try to display the path, and if we fail, we return an error. The only strange thing is that if everything goes fine, we have to return PATHNAMECreated. This RFC is really strange...

Sorry, this was the last *simple* command. Now we'll go deeper into the FTP and its strange RFC. The following command is just a nice introduction to what's coming next. (I hope I didn't scare you!)

Implementing the TYPE command

For now, we'll have an implementation of the TYPE command that does nothing. We'll come back to it in the following chapters. However, a bit of explanation will come in handy, I assume.

TYPE stands for the representation type. When you're transferring data over the data connection (which is different from the command connection, which is the only one we've been using until now), you can transfer data differently.

By default, the transfer type is ASCII (the main difference is that all " " have to be transformed into " "). We'll use the image one (where you send data as you have it) to make our lives easier.

Once again, we'll go back to this implementation in later chapters.

For now, let's just add a `Type` command that doesn't take any argument:

```
Command::Type => send_cmd(&mut self.stream, ResultCode::Ok,
    "Transfer type changed successfully"),
```

OK, we're lying a bit, but we'll have to deal with it for the moment.

We're almost at the end of the basics, but there's one last command to implement before you can try accessing the server using an FTP client.

Implementing the LIST command

The `LIST` command returns a list of the current files and folders of the current folder or at the given parameter path. This is already very difficult itself because you need to check that the *final* path is accessible to the user (for example, if you receive `foo/../../` when you're at "/", there's an issue). But that's not all! When you're transferring the files and folders list, there is no official way to format it! Fun, right? Luckily, most of the FTP clients follow some kind of non-official RFC for this case, and we'll use it.

In addition to all of this, this command is the first one that we'll implement that uses the data connection. This requires you to add another command: `PASV`.

Implementing the PASV command

To be able to make this command work, we need to add a few new fields in our `Client` struct:

```
struct Client {
    cwd: PathBuf,
    stream: TcpStream,
    name: Option<String>,
    data_writer: Option<TcpStream>,
}
```

We now need to update the `Client::new` method as well:

```
fn new(stream: TcpStream) -> Client {
    Client {
        cwd: PathBuf::from("/"),
        stream: stream,
        name: None,
        data_writer: None,
    }
}
```

The PASV command doesn't take arguments, so I'll let you add it to the structures and everything. Let's focus on the interesting part:

```
// Adding some new imports:
use std::net::{IpAddr, Ipv4Addr, SocketAddr};

Command::Pasv => {
    if self.data_writer.is_some() {
        send_cmd(&mut self.stream,
ResultCode::DataConnectionAlreadyOpen, "Already
        listening...")
    } else {
        let port = 43210;
        send_cmd(&mut self.stream, ResultCode::EnteringPassiveMode,
            &format!("127,0,0,1,{},{}", port >> 8, port & 0xFF));
        let addr = SocketAddr::new(IpAddr::V4(Ipv4Addr::new(127, 0,
        0, 1)), port);
        let listener = TcpListener::bind(&addr).unwrap();
        match listener.incoming().next() {
            Some(Ok(client)) => {
                self.data_writer = Some(client);
            }
            _ => {
                send_cmd(&mut self.stream,
ResultCode::ServiceNotAvailable, "issues
                happen...");
            }
        }
    }
}
```

Phew... Let's explain all this:

```
if self.data_writer.is_some() {
    send_cmd(&mut self.stream,
ResultCode::DataConnectionAlreadyOpen, "Already listening...")
}
```

If we already have a data connection with this client, there's no need to open a new one, so we don't do anything else:

```
let port: u16 = 43210;
send_cmd(&mut self.stream, ResultCode::EnteringPassiveMode,
        &format!("127,0,0,1,{},{}", port >> 8, port & 0xFF));
```

This part is a bit more tricky. First, we pick a port (the best way would be to check if the port is available first; we'll do this in later chapters). Then, we have to tell the client *where* it should connect to.

This is where things get a bit more complicated. We have to transfer the address as follows:

```
ip1,ip2,ip3,ip4,port1,port2
```

Every `ip` part has to be 8-bits long (so 1-byte long), whereas, each `port` part has to be 16-bits long (so, 2 bytes). The first part is easy; we just print localhost. However, the second part requires you to perform some binary operation.

To get the first byte only is simple; we just have to move 8 bits to the right. To sum this up, take a look at this:

```
1010 1010 1111 1111
```

This is our `u16`. We now shift 8 bits to the right:

```
0000 0000 1010 1010
```

Tadaa!

For the second part, we could move 8 bits to the left and then 8 bits to the right, or we could just use the and binary operator. Here's a little scheme to explain this:

```
1 & 1 == 1
1 & 0 == 0
```

Now let's take a nice binary to the hexadecimal converter and check the result:

```
0000 0000 1111 1111 == 0xFF
```

Now if we perform this operation, we get the following:

```
1111 1111 1010 1010 & 0xFF
=>
0000 0000 1010 1010
```

Now we have the last 8 bits only. Great! The last part of the command handling is very easy:

```
let addr = SocketAddr::new(IpAddr::V4(Ipv4Addr::new(127, 0, 0, 1)),
port);
let listener = TcpListener::bind(&addr).unwrap();
match listener.incoming().next() {
    Some(Ok(client)) => {
        self.data_writer = Some(client);
    }
    _ => {
        send_cmd(&mut self.stream, ResultCode::ServiceNotAvailable,
"issues
        happen...");
    }
}
```

We bind the address and port, wait for a client to connect, and then assign it to our data writer. There's nothing problematic in this.

Back to the LIST command

Now that we can handle a data connection, let's implement the LIST! For now, let's implement it without parameters (once again, we'll see in later chapters how to handle the LIST parameter). As usual, I'll let you add everything where it's needed and we'll just focus on the command handling:

```
Command::List => {
    if let Some(ref mut data_writer) = self.data_writer {
        let mut tmp = PathBuf::from(".");
        send_cmd(&mut self.stream,
ResultCode::DataConnectionAlreadyOpen,
                "Starting to list directory...");
        let mut out = String::new();
        for entry in read_dir(tmp).unwrap() {
            for entry in dir {
                if let Ok(entry) = entry {
                    add_file_info(entry.path(), &mut out);
                }
            }
```

```
                    send_data(data_writer, &out)
            }
        } else {
            send_cmd(&mut self.stream, ResultCode::ConnectionClosed,
              "No opened data connection");
        }
        if self.data_writer.is_some() {
            self.data_writer = None;
            send_cmd(&mut self.stream,
    ResultCode::ClosingDataConnection, "Transfer
            done");
        }
    }
```

There's nothing complicated here either too. Once the transfer is over, we close the client socket and move on. What remains to be added are the send_data and the add_file_info functions. Let's start with the first one:

```
fn send_data(stream: &mut TcpStream, s: &str) {
    write!(stream, "{}", s).unwrap();
}
```

Easy, there's no error handling, so it just stands on one line. Now let's see the add_file_info function:

```
fn add_file_info(path: PathBuf, out: &mut String) {
    let extra = if path.is_dir() { "/" } else { "" };
    let is_dir = if path.is_dir() { "d" } else { "-" };

    let meta = match ::std::fs::metadata(&path) {
        Ok(meta) => meta,
        _ => return,
    };
    let (time, file_size) = get_file_info(&meta);
    let path = match path.to_str() {
        Some(path) => match path.split("/").last() {
            Some(path) => path,
            _ => return,
        },
        _ => return,
    };
    let rights = if meta.permissions().readonly() {
        "r--r--r--"
    } else {
        "rw-rw-rw-"
    };
    let file_str = format!("{is_dir}{rights} {links} {owner}
```

```
            {group} {size} {month}
                {day} {hour}:{min} {path}{extra}\r\n",
                                    is_dir=is_dir,
                                    rights=rights,
                                    links=1, // number of links
                                    owner="anonymous", // owner name
                                    group="anonymous", // group name
                                    size=file_size,
                                    month=MONTHS[time.tm_mon as usize],
                                    day=time.tm_mday,
                                    hour=time.tm_hour,
                                    min=time.tm_min,
                                    path=path,
                                    extra=extra);
            out.push_str(&file_str);
            println!("==> {:?}", &file_str);
        }
```

To make this code work, you'll also need the following:

```
        #[macro_use]
        extern crate cfg_if;

        cfg_if! {
            if #[cfg(windows)] {
                fn get_file_info(meta: &Metadata) -> (time::Tm, u64) {
                    use std::os::windows::prelude::*;
                    (time::at(time::Timespec::new(meta.last_write_time())),
                     meta.file_size())
                }
            } else {
                fn get_file_info(meta: &Metadata) -> (time::Tm, u64) {
                    use std::os::unix::prelude::*;
                    (time::at(time::Timespec::new(meta.mtime(), 0)),
                     meta.size())
                }
            }
        }
```

Don't forget to add `cfg_if` in your `Cargo.toml`:

```
        cfg-if = "0.1.2"
```

`cfg-if` is really good at help you do conditional compilation in a more easily readable way. A point to note about the `get_file_info` function now—this is one of the rare things that can't be performed in the same way on all systems.

Here, Windows has its own version and Unix has another. However, the two functions take the same argument (the import), and one function call changes. Let's go back to the `add_file_info` function now:

I suppose you recognized the output of the `ls` command, right? Apparently, the non-official RFC is working as follows:

```
dr--r--r-- 1 me me 1024 Jan 7 12:42 foo/
-rw-rw-rw- 1 me me 4 Mar 3 23:42 some_file
```

First, `d` if it's a directory or `-` if it isn't. Then, the rights (just like on Unix platforms):

```
[rwx][rwx][rwx]
```

The first `rwx` is for the owner, the second is about the group, and the last one is about everyone. Here, `r` stands for read access, `w` stands for write access, and `x` stands for execution access.

The rest seems explicit enough on its own, so there's no need to explain it.

Implementing the CWD command

The `CWD` command allows the user to change its current folder location. However, it's far from easy to do.

Before going into the implementation of this command, we'll need to discuss a potential security issue: paths.

Imagine the user is at the `"/"` location (which will corresponds to, say, `/home/someone/somewhere`) and requests `foo/../../.`. If we just accept the path and move the user to this location, it'll end up at `/home/someone`. This means that the users could access all of your computer without issue. You see the problem now?

Luckily for us, `Rust` has a nice method on `Path` that allows us to fix this huge security issue. I'm talking about `Path::canonicalize` (which is an alias of the `fs::canonicalize` function).

So, what does this function do? Let's take an example:

```
let path = Path::new("/foo/test/../bar.rs");
assert_eq!(path.canonicalize().unwrap(),
PathBuf::from("/foo/bar.rs"));
```

As you can see, it interprets the path, normalizes everything (. . removes the folder component), and resolves symbolic links as well. Quite magical, right?

Of course, all good things have a downside, and so does `canonicalize.`: it can only work on *real* paths. If a part of the path doesn't exist, the function will just fail. It's pretty easy to get through it when you know it, but it can sound surprising at first.

So, how do we fix this? Well, we need to play with a real path. So first, we need to append the user's server path to the real server path (the one it has on the computer). Once this is done, we just append the path requested by the user and call `canonicalize.`

That's not very complicated, but is a bit annoying to play with at first. Don't worry, though, the code is coming!

If you wonder why we're not just using the `chroot` function (which would solve all problems), remember that this FTP server is supposed to work on every platform.

So first, let's add a new command entry to the `enum Command`:

```
Cwd(PathBuf),
```

Good, now let's add it to the `Command::new` method matching:

```
b"CWD" => Command::Cwd(data.map(|bytes|
Path::new(str::from_utf8(bytes).unwrap()).to_path_buf()).unwrap()),
```

Perfect! I'll let you add it into the `AsRef` implementation as well. Now it's time to go into the *real* implementation:

```
Command::Cwd(directory) => self.cwd(directory),
```

For once, to make our life easier, we'll create a new method in our `Client`, so all the code from the `CWD` command won't fill the `enum`:

```
fn complete_path(&self, path: PathBuf, server_root: &PathBuf) ->
Result<PathBuf, io::Error> {
    let directory = server_root.join(if path.has_root() {
        path.iter().skip(1).collect()
    } else {
        path
    });
    let dir = directory.canonicalize();
    if let Ok(ref dir) = dir {
        if !dir.starts_with(&server_root) {
            return Err(io::ErrorKind::PermissionDenied.into());
        }
    }
```

```
        }
        dir
    }

    fn cwd(mut self, directory: PathBuf) {
        let server_root = env::current_dir().unwrap();
        let path = self.cwd.join(&directory);
        if let Ok(dir) = self.complete_path(path, &server_root) {
            if let Ok(prefix) = dir.strip_prefix(&server_root)
                                    .map(|p| p.to_path_buf()) {
                self.cwd = prefix.to_path_buf();
                send_cmd(&mut self.stream, ResultCode::Ok,
                        &format!("Directory changed to \"{}\"",
directory.display())));
                return
            }
        }
        send_cmd(&mut self.stream, ResultCode::FileNotFound, "No such
file or directory");
    }
```

OK, that's a lot of code. Let's now go through the execution flow:

```
    let server_root = env::current_dir().unwrap();
```

For now, you can't set which folder the server is running on; it'll be changed later on:

```
    let path = self.cwd.join(&directory);
```

First, we join the requested directory to the current directory of the user:

```
    if let Ok(dir) = self.complete_path(path, &server_root) {
```

Things start to get funny in here. The whole canonicalization process is in there.

Now let's append the user path to the (real) server path:

```
    let directory = server_root.join(if path.has_root() {
        path.iter().skip(1).collect()
    } else {
        path
    });
```

So, if the path is an absolute one (starting with "/" on Unix or a prefix on Windows such as c:), we need to remove the first component of the path, otherwise, we just append it.

We now have a full and potentially existent path. Let's canonicalize it:

```
let dir = directory.canonicalize();
```

Now we have one more thing to check—if the path doesn't start with the server root, then it means that the user tried to cheat on us and tried to access non-accessible folders. Here is how we do it:

```
if let Ok(ref dir) = dir {
    if !dir.starts_with(&server_root) {
        return Err(io::ErrorKind::PermissionDenied.into());
    }
}
```

In the case that `canonicalize` returned an error, there's no need to check if it did (since it's already an error). If it succeeded but doesn't start with `server_root`, then we return an error.

That's it for this function. Now, we'll return the result to the caller and can go back to the `cwd` method:

```
if let Ok(dir) = self.complete_path(path, &server_root) {
    if let Ok(prefix) = dir.strip_prefix(&server_root)
                        .map(|p| p.to_path_buf()) {
        // ...
    }
}
```

Once we get the full directory path and have confirmed it was okay, we need to remove the `server_root` prefix to get the path from our server root:

```
self.cwd = prefix.to_path_buf();
send_cmd(&mut self.stream, ResultCode::Ok,
        &format!("Directory changed to \"{}\"",
directory.display()));
return
```

Finally, once this is done, we can just set the path to the user and send back a message that the command succeeded (and return to avoid sending back that we failed!).

If anything goes wrong, we send back the following:

```
send_cmd(&mut self.stream, ResultCode::FileNotFound, "No such file
or directory");
```

That's it for this command! You now know how to avoid a security issue by checking received paths provided by the clients.

Implementing the CDUP command

CDUP is used to go up to the parent directory. In comparison to the CWD command implementation, it'll be a piece of cake! The CDUP command doesn't take arguments, so I'll let you add it to enums. Now, let's focus on the command implementation:

```
Command::CdUp => {
    if let Some(path) = self.cwd.parent().map(Path::to_path_buf) {
        self.cwd = path;
    }
    send_cmd(&mut self.stream, ResultCode::Ok, "Done");
}
```

And that's it. There's need to check if the parent folder exists, as it does. And if we're already at the root, then there's no need to do anything. Isn't it wonderful?

Full implementation of the LIST command

Now that we know how to play with paths nicely, it'd be a shame not fully implement the LIST command, right?

To complete it, you'll need to update the Command::List variant in order to make it accept PathBuf as an argument.

So, we currently have the following code:

```
Command::List => {
    if let Some(ref mut data_writer) = self.data_writer {
        let mut tmp = PathBuf::from(".");
        send_cmd(&mut self.stream,
ResultCode::DataConnectionAlreadyOpen,
                "Starting to list directory...");
        let mut out = String::new();
        for entry in read_dir(tmp).unwrap() {
            for entry in dir {
                if let Ok(entry) = entry {
                    add_file_info(entry.path(), &mut out);
                }
            }
            send_data(data_writer, &out)
        }
    } else {
        send_cmd(&mut self.stream, ResultCode::ConnectionClosed,
"No opened data
            connection");
```

```
        }
    if self.data_writer.is_some() {
        self.data_writer = None;
        send_cmd(&mut self.stream,
ResultCode::ClosingDataConnection, "Transfer
            done");
    }
}
```

Let's update it as follows:

```
Command::List(path) => {
    if let Some(ref mut data_writer) = self.data_writer {
        let server_root = env::current_dir().unwrap();
        let path = self.cwd.join(path.unwrap_or_default());
        let directory = PathBuf::from(&path);
        if let Ok(path) = self.complete_path(directory,
          &server_root) {
            send_cmd(&mut self.stream,
              ResultCode::DataConnectionAlreadyOpen,
              "Starting to list directory...");
            let mut out = String::new();
            for entry in read_dir(path).unwrap() {
                for entry in dir {
                    if let Ok(entry) = entry {
                        add_file_info(entry.path(), &mut out);
                    }
                }
                send_data(data_writer, &out)
            }
        } else {
            send_cmd(&mut self.stream,
ResultCode::InvalidParameterOrArgument,
                    "No such file or directory...");
        }
    } else {
        send_cmd(&mut self.stream, ResultCode::ConnectionClosed,
          "No opened data connection");
    }
    if self.data_writer.is_some() {
        self.data_writer = None;
        send_cmd(&mut self.stream,
          ResultCode::ClosingDataConnection, "Transfer done");
    }
}
```

To put it simply, we just added the following line:

```
let path = self.cwd.join(path.unwrap_or_default());
let directory = PathBuf::from(&path);
if let Ok(path) = self.complete_path(directory, &server_root) {
    // ...
} else {
    send_cmd(&mut self.stream,
ResultCode::InvalidParameterOrArgument,
            "No such file or directory...");
}
```

Thanks to the `Client::complete_path` method, things were pretty easy with the path manipulation. So, what happens if the given path is a file? We don't check such a case but we should! Let's replace the following lines:

```
for entry in read_dir(path).unwrap() {
    for entry in dir {
        if let Ok(entry) = entry {
            add_file_info(entry.path(), &mut out);
        }
    }
    send_data(data_writer, &out)
}
```

With:

```
if path.is_dir() {
    for entry in read_dir(path).unwrap() {
        for entry in dir {
            if let Ok(entry) = entry {
                add_file_info(entry.path(), &mut out);
            }
        }
        send_data(data_writer, &out)
    }
} else {
    add_file_info(path, &mut out);
}
```

And that's it! Luckily for us, we did things correctly the first time, so *it just works*.

Implementing the MKD command

The MKD stands for make directory (yes, exactly like the Unix command but shorter). Just like LIST and CWD, it takes PathBuf as an argument. I'll let you handle the other adds as usual and focus on the command implementation:

```
Command::Mkd(path) => self.mkd(path),
```

Just like last time, we'll create a new method:

```
use std::fs::create_dir;

fn mkd(&self, path: PathBuf) {
    let server_root = env::current_dir().unwrap();
    let path = self.cwd.join(&path);
    if let Some(parent) = path.parent().map(|p| p.to_path_buf()) {
        if let Ok(mut dir) = self.complete_path(parent,
            &server_root) {
            if dir.is_dir() {
                if let Some(filename) = path.file_name().map(|p|
                    p.to_os_string()) {
                    dir.push(filename);
                    if create_dir(dir).is_ok() {
                        send_cmd(&mut self.stream,
                          ResultCode::PATHNAMECreated,
                           "Folder successfully created!");
                        return
                    }
                }
            }
        }
    }
    send_cmd(&mut self.stream, ResultCode::FileNotFound,
            "Couldn't create folder");
}
```

Once again, a few things have to be done before even actually trying to make the directory.

First, we need to check whether all the elements of the given path are folders (well, only the last one in fact since otherwise, the Client::complete_path method will fail otherwise).

Then we need to once again, canonicalize this path (by calling the Client::complete_path method). Finally, we push the filename to the received path.

The main difference here is that we don't strip the `server_root` path from the path returned by `Client::complete_path`.

Once all of this is done, we can try to create the folder by using the `create_dir` function. If it goes well, we then return `ResultCode::PATHNAMECreated` (and for once it makes sense!).

If any error occurs at any level, we just send that the path was incorrect.

That's it for this command!

Implementing the RMD command

Now that we can create folders, it'd be nice to be able to remove them, right? That's what RMD (which stands for *remove directory*) is supposed to do!

Just like MKD (and the others), RMD takes `PathBuf` as an argument. Once again, and as usual, I'll let you handle the `Command` part so we can focus on the command implementation:

```
Command::Rmd(path) => self.rmd(path),
```

Yep, it's a new method once again. It becomes a habit at this point I suppose?

```
use std::fs::remove_dir_all;

fn rmd(&self, path: PathBuf) {
    let server_root = env::current_dir().unwrap();
    if let Ok(path) = self.complete_path(path, &server_root) {
        if remove_dir_all(path).is_ok() {
            send_cmd(&mut self.stream,
                    ResultCode::RequestedFileActionOkay,
                    "Folder successfully removed!");
            return
        }
    }
    send_cmd(&mut self.stream, ResultCode::FileNotFound,
        "Couldn't remove folder!");
}
```

And that's it! This is even easier than MKD since we don't need to check if the last potential parent is a folder. Once we have confirmed that the path was an authorized one, we can just remove it.

With all these commands, I think we can say that we have a very fine base to build upon in order to make a complete FTP server.

Testing it

You now have a (very) basic FTP server implementation. You can connect to the server and list the files and folders in the current folder.

Start it with `cargo run` and give it a try! I recommend that you use `FileZilla`. This is a great FTP client. Connect to `localhost` on the port `1234` and use the `anonymous` username (or none), and you should be able to have a bit of fun already:

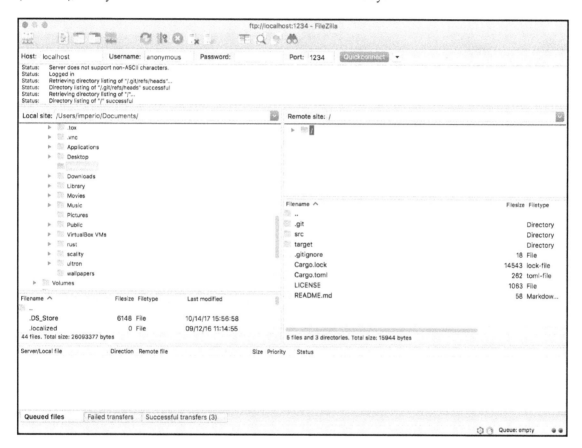

Figure 8.1

Information on the file transfers and additional commands will be covered in later chapters.

Summary

In this chapter, we looked at the basics of the FTP. We now have a simple (synchronous) server implementation, and you should have a good idea about how all of this is working. We also looked at a potential security issue and how to fix it.

The following chapters will introduce you to asynchronous programming in Rust. Thanks to this chapter, it'll go a lot quicker on the FTP RFC side so we can focus on the asynchronous part.

9

Implementing an Asynchronous FTP Server

In the previous chapter, we wrote a synchronous FTP server. Now, we'll write an asynchronous version with `tokio`, the asynchronous IO (Input/Output) library for Rust. We'll cover the following topics:

- Asynchronous servers
- Futures
- Streams
- Tokio
- Async/await
- Error handling

Advantages of asynchronous IO

Asynchronous IO allows us to send a request without waiting for its result, we'll get notified somehow later when we receive the response. This enables our programs to be more concurrent and scale better.

In the previous chapter, we used threads in order to avoid blocking other clients while we wait for a response. Using threads has a cost, though, besides the fact that threads require more memory, they also impose a performance cost because they require a context switch when the code goes from one thread to the other.

Disadvantages of asynchronous IO

However, using asynchronous IO does not come without drawbacks. Using asynchronous IO is harder than using synchronous IO. With asynchronous IO, we also need a way to know when an event has terminated. So, we need to learn a new way to manage the IO events and it'll take more time to implement the same software that we wrote in the previous chapter.

Creating the new project

Let's start by creating a new binary project, as usual:

```
cargo new --bin ftp-server
```

We'll add the following dependencies in the `Cargo.toml` file:

```
[dependencies]
bytes = "^0.4.5"
tokio-core = "^0.1.10"
tokio-io = "^0.1.3"

[dependencies.futures-await]
git = "https://github.com/alexcrichton/futures-await"
```

As you can see here, we specify a dependency via a Git URL. This dependency is using nightly-only features, so make sure you're using the nightly compiler by running this command:

```
rustup default nightly
```

Let's start our `main` module by adding the required `extern crate` statements:

```
#![feature(proc_macro, conservative_impl_trait, generators)]

extern crate bytes;
extern crate futures_await as futures;
extern crate tokio_core;
extern crate tokio_io;
```

As you can see, we're using some nightly features. These are needed by the `futures-await` crate. We also decided to import this crate under another name, `futures`, because it exports the same types and functions as the `futures` crate itself.

We'll copy some code from the previous chapter and put them in the new module, for better organization. Here are the new modules:

```
mod cmd;
mod ftp;
```

In a new file, called `src/cmd.rs`, put the following code:

```
use std::path::{Path, PathBuf};
use std::str::{self, FromStr};

use error::{Error, Result};

#[derive(Clone, Debug)]
pub enum Command {
    Auth,
    Cwd(PathBuf),
    List(Option<PathBuf>),
    Mkd(PathBuf),
    NoOp,
    Port(u16),
    Pasv,
    Pwd,
    Quit,
    Retr(PathBuf),
    Rmd(PathBuf),
    Stor(PathBuf),
    Syst,
    Type(TransferType),
    CdUp,
    Unknown(String),
    User(String),
}
```

We first have an enumeration representing the different commands and their parameters:

```
impl AsRef<str> for Command {
    fn as_ref(&self) -> &str {
        match *self {
            Command::Auth => "AUTH",
            Command::Cwd(_) => "CWD",
            Command::List(_) => "LIST",
            Command::Pasv => "PASV",
            Command::Port(_) => "PORT",
            Command::Pwd => "PWD",
            Command::Quit => "QUIT",
            Command::Retr(_) => "RETR",
            Command::Stor(_) => "STOR",
```

```
                    Command::Syst => "SYST",
                    Command::Type(_) => "TYPE",
                    Command::User(_) => "USER",
                    Command::CdUp => "CDUP",
                    Command::Mkd(_) => "MKD",
                    Command::Rmd(_) => "RMD",
                    Command::NoOp => "NOOP",
                    Command::Unknown(_) => "UNKN", // doesn't exist
            }
        }
    }
```

Here, we create a method to get the string representation of a command:

```
impl Command {
    pub fn new(input: Vec<u8>) -> Result<Self> {
        let mut iter = input.split(|&byte| byte == b' ');
        let mut command = iter.next().ok_or_else(
         || Error::Msg("empty command".to_string()))?.to_vec();
        to_uppercase(&mut command);
        let data = iter.next().ok_or_else(|| Error::Msg("no command
         parameter".to_string()));
        let command =
            match command.as_slice() {
                b"AUTH" => Command::Auth,
                b"CWD" => Command::Cwd(data.and_then(|bytes|
Ok(Path::new(str::from_utf8(bytes)?).to_path_buf()))?),
                b"LIST" => Command::List(data.and_then(|bytes|
Ok(Path::new(str::from_utf8(bytes)?).to_path_buf())).ok()),
                b"PASV" => Command::Pasv,
                b"PORT" => {
                    let addr = data?.split(|&byte| byte == b',')
                        .filter_map(|bytes|
                         str::from_utf8(bytes).ok()
                         .and_then(|string|
u8::from_str(string).ok()))
                        .collect::<Vec<u8>>();
                    if addr.len() != 6 {
                        return Err("Invalid address/port".into());
                    }

                    let port = (addr[4] as u16) << 8 | (addr[5] as
                     u16);
                    if port <= 1024 {
                        return Err("Port can't be less than
                         10025".into());
                    }
                    Command::Port(port)
```

```
            },
            b"PWD" => Command::Pwd,
            b"QUIT" => Command::Quit,
            b"RETR" => Command::Retr(data.and_then(|bytes|
Ok(Path::new(str::from_utf8(bytes)?).to_path_buf()))?),
            b"STOR" => Command::Stor(data.and_then(|bytes|
Ok(Path::new(str::from_utf8(bytes)?).to_path_buf()))?),
            b"SYST" => Command::Syst,
            b"TYPE" => {
                match TransferType::from(data?[0]) {
                    TransferType::Unknown => return
                     Err("command not implemented
                     for that parameter".into()),
                    typ => {
                        Command::Type(typ)
                    },
                }
            },
            b"CDUP" => Command::CdUp,
            b"MKD" => Command::Mkd(data.and_then(|bytes|
Ok(Path::new(str::from_utf8(bytes)?).to_path_buf()))?),
            b"RMD" => Command::Rmd(data.and_then(|bytes|
Ok(Path::new(str::from_utf8(bytes)?).to_path_buf()))?),
            b"USER" => Command::User(data.and_then(|bytes|
String::from_utf8(bytes.to_vec()).map_err(Into::into))?),
            b"NOOP" => Command::NoOp,
            s =>
Command::Unknown(str::from_utf8(s).unwrap_or("").to_owned()),
        };
    Ok(command)
    }
}
```

This constructor parses a byte string as a `Command`. This requires a function to convert a byte string to uppercase:

```
fn to_uppercase(data: &mut [u8]) {
    for byte in data {
        if *byte >= 'a' as u8 && *byte <= 'z' as u8 {
            *byte -= 32;
        }
    }
}
```

We simply decrement all lowercase letters by 32 to convert them to uppercase:

```
#[derive(Clone, Copy, Debug)]
pub enum TransferType {
    Ascii,
    Image,
    Unknown,
}

impl From<u8> for TransferType {
    fn from(c: u8) -> TransferType {
        match c {
            b'A' => TransferType::Ascii,
            b'I' => TransferType::Image,
            _ => TransferType::Unknown,
        }
    }
}
```

Here, we have an enumeration for the transfer type and a function to parse a byte character to this type. And in another file, `src/ftp.rs`, let's write the following:

```
pub struct Answer {
    pub code: ResultCode,
    pub message: String,
}

impl Answer {
    pub fn new(code: ResultCode, message: &str) -> Self {
        Answer {
            code,
            message: message.to_string(),
        }
    }
}

#[derive(Debug, Clone, Copy)]
#[repr(u32)]
#[allow(dead_code)]
pub enum ResultCode {
    RestartMarkerReply = 110,
    ServiceReadInXXXMinutes = 120,
    DataConnectionAlreadyOpen = 125,
    FileStatusOk = 150,
    Ok = 200,
    CommandNotImplementedSuperfluousAtThisSite = 202,
    SystemStatus = 211,
```

```
        DirectoryStatus = 212,
        FileStatus = 213,
        HelpMessage = 214,
        SystemType = 215,
        ServiceReadyForNewUser = 220,
        ServiceClosingControlConnection = 221,
        DataConnectionOpen = 225,
        ClosingDataConnection = 226,
        EnteringPassiveMode = 227,
        UserLoggedIn = 230,
        RequestedFileActionOkay = 250,
        PATHNAMECreated = 257,
        UserNameOkayNeedPassword = 331,
        NeedAccountForLogin = 332,
        RequestedFileActionPendingFurtherInformation = 350,
        ServiceNotAvailable = 421,
        CantOpenDataConnection = 425,
        ConnectionClosed = 426,
        FileBusy = 450,
        LocalErrorInProcessing = 451,
        InsufficientStorageSpace = 452,
        UnknownCommand = 500,
        InvalidParameterOrArgument = 501,
        CommandNotImplemented = 502,
        BadSequenceOfCommands = 503,
        CommandNotImplementedForThatParameter = 504,
        NotLoggedIn = 530,
        NeedAccountForStoringFiles = 532,
        FileNotFound = 550,
        PageTypeUnknown = 551,
        ExceededStorageAllocation = 552,
        FileNameNotAllowed = 553,
    }
```

We're now ready to start working on the FTP server itself.

Using Tokio

Tokio is based on the lower-level crate mio, which is itself directly based on system calls such as `epoll` (Linux), `kqueue` (FreeBSD), and IOCP (Windows). This crate is also based on the `futures` crate, which provides abstractions to reason about a value (or multiple values) that will be available later. As I told you when using asynchronous I/O, the calls do not block so we need a way to know when the result of a read is available. This is where `Future` and `Stream`, two abstractions from the `futures` crate, come into play.

Tokio event loop

Tokio also provides an event loop, on which we will be able to execute some code (with `futures`) that will be executed when some I/O events happen, such as when the result of a socket read is ready. To do so, the event loop will register events on specific file descriptors that represent sockets. It registers these events using the aforementioned system calls and then waits for any of the registered events to happen. The file descriptors and the system calls are low-level stuff that we do not need to know to use `tokio`, but it is important to understand how it works at the lower level. For instance, `epoll` does not support regular files, so if you try to wait for an event to happen on a regular file, it could block even though we're using asynchronous I/O which should not block.

Using futures

A `future` represents a value that will be available later, or an error, similar to the `Result` type. A `stream` represents multiple values (or errors) that will be available at different times in the `future`, similar to an `Iterator<Result<T>>`. This crate provides many combinators such as `and_then()`, `map()`, and others similar to the one available on the `Result` type. But, we won't use them, preferring the `async/await` syntax that we'll see later.

Handling errors

Before we start coding the FTP server, let's talk about how we'll be handling the errors.

Unwrapping

In the previous projects, we used the `unwrap()` or `expect()` methods a lot. These methods are handy for fast prototyping, but when we want to write high-quality software, we should avoid them in most cases. Since we're writing an FTP server, a software that must keep running for a long time, we don't want it to crash because we called `unwrap()` and a client sent a bad command. So, we'll do proper error handling.

Custom error type

Since we can get different types of errors and we want to keep track of all of them, we'll create a custom error type. Let's create a new module in which we'll put this new type:

```
mod error;
```

Add it to the `src/error.rs` file:

```
use std::io;
use std::str::Utf8Error;
use std::string::FromUtf8Error;

pub enum Error {
    FromUtf8(FromUtf8Error),
    Io(io::Error),
    Msg(String),
    Utf8(Utf8Error),
}
```

Here, we have an enum representing the different errors that can happen in our FTP server to be implemented. There are UTF-8 errors since FTP is a string-based protocol and I/O errors because we communicate over the network and communication issues can happen. We created variants for error types coming from the standard library, which will be helpful later when we want to compose different types of errors. We also created a variant `Msg` for our own errors and we represent them as a `String` since we only want to show them in the terminal (we could also log them to `syslog`, for instance).

This is the standard way in Rust to represent an error type. It's a good practice to create this type, especially if your crate is a library, so that the users of your crate can know exactly why an error happened.

Displaying the error

Since we want to print the error to the terminal, we'll implement the `Display` trait for our `Error` type:

```
use std::fmt::{self, Display, Formatter};

use self::Error::*;

impl Display for Error {
    fn fmt(&self, formatter: &mut Formatter) -> fmt::Result {
        match *self {
```

```
            FromUtf8(ref error) => error.fmt(formatter),
            Io(ref error) => error.fmt(formatter),
            Utf8(ref error) => error.fmt(formatter),
            Msg(ref msg) => write!(formatter, "{}", msg),
        }
    }
}
```

For the three cases where we wrap an error from another type, we just call the corresponding `fmt()` method of these errors. In the case that it is a `Msg`, we write the string using the `write!` macro. This macro is a bit similar to `print!`, but needs a parameter to specify where to write the formatted data.

It is not very helpful in our case, but it is recommended to also implement the `Error` trait for custom error types:

```
use std::error;

impl error::Error for Error {
    fn description(&self) -> &str {
        match *self {
            FromUtf8(ref error) => error.description(),
            Io(ref error) => error.description(),
            Utf8(ref error) => error.description(),
            Msg(ref msg) => msg,
        }
    }

    fn cause(&self) -> Option<&error::Error> {
        let cause: &error::Error =
            match *self {
                FromUtf8(ref error) => error,
                Io(ref error) => error,
                Utf8(ref error) => error,
                Msg(_) => return None,
            };
        Some(cause)
    }
}
```

The only required method of this trait is `description()`, which returns a short description of the error. Again, in the three cases, we just call the `description()` method from the wrapped type itself. And, for our `Msg` variant, we return the wrapped message.

It is possible that we don't have a string to return from this method. If it is the case, we can just return &'static str, like this:

```
Io(_) => "IO error",
```

The cause() method is optional and is used to return the cause of the error. Here, we return the inner error when there's one in the variant and return None for our Msg variant.

The trait Error requires the Self type to implement both Display and Debug. We implemented Display earlier, but we don't implement Debug yet. Let's fix that by adding an attribute in front of the type declaration:

```
#[derive(Debug)]
pub enum Error {
    FromUtf8(FromUtf8Error),
    Io(io::Error),
    Msg(String),
    Utf8(Utf8Error),
}
```

It is good practice to provide a type alias named Result that is specialized for our error type. Let's write one:

```
use std::result;

pub type Result<T> = result::Result<T, Error>;
```

By doing so, we hide the original Result type from the standard library. That's why we're specifying a qualified version of this type. Otherwise, the compiler will assume that it is a recursive type, which is not the case here. We'll have to be careful when we import this type in other modules, because it hides the Result type. In case we want to use the original Result type, we'll have to use the same trick; qualifying it.

Composing error types

The last thing we need to do in order to use all the good practices for error types in Rust is to make them easy to compose, because, for now, if we have another error type, such as io::Error, we would need to use the following code every time we have another type:

```
let val =
    match result {
        Ok(val) => val,
        Err(error) => return Err(Error::Io(error)),
    };
```

This can quickly become cumbersome. To improve that, we'll implement the From trait for different error types:

```
impl From<io::Error> for Error {
    fn from(error: io::Error) -> Self {
        Io(error)
    }
}

impl<'a> From<&'a str> for Error {
    fn from(message: &'a str) -> Self {
        Msg(message.to_string())
    }
}

impl From<Utf8Error> for Error {
    fn from(error: Utf8Error) -> Self {
        Utf8(error)
    }
}

impl From<FromUtf8Error> for Error {
    fn from(error: FromUtf8Error) -> Self {
        FromUtf8(error)
    }
}
```

These implementations are easy to understand: if we have an io::Error, we just wrap them in the corresponding variant. We also added a convenient conversion from the &str type.

This will allow us to use the following, which is not really better, but the good old ? operator will help us to reduce the boilerplate:

```
let val =
    match result {
        Ok(val) => val,
        Err(error) => return Err(error.into()),
    };
```

The ? operator, revisited

This operator will not only return the error if there is one, but will also convert it to the required type. It converts it with a call to `Into::into()`, `Into` being a trait. But why did we implement the `From` trait, instead of `Into`? Because there's a generic implementation of `Into` which is based on `From`:

```
impl<T, U> Into<U> for T
where U: From<T>,
```

Thanks to this implementation, we rarely need to implement the `Into` trait ourselves. We only need to implement the `From` trait.

This means that we can rewrite the previous code as follows:

```
let val = result?;
```

And it will behave exactly the same as before.

Starting the Tokio event loop

In `tokio`, the object we need to use to manage an event loop is `Core`. Here's how we start an event loop using `tokio` (in the `main` module):

```
use tokio_core::reactor::Core;

fn main() {
    let mut core = Core::new().expect("Cannot create tokio Core");
    if let Err(error) = core.run(server()) {
        println!("Error running the server: {}", error);
    }
}
```

We first create a new `Core` object, and then call the `run()` method to start the event loop. The latter method will return when the provided future ends. Here, we call `server()` to get the future, so let's write this function:

```
use std::io;

use futures::prelude::async;

#[async]
fn server() -> io::Result<()> {
    Ok(())
```

```
    }
```

As you can see, we use the `#[async]` attribute. Since attributes are currently instable in Rust, we had to specify that we are using the `proc_macro` feature. We also import the `async` attribute from the `futures_await` crate (which was imported under the name `futures`). So don't forget the `#![feature]` attribute and the `extern crate` statements at the top.

This attribute allows us to write a normal function, returning a `Result`, and will convert this function to actually return a `Future`. This function does nothing and returns `Ok(())`, so when you run the program, it will end immediately.

There's another syntax we could have used that is provided by the `futures-await` crate:

```
use futures::prelude::async_block;

fn main() {
    let mut core = Core::new().expect("Cannot create tokio Core");
    let server = async_block! {
        Ok(())
    };
    let result: Result<_, io::Error> = core.run(server);
    if let Err(error) = result {
        println!("Error running the server: {}", error);
    }
}
```

We won't use this syntax in our FTP server, but it is worth knowing about. By using an `async_block`, we are not required to create a new function.

Starting the server

The program we just wrote does absolutely nothing, so let's update it so that it at least starts a server, using `tokio`. Let's write an actual body to our `server()` function:

```
use std::net::{IpAddr, Ipv4Addr, SocketAddr};

use tokio_core::reactor::Handle;
use tokio_core::net::TcpListener;

#[async]
fn server(handle: Handle) -> io::Result<()> {
    let port = 1234;
    let addr = SocketAddr::new(IpAddr::V4(Ipv4Addr::new(127, 0, 0,
```

```
1)), port);
    let listener = TcpListener::bind(&addr, &handle)?;

    println!("Waiting clients on port {}...", port);
    #[async]
    for (stream, addr) in listener.incoming() {
        let address = format!("[address : {}]", addr);
        println!("New client: {}", address);
        handle.spawn(handle_client(stream));
        println!("Waiting another client...");
    }
    Ok(())
}
```

The function now takes a `Handle`, which will be useful to specify on which event loop the server must run. We start this function by specifying on which port we want to start the server by creating a `SocketAddr`. Then, we create a `TcpListener` in a similar way to how we would create a synchronous `TcpListener` from the standard library. The difference here is that we also send the `handle` as an argument to specify on which event loop we want the server to run. After that, we use the `#[async]` attribute again, but on a `for` loop this time.

Async `for` loops are used to iterate over a `Stream`, returning an error if there is one. These async loops can only be used in an `#[async]` function. In the loop, we spawn the future returned by `handle_client()`. Spawning a future means that it will be executed and handled by the event loop. The difference with `Core::run()` is that the future must return `()` and the error should also be `()`.

Now that this function takes an argument, we'll need to update the `main` function:

```
fn main() {
    let mut core = Core::new().expect("Cannot create tokio Core");
    let handle = core.handle();
    if let Err(error) = core.run(server(handle)) {
        println!("Error running the server: {}", error);
    }
}
```

Handling clients

Let's now see the `handle_client()` function we've just mentioned:

```
use std::result;

use futures::prelude::await;

#[async]
use tokio_core::net::TcpStream;

fn handle_client(stream: TcpStream) -> result::Result<(), ()> {
    await!(client(stream))
        .map_err(|error| println!("Error handling client: {}",
error))
}
```

It is a simple wrapper over the `client` future. Here, we used a new macro, `await!`, which allows us to write asynchronous code in an asynchronous way. When the result of the future inside `await!()` is not ready, the event loop will execute other stuff, and when it's ready it will continue executing the code after the `await!()`. In this case, we print the error returned by the `client` future. This is why we needed a wrapper.

Now, let's write this `client` future:

```
use futures::{Sink, Stream};
use futures::stream::SplitSink;
use tokio_io::AsyncRead;
use tokio_io::codec::Framed;

use codec::FtpCodec;
use error::Result;
use ftp::{Answer, ResultCode};

#[async]
fn client(stream: TcpStream) -> Result<()> {
    let (writer, reader) = stream.framed(FtpCodec).split();
    let writer =
await!(writer.send(Answer::new(ResultCode::ServiceReadyForNewUser,
    "Welcome to this FTP server!")))?;
    let mut client = Client::new(writer);
    #[async]
    for cmd in reader {
        client = await!(client.handle_cmd(cmd))?;
    }
    println!("Client closed");
```

```
        Ok(())
    }
```

Here, we specify that the `stream` will be handled by a `FtpCodec`, which means that we'll be able to encode and decode structured data instead of dealing with bytes directly. We'll write this `FtpCodec` soon. Then, we split the stream between a `reader` and a `writer`. This `split()` method is very useful in Rust, because of ownership: we cannot have two owners, one that will write to the socket and another that will read to it. To fix this issue, we split the stream and we can now have an owner for the `reader` and another owner for the `writer`.

Then, we use the `writer` to send a welcome message. Again, we use the `await!` macro to specify that the code after will be executed when the message is sent (but without blocking the whole program, thanks to asynchronous I/O). Next, we create a `Client` which will be the object that will manage a client, by executing the appropriate actions when it receives commands and sending the right responses.

After that, we use again an `#[async]` `for` loop to iterate over a stream; here, we iterate over the stream of the data received by this specific client. In the `for` loop, we call the `handle_cmd()` method that we will soon write. This method, as its name indicates, will handle the command received from this FTP client, act accordingly, and send a response back. Here, we use `await!()?` with a question mark at the end. The `futures-await` crate allows us to do so; this means that if the future returned an error, this error will propagate to the `client` future, which is the same semantic for the normal `?` operator used in a function returning a `Result`. We'll see why we reassign the result to `client` when we write the `handle_cmd()` method.

Handling commands

To handle the commands received by the FTP server, we'll have a `Client` struct:

```
type Writer = SplitSink<Framed<TcpStream, FtpCodec>>;

struct Client {
    writer: Writer,
}
```

The client contains a `Writer` object that will be useful to send messages to the client. The `Writer` type represents a `Sink` that has been split, and uses the `FtpCodec` on a `TcpStream`. A `Sink` is the opposite of a `Stream`: instead of representing a sequence of values that are received, it represents a sequence of values that are sent.

We used two methods on `Client`, so let's write them:

```
use cmd::Command;

impl Client {
    fn new(writer: Writer) -> Client {
        Client {
            writer,
        }
    }

    #[async]
    fn handle_cmd(mut self, cmd: Command) -> Result<Self> {
        Ok(self)
    }
}
```

The constructor is very simple and creates the `struct` with the provided argument. The `handle_cmd()` receives the command sent to the FTP server by this specific client and will handle them; we'll write the code to handle them progressively in this chapter and the next. For now, it only returns `self`. Also, take note that this method receives `self` by move, instead of by `reference`. This is due to a current limitation of the `futures-await` crate: for now, async functions cannot take a reference. This issue will probably be fixed later, which will make the code even better. This is why we reassigned to the `client` variable in the `client` function:

```
client = await!(client.handle_cmd(cmd))?;
```

FTP codec

The only remaining thing to code before we can try our FTP server is the `codec`. So, let's create a new module for the `codec`:

```
mod codec;
```

In the `src/codec.rs` file, we'll create our FTP `codec`:

```
pub struct FtpCodec;
```

To create a `codec`, we must implement the traits `Decoder` and `Encoder`. These traits come from the `tokio-io` crate:

```
use tokio_io::codec::{Decoder, Encoder};
```

Decoding FTP commands

Let's first write the decoder:

```
use std::io;

use bytes::BytesMut;

use cmd::Command;
use error::Error;

impl Decoder for FtpCodec {
    type Item = Command;
    type Error = io::Error;

    fn decode(&mut self, buf: &mut BytesMut) ->
    io::Result<Option<Command>> {
        if let Some(index) = find_crlf(buf) {
            let line = buf.split_to(index);
            buf.split_to(2); // Remove \r\n.
            Command::new(line.to_vec())
                .map(|command| Some(command))
                .map_err(Error::to_io_error)
        } else {
            Ok(None)
        }
    }
}
```

The `Decoder` trait has two associated types, `Item` and `Error`. The former is the type produced when we're able to decode a sequence of bytes. The latter is the type of the error. We first check if there the bytes CR and LF. If we don't find them, we return `Ok(None)` to indicate that we need more bytes to parse the command. If we find them, we get the line of the command, excluding these bytes. Then, we skip these bytes so that the next parsing does not see them. Finally, we parse the line with `Command::new()`.

We used two new functions here that we must implement. The first one is the `Error::to_io_error()` method that we'll add to the `error` module:

```
impl Error {
    pub fn to_io_error(self) -> io::Error {
        match self {
            Io(error) => error,
            FromUtf8(_) | Msg(_) | Utf8(_) =>
                io::ErrorKind::Other.into(),
        }
    }
}
```

If we have an `Io` error, we return it. Otherwise, we return the `Other` kind of I/O error.

The `decode()` methods also uses the following function:

```
fn find_crlf(buf: &mut BytesMut) -> Option<usize> {
    buf.windows(2)
        .position(|bytes| bytes == b"\r\n")
}
```

This returns the position of the byte string `"\r\n"` if it is present. Remember that this string is the delimiter in the FTP protocol.

Encoding FTP commands

We still need to write an `Encoder` in order to have a `codec` that can send commands to FTP clients:

```
use ftp::Answer;

impl Encoder for FtpCodec {
    type Item = Answer;
    type Error = io::Error;

    fn encode(&mut self, answer: Answer, buf: &mut BytesMut) ->
io::Result<()> {
        let answer =
            if answer.message.is_empty() {
                format!("{}\r\n", answer.code as u32)
            } else {
                format!("{} {}\r\n", answer.code as u32,
                answer.message)
            };
        buf.extend(answer.as_bytes());
```

```
                        Ok(())
                }
        }
```

Here, if we have a non-empty message, we push it to the buffer, preceded by the FTP code number. Otherwise, we only push this code number to the buffer.

We can now try the FTP server in FileZilla to see the following result:

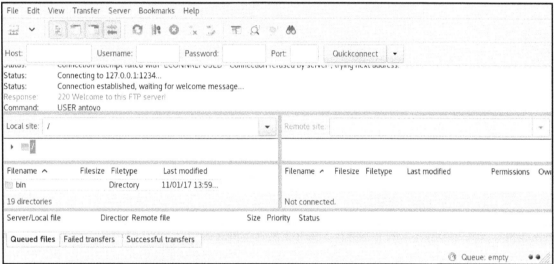

Figure 9.1

Handling commands

Our `handle_cmd()` method does nothing, for now, so let's update it. First of all, we'll need a method to send a response to a client:

```
impl Client {
    #[async]
    fn send(mut self, answer: Answer) -> Result<Self> {
        self.writer = await!(self.writer.send(answer))?;
        Ok(self)
    }
}
```

This simply calls the send() method of the writer. Since it consumes it, we reassign the result to the attribute.

Now, we'll handle the USER FTP command:

```
#[async]
fn handle_cmd(mut self, cmd: Command) -> Result<Self> {
    println!("Received command: {:?}", cmd);
    match cmd {
        Command::User(content) => {
            if content.is_empty() {
                self = await!
(self.send(Answer::new(ResultCode::InvalidParameterOrArgument,
"Invalid
                username")))?;
            } else {
                self =
await!(self.send(Answer::new(ResultCode::UserLoggedIn,
                &format!("Welcome {}!", content))))?;
            }
        }
        Command::Unknown(s) =>
                self =
await!(self.send(Answer::new(ResultCode::UnknownCommand,
                &format!("\"{}\": Not implemented", s))))? ,
        _ => self =
await!(self.send(Answer::new(ResultCode::CommandNotImplemented,
            "Not implemented")))?,
    }
    Ok(self)
}
```

Here, we pattern match to know which command was sent by the client. If it is not User, we send a response to say that the command is not implemented. If it is User, we check the content and if it is good, we send the welcome message. This is very similar to what we did in the previous chapter.

If we run the server again, we'll see the following:

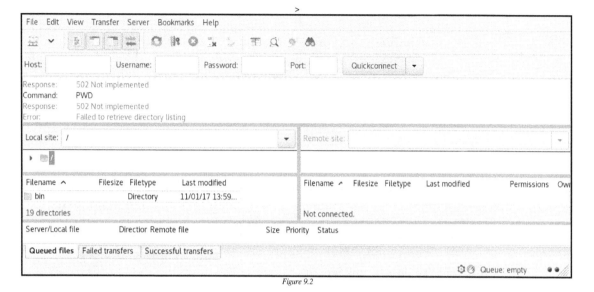

Figure 9.2

Managing the current working directory

There are still a few commands missing before we can see the files in the FTP client. Let's now add the command to print the current directory and to change it.

Printing the current directory

First of all, we'll need a new attribute for our `Client` structure to specify what the current directory is:

```
use std::path::PathBuf;

struct Client {
    cwd: PathBuf,
    writer: Writer,
}
```

The cwd attribute stands for current working directory. We also need to update the Client constructor accordingly:

```
impl Client {
    fn new(writer: Writer) -> Client {
        Client {
            cwd: PathBuf::from("/"),
            writer,
        }
    }
}
```

Now, we can add the handler for the PWD command:

```
#[async]
fn handle_cmd(mut self, cmd: Command) -> Result<Self> {
    println!("Received command: {:?}", cmd);
    match cmd {
        Command::Pwd => {
            let msg = format!("{}",
self.cwd.to_str().unwrap_or(""));
            if !msg.is_empty() {
                let message = format!("\"/{}\" ", msg);
                self =
await!(self.send(Answer::new(ResultCode::PATHNAMECreated,
                &message)))?;
            } else {
                self =
await!(self.send(Answer::new(ResultCode::FileNotFound, "No
                such file or directory")))?;
            }
        }
        // ...
    }
}
```

So, again, we have a code similar to the previous chapter.

Changing the current directory

Let's add another case in our match expression in the handle_cmd() method:

```
#[async]
fn handle_cmd(mut self, cmd: Command) -> Result<Self> {
    match cmd {
        Command::Cwd(directory) => self =
```

```
        await!(self.cwd(directory))?,
            // ...
        }
    }
```

It simply calls the following method:

```
    #[async]
    fn cwd(mut self, directory: PathBuf) -> Result<Self> {
        let path = self.cwd.join(&directory);
        let (new_self, res) = self.complete_path(path);
        self = new_self;
        if let Ok(dir) = res {
            let (new_self, res) = self.strip_prefix(dir);
            self = new_self;
            if let Ok(prefix) = res {
                self.cwd = prefix.to_path_buf();
                self = await!(self.send(Answer::new(ResultCode::Ok,
                                        &format!("Directory
changed to \"
                    {}\"", directory.display()))))?;
                return Ok(self)
            }
        }
        self = await!(self.send(Answer::new(ResultCode::FileNotFound,
                                        "No such file or
directory")))?;
        Ok(self)
    }
```

This code uses the following two methods, which are similar to those in the previous chapter:

```
    use std::path::StripPrefixError;

    fn complete_path(self, path: PathBuf) -> (Self,
    result::Result<PathBuf, io::Error>) {
        let directory = self.server_root.join(if path.has_root() {
            path.iter().skip(1).collect()
        } else {
            path
        });
        let dir = directory.canonicalize();
        if let Ok(ref dir) = dir {
            if !dir.starts_with(&self.server_root) {
                return (self,
                    Err(io::ErrorKind::PermissionDenied.into()));
            }
```

```
        }
        (self, dir)
    }

    fn strip_prefix(self, dir: PathBuf) -> (Self,
    result::Result<PathBuf, StripPrefixError>) {
        let res = dir.strip_prefix(&self.server_root).map(|p|
    p.to_path_buf());
        (self, res)
    }
```

Since it uses a new attribute, let's add it to the Client structure:

```
struct Client {
    cwd: PathBuf,
    server_root: PathBuf,
    writer: Writer,
}
```

We also add its constructor:

```
impl Client {
    fn new(writer: Writer, server_root: PathBuf) -> Client {
        Client {
            cwd: PathBuf::from("/"),
            server_root,
            writer,
        }
    }
}
```

We also need to pass this value in a few places, first, in the client function and its wrapper:

```
#[async]
fn client(stream: TcpStream, server_root: PathBuf) -> Result<()> {
    // ...
    let mut client = Client::new(writer, server_root);
    // ...
}

#[async]
fn handle_client(stream: TcpStream, server_root: PathBuf) ->
result::Result<(), ()> {
    await!(client(stream, server_root))
        .map_err(|error| println!("Error handling client: {}",
        error))
}
```

Then, we need to update the `server` function:

```
#[async]
fn server(handle: Handle, server_root: PathBuf) -> io::Result<()> {
    // ...
    #[async]
    for (stream, addr) in listener.incoming() {
        let address = format!("[address : {}]", addr);
        println!("New client: {}", address);
        handle.spawn(handle_client(stream, server_root.clone()));
        println!("Waiting another client...");
    }
    Ok(())
}
```

To send the server root to the `handle_client` function call.

And finally, we'll update the main function to send it to the `server` function:

```
use std::env;

fn main() {
    let mut core = Core::new().expect("Cannot create tokio Core");
    let handle = core.handle();

    match env::current_dir() {
        Ok(server_root) => {
            if let Err(error) = core.run(server(handle,
            server_root)) {
                println!("Error running the server: {}", error);
            }
        }
        Err(e) => println!("Couldn't start server: {:?}", e),
    }
}
```

Here, we send the current directory as the server root.

Setting the transfer type

Let's add a new command before we test our server again:

```
use cmd::TransferType;

#[async]
fn handle_cmd(mut self, cmd: Command) -> Result<Self> {
```

```
match cmd {
    // ...
    Command::Type(typ) => {
        self.transfer_type = typ;
        self = await!(self.send(Answer::new(ResultCode::Ok,
"Transfer type
        changed successfully")))?;
    }
    // ...
}
```

This requires a new attribute for our `Client` structure:

```
struct Client {
    cwd: PathBuf,
    server_root: PathBuf,
    transfer_type: TransferType,
    writer: Writer,
}
```

And we need to update the constructor:

```
impl Client {
    fn new(writer: Writer, server_root: PathBuf) -> Client {
        Client {
            cwd: PathBuf::from("/"),
            server_root,
            transfer_type: TransferType::Ascii,
            writer,
        }
    }
}
```

If we run this new server and connect to it through FileZilla, we'll see the following:

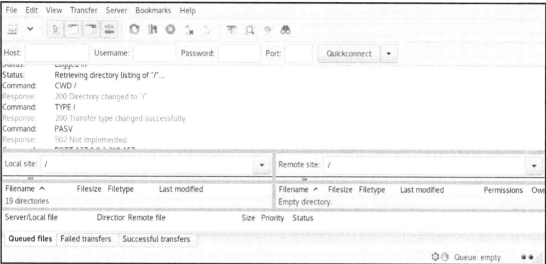

Figure 9.3

Entering passive mode

Let's now write the code to handle the PASV command. Add the following case in
handle_cmd():

```
#[async]
fn handle_cmd(mut self, cmd: Command) -> Result<Self> {
    match cmd {
        // ...
        Command::Pasv => self = await!(self.pasv())?,
        // ...
    }
}
```

For the following, we'll need four new fields in the Client structure:

```
use futures::stream::SplitStream;

use codec::BytesCodec;

type DataReader = SplitStream<Framed<TcpStream, BytesCodec>>;
type DataWriter = SplitSink<Framed<TcpStream, BytesCodec>>;
```

```
struct Client {
    data_port: Option<u16>,
    data_reader: Option<DataReader>,
    data_writer: Option<DataWriter>,
    handle: Handle,
    // ...
}
```

And all of them are initialized to None:

```
impl Client {
    fn new(handle: Handle, writer: Writer, server_root: PathBuf) ->
Client {
        Client {
            data_port: None,
            data_reader: None,
            data_writer: None,
            handle,
            // ...
        }
    }
}
```

This requires changing a few other functions to send the Handle to the Client constructor. First, the client function now requires a new handle parameter:

```
#[async]
fn client(stream: TcpStream, handle: Handle, server_root: PathBuf)
-> Result<()> {
    let (writer, reader) = stream.framed(FtpCodec).split();
    let writer =
await!(writer.send(Answer::new(ResultCode::ServiceReadyForNewUser,
        "Welcome to this FTP server!")))?;
    let mut client = Client::new(handle, writer, server_root);
    // ...
}
```

The handle_client() method also needs to take a new parameter:

```
#[async]
fn handle_client(stream: TcpStream, handle: Handle, server_root:
PathBuf) -> result::Result<(), ()> {
    await!(client(stream, handle, server_root))
        .map_err(|error| println!("Error handling client: {}",
error))
}
```

And in the `server()` function, you need to send the `handler` to the `handle_client()` function:

```
#[async]
fn server(handle: Handle, server_root: PathBuf) -> io::Result<()> {
    // ...
    #[async]
    for (stream, addr) in listener.incoming() {
        // ...
        handle.spawn(handle_client(stream, handle.clone(),
server_root.clone()));
    }
}
```

And here is the start of the method that does the real stuff for the PASV command:

```
#[async]
fn pasv(mut self) -> Result<Self> {
    let port =
        if let Some(port) = self.data_port {
            port
        } else {
            0
        };
    if self.data_writer.is_some() {
        self =
await!(self.send(Answer::new(ResultCode::DataConnectionAlreadyOpen,
            "Already listening...")))?;
        return Ok(self);
    }

    // ...
```

If a port was set by an earlier command, we use it, otherwise, we use zero to ask the system to choose one. As you know from the previous chapter, there are two channels in FTP—the command channel and the data channel. So, here, we check whether the data channel is already open. If that is the case, we send the appropriate response and end the function by returning. Here's the rest of the method:

```
    // ...

    let addr = SocketAddr::new(IpAddr::V4(Ipv4Addr::new(127, 0, 0, 1)),
port);
    let listener = TcpListener::bind(&addr, &self.handle)?;
    let port = listener.local_addr()?.port();

    self =
```

```
await!(self.send(Answer::new(ResultCode::EnteringPassiveMode,
                             &format!("127,0,0,1,{},{}", port >> 8, port &
0xFF)))?;

    println!("Waiting clients on port {}...", port);
    #[async]
    for (stream, _rest) in listener.incoming() {
        let (writer, reader) = stream.framed(BytesCodec).split();
        self.data_writer = Some(writer);
        self.data_reader = Some(reader);
        break;
    }
    Ok(self)
}
```

We start by starting the listener for the data channel. See the following line:

```
let port = listener.local_addr()?.port();
```

This is used to get the port that was chosen by the system, if we specified port 0 to let the operating system choose a port. Then, we use an `async for` loop that breaks immediately after the first iteration because we only have one client that will connect to this new channel. In the loop, we're using the same split trick again; after saying that our stream uses the `BytesCodec`, we split the stream between the `writer` and the `reader`. We'll describe this new `codec` shortly. We then same both the data `writer` and `reader`.

Bytes codec

We start by creating an empty structure for the `codec`:

```
pub struct BytesCodec;
```

Decoding data bytes

Then, we implement the `Decoder` trait like we did for the `FtpCodec`:

```
impl Decoder for BytesCodec {
    type Item = Vec<u8>;
    type Error = io::Error;

    fn decode(&mut self, buf: &mut BytesMut) ->
io::Result<Option<Vec<u8>>> {
        if buf.len() == 0 {
            return Ok(None);
```

```
        }
        let data = buf.to_vec();
        buf.clear();
        Ok(Some(data))
    }
}
```

Since the data of a transmitted file can be binary, we cannot use an `Item` of type `String`. We instead use `Vec<u8>`, which we can contain every possible byte. If the buffer is empty, we return `Ok(None)` to indicate to `tokio` that we need more data. Otherwise, we convert it to a vector, clear the buffer and return the vector.

Encoding data bytes

Let's now see how to encode data; it's even simpler:

```
impl Encoder for BytesCodec {
    type Item = Vec<u8>;
    type Error = io::Error;

    fn encode(&mut self, data: Vec<u8>, buf: &mut BytesMut) ->
io::Result<()> {
        buf.extend(data);
        Ok(())
    }
}
```

We just extend the buffer with the data.

Quitting

Let's now implement the `QUIT` command. As always, we need to add a case in the `handle_cmd()` method:

```
#[async]
fn handle_cmd(mut self, cmd: Command) -> Result<Self> {
    match cmd {
        Command::Quit => self = await!(self.quit())?,
        // ...
    }
}
```

And here is the code of the `quit()` method:

```
#[async]
fn quit(mut self) -> Result<Self> {
    if self.data_writer.is_some() {
        unimplemented!();
    } else {
        self =
await!(self.send(Answer::new(ResultCode::ServiceClosingControlConne
ction, "Closing connection...")))?;
        self.writer.close()?;
    }
    Ok(self)
}
```

So, we send a response back to the client and `close()` the `writer`.

To finish this chapter, let's implement the command to create and delete directories.

Creating directories

We'll start by handling the command to create a new directory. So, we add a case in `handle_cmd()`:

```
#[async]
fn handle_cmd(mut self, cmd: Command) -> Result<Self> {
    match cmd {
        Command::Mkd(path) => self = await!(self.mkd(path))?,
        // ...
    }
}
```

And the function handling this command is:

```
use std::fs::create_dir;

#[async]
fn mkd(mut self, path: PathBuf) -> Result<Self> {
    let path = self.cwd.join(&path);
    let parent = get_parent(path.clone());
    if let Some(parent) = parent {
        let parent = parent.to_path_buf();
        let (new_self, res) = self.complete_path(parent);
        self = new_self;
        if let Ok(mut dir) = res {
```

We first check that the `parent` directory is valid and under the server root:

```
if dir.is_dir() {
    let filename = get_filename(path);
    if let Some(filename) = filename {
        dir.push(filename);
        if create_dir(dir).is_ok() {
            self = await!
    (self.send(Answer::new(ResultCode::PATHNAMECreated,
    "Folder successfully created!")))?;
            return Ok(self);
        }
    }
}
self = await!(self.send(Answer::new(ResultCode::FileNotFound,
                                "Couldn't create folder")))?;
Ok(self)
}
```

If it is, we create the directory. Otherwise, we send an error.

This requires two new functions:

```
use std::ffi::OsString;

fn get_parent(path: PathBuf) -> Option<PathBuf> {
    path.parent().map(|p| p.to_path_buf())
}

fn get_filename(path: PathBuf) -> Option<OsString> {
    path.file_name().map(|p| p.to_os_string())
}
```

These are simple wrappers over the methods from the standard library, doing type conversion.

Removing directories

Finally, let's see the code to remove directories:

```
#[async]
fn handle_cmd(mut self, cmd: Command) -> Result<Self> {
    match cmd {
```

```
        Command::Rmd(path) => self = await!(self.rmd(path))?,
        // ...
    }
}
```

Like for the previous commands, we add a new case that calls the method that will handle it:

```
use std::fs::remove_dir_all;

#[async]
fn rmd(mut self, directory: PathBuf) -> Result<Self> {
    let path = self.cwd.join(&directory);
    let (new_self, res) = self.complete_path(path);
    self = new_self;
    if let Ok(dir) = res {
        if remove_dir_all(dir).is_ok() {
            self =
await!(self.send(Answer::new(ResultCode::RequestedFileActionOkay,
                                         "Folder
successfully removed")))?;
            return Ok(self);
        }
    }
    self = await!(self.send(Answer::new(ResultCode::FileNotFound,
                                         "Couldn't remove
folder")))?;
    Ok(self)
}
```

Here again, we check that the directory is valid and under the server root, and delete it if that is the case. Otherwise, we send an error message.

Summary

In this chapter, we implemented a lot of commands for our asynchronous FTP server and learned about using tokio. We also saw in more detail what asynchronous I/O is, and its advantages and disadvantages. We used the new async/await syntax to simplify the code using tokio. We learned what futures and streams are, and how they interact with tokio. We also saw how to do proper error handling and how to do it concisely. In the next chapter, we'll complete the implementation of the FTP server and see how to test it.

10
Implementing Asynchronous File Transfer

In the previous chapter, we started to write an asynchronous FTP server using `tokio`. Now, we'll start using the second channel used in the FTP protocol: the data channel. We'll cover the following topics:

- Unit tests
- Integration tests
- Backtraces
- Documentation
- Documentation tests
- Fuzzing tests

Listing files

We'll start this chapter by implementing the command to list files. This will allow us to actually see the files in an FTP client, and we'll be able to tests some commands from the previous chapter by navigating in the directories. So, let's add a case in the `Client::handle_cmd()` method:

```
#[async]
fn handle_cmd(mut self, cmd: Command) -> Result<Self> {
    match cmd {
        Command::List(path) => self = await!(self.list(path))?,
        // ...
    }
}
```

This simply calls the `list()` method, which begins as follows:

```
use std::fs::read_dir;

#[async]
fn list(mut self, path: Option<PathBuf>) -> Result<Self> {
    if self.data_writer.is_some() {
        let path = self.cwd.join(path.unwrap_or_default());
        let directory = PathBuf::from(&path);
        let (new_self, res) = self.complete_path(directory);
        self = new_self;
        if let Ok(path) = res {
            self = await!
(self.send(Answer::new(ResultCode::DataConnectionAlreadyOpen,
                                    "Starting to list
directory...")))?;
```

We first check that the data channel is opened and, if this is the case, we check that the provided optional path is valid. If it is, we send a response that indicates to the client that we're about to send it the data. The next part of the method is as follows:

```
let mut out = vec![];
if path.is_dir() {
    if let Ok(dir) = read_dir(path) {
        for entry in dir {
            if let Ok(entry) = entry {
                add_file_info(entry.path(), &mut out);
            }
        }
    } else {
        self = await!
(self.send(Answer::new(ResultCode::InvalidParameterOrArgument,
                                    "No such file or
                                    directory")))?;
        return Ok(self);
    }
} else {
    add_file_info(path, &mut out);
}
```

We first create a variable, out, that will contain the data to send to the client. If the specified path is a directory, we use the read_dir() function from the standard library. We then iterate over all files in the directory to gather the info about every file. If we were unable to open the directory, we send an error back to the client. If the path is not a directory, for example, if it is a file, we only get the info for this single file. Here's the end of the method:

```
            self = await!(self.send_data(out))?;
            println!("-> and done!");
        } else {
            self = await!
    (self.send(Answer::new(ResultCode::InvalidParameterOrArgument,
                                                "No such file or
        directory")))?;
            }
        } else {
            self =
    await!(self.send(Answer::new(ResultCode::ConnectionClosed, "No
    opened
            data connection")))?;
        }
        if self.data_writer.is_some() {
            self.close_data_connection();
            self =
    await!(self.send(Answer::new(ResultCode::ClosingDataConnection,
                        "Transfer done")))?;
        }
        Ok(self)
    }
```

We then send the data in the right channel using the send_data() method that we'll see later. If there was another error, we send the appropriate response to the client. If we successfully sent the data, we close the connection and indicate this action to the client. This code used a few new methods, so let's implement them.

First, here's the method that sends data in the data channel:

```
#[async]
fn send_data(mut self, data: Vec<u8>) -> Result<Self> {
    if let Some(writer) = self.data_writer {
        self.data_writer = Some(await!(writer.send(data))?);
    }
    Ok(self)
}
```

It is very similar to the `send()` method, but this one only sends the data if the data socket is opened. Another method that is needed is the one that closes the connection:

```
fn close_data_connection(&mut self) {
    self.data_reader = None;
    self.data_writer = None;
}
```

We need to implement the method to gather the info about a file. Here is how it starts:

```
const MONTHS: [&'static str; 12] = ["Jan", "Feb", "Mar", "Apr",
"May", "Jun",
                                    "Jul", "Aug", "Sep", "Oct",
"Nov", "Dec"];

fn add_file_info(path: PathBuf, out: &mut Vec<u8>) {
    let extra = if path.is_dir() { "/" } else { "" };
    let is_dir = if path.is_dir() { "d" } else { "-" };

    let meta = match ::std::fs::metadata(&path) {
        Ok(meta) => meta,
        _ => return,
    };
    let (time, file_size) = get_file_info(&meta);
    let path = match path.to_str() {
        Some(path) => match path.split("/").last() {
            Some(path) => path,
            _ => return,
        },
        _ => return,
    };
    let rights = if meta.permissions().readonly() {
        "r--r--r--"
    } else {
        "rw-rw-rw-"
    };
```

The parameter `out` is a mutable reference, because we'll append the info in this variable. Then, we gather the different required info and permissions of the file. Here's the rest of the function:

```
    let file_str = format!("{is_dir}{rights} {links} {owner}
{group} {size} {month}
    {day} {hour}:{min} {path}{extra}\r\n",
                           is_dir=is_dir,
                           rights=rights,
                           links=1, // number of links
```

```
                        owner="anonymous", // owner name
                        group="anonymous", // group name
                        size=file_size,
                        month=MONTHS[time.tm_mon as usize],
                        day=time.tm_mday,
                        hour=time.tm_hour,
                        min=time.tm_min,
                        path=path,
                        extra=extra);
        out.extend(file_str.as_bytes());
        println!("==> {:?}", &file_str);
    }
```

It formats the info and appends it to the variable `out`.

This function uses another one:

```
        extern crate time;

        use std::fs::Metadata;

        #[cfg(windows)]
        fn get_file_info(meta: &Metadata) -> (time::Tm, u64) {
            use std::os::windows::prelude::*;
            (time::at(time::Timespec::new(meta.last_write_time())),
        meta.file_size())
        }

        #[cfg(not(windows))]
        fn get_file_info(meta: &Metadata) -> (time::Tm, u64) {
            use std::os::unix::prelude::*;
            (time::at(time::Timespec::new(meta.mtime(), 0)), meta.size())
        }
```

Here, we have two versions of `get_file_info()`: one for Windows and the other for all non-Windows operating systems. Since we use a new crate, we need to add this line in `Cargo.toml`:

```
        time = "0.1.38"
```

We can now test, in the FTP client, that the files are indeed listed (on the right):

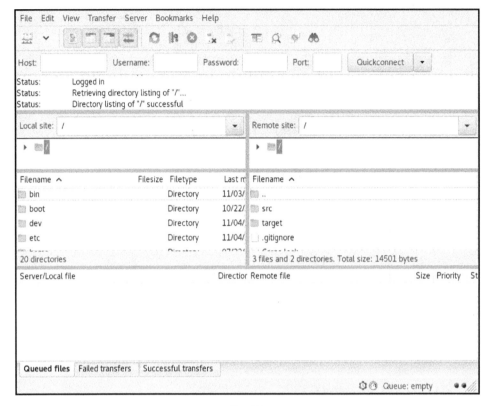

Figure 10.1

If we double-click on a directory, for instance, **src**, the FTP client will update its content:

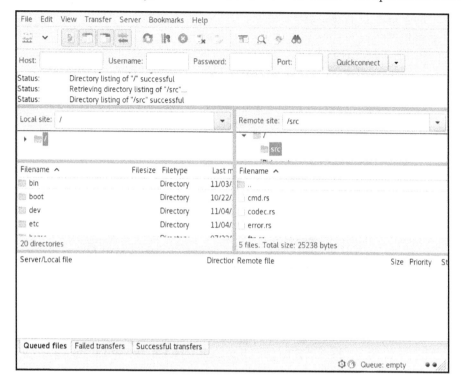

Figure 10.2

Downloading a file

A very useful feature of an FTP server is the ability to download files. So, it's time to add the command to do so.

First of all, we add the case in the `handle_cmd()` method:

```
#[async]
fn handle_cmd(mut self, cmd: Command) -> Result<Self> {
    match cmd {
        Command::Retr(file) => self = await!(self.retr(file))?,
        // ...
    }
}
```

Here is the start of the `retr()` function:

```
use std::fs::File;
use std::io::Read;

use error::Error;

#[async]
fn retr(mut self, path: PathBuf) -> Result<Self> {
    if self.data_writer.is_some() {
        let path = self.cwd.join(path);
        let (new_self, res) = self.complete_path(path.clone());
        self = new_self;
        if let Ok(path) = res {
            if path.is_file() {
                self =
await!(self.send(Answer::new(ResultCode::DataConnectionAlreadyOpen,
"Starting to send file...")))?;
                let mut file = File::open(path)?;
                let mut out = vec![];
                file.read_to_end(&mut out)?;
                self = await!(self.send_data(out))?;
                println!("-> file transfer done!");
```

Again, we check that the data channel is opened and we check the path. If it is a file, we open it, read its content, and send it to the client. Otherwise, we send the appropriate error:

```
            } else {
                self =
await!(self.send(Answer::new(ResultCode::LocalErrorInProcessing,
                            &format!("\"{}\" doesn't exist",
                            path.to_str().ok_or_else(|| Error::Msg("No
                            path".to_string()))?))))?;
            }
        } else {
            self =
await!(self.send(Answer::new(ResultCode::LocalErrorInProcessing,
                        &format!("\"{}\" doesn't exist",
                        path.to_str().ok_or_else(|| Error::Msg("No
                        path".to_string()))?))))?;
        }
    } else {
        self = await!
```

```
(self.send(Answer::new(ResultCode::ConnectionClosed, "No opened
    data connection")))?;
}
```

Here, we use this pattern:

```
.ok_or_else(|| Error::Msg("No path".to_string()))?
```

This converts the `Option` into a `Result`, and returns the error if there is one.

And finally, we close the data socket if we successfully sent the file:

```
if self.data_writer.is_some() {
    self.close_data_connection();
    self =
await!(self.send(Answer::new(ResultCode::ClosingDataConnection,
        "Transfer done")))?;
}
Ok(self)
}
```

Let's download a file in FileZilla to check that it works:

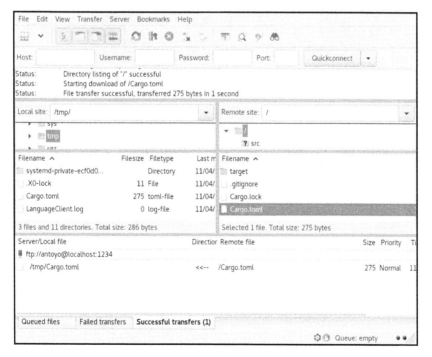

Figure 10.3

Uploading files

Now, let's do the opposite command: STOR to upload a file on the server.

As always, we'll add a case in the handle_cmd() method:

```
#[async]
fn handle_cmd(mut self, cmd: Command) -> Result<Self> {
    match cmd {
        Command::Stor(file) => self = await!(self.stor(file))?,
        // ...
    }
}
```

Here is the start of the corresponding method:

```
use std::io::Write;

#[async]
fn stor(mut self, path: PathBuf) -> Result<Self> {
    if self.data_reader.is_some() {
        if invalid_path(&path) {
            let error: io::Error =
io::ErrorKind::PermissionDenied.into();
            return Err(error.into());
        }
        let path = self.cwd.join(path);
        self =
await!(self.send(Answer::new(ResultCode::DataConnectionAlreadyOpen,
            "Starting to send file...")))?;
```

Once again, we check that the data channel is opened. Then, we use a new function to check that the path is valid, by which we mean it does not contain ... In the other cases, we used another method, canonicalize(), and checked that the path was under the server root, but we cannot do so here since there exists no file to upload yet. Here's the end of the method:

```
        let (data, new_self) = await!(self.receive_data())?;
        self = new_self;
        let mut file = File::create(path)?;
        file.write_all(&data)?;
        println!("-> file transfer done!");
        self.close_data_connection();
        self =
await!(self.send(Answer::new(ResultCode::ClosingDataConnection,
            "Transfer done")))?;
```

```
    } else {
        self = await!(self.send(Answer::new(ResultCode::ConnectionClosed,
          "No opened data connection")))?;
    }
    Ok(self)
}
```

Here, we call `receive_data()`, which is a `Future` that will resolve to the data received from the client. Then, we write this content in a new file. Finally, we close the connection and send the response to indicate that the transfer is done.

Here's the method to read the data from the data socket:

```
#[async]
fn receive_data(mut self) -> Result<(Vec<u8>, Self)> {
    let mut file_data = vec![];
    if self.data_reader.is_none() {
        return Ok((vec![], self));
    }
    let reader = self.data_reader.take().ok_or_else(||
Error::Msg("No data
      reader".to_string()))?;
    #[async]
    for data in reader {
        file_data.extend(&data);
    }
    Ok((file_data, self))
}
```

Here, we take the `data_reader` attribute, which means it will be `None` after this statement. And we iterate, using an `async  for` loop, over the reader stream. At every iteration, we add the data to the vector that is returned at the end.

This is the method to check if the path is valid:

```
use std::path::Component;

fn invalid_path(path: &Path) -> bool {
    for component in path.components() {
        if let Component::ParentDir = component {
            return true;
        }
    }
    false
}
```

Let's check that the upload does indeed work:

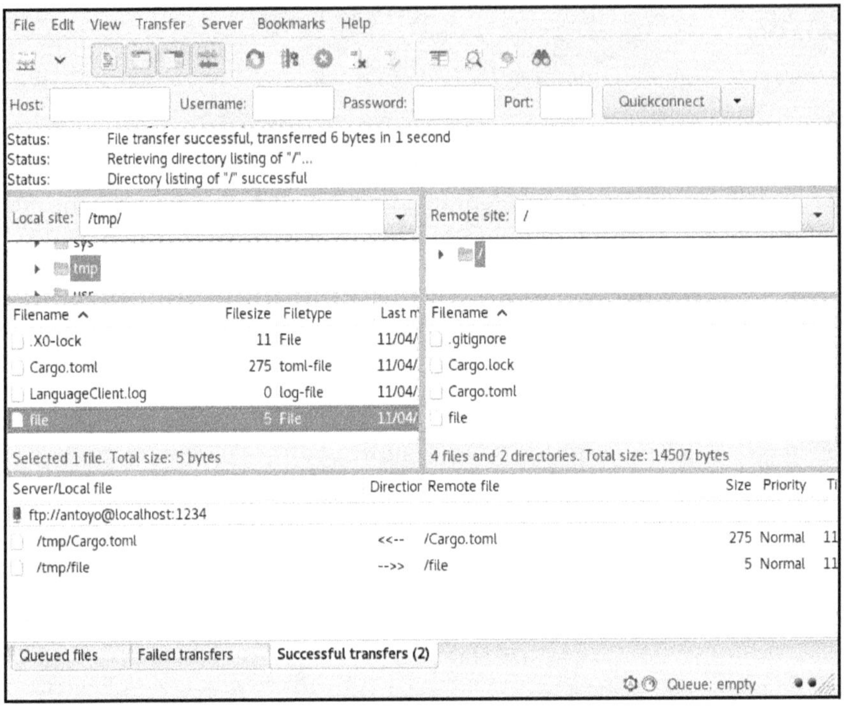

Figure 10.4

Going further!

Adding a bit of configuration would be nice, don't you think? Adding user authentication would be nice as well. Let's start with the configuration!

Configuration

First, let's create a new file in `src/` called `config.rs`. To make things easier, we'll use the TOML format for our configuration file. Luckily for us, there is a crate for handling TOML files in Rust, called `toml`. In addition to this one, we'll use `serde` to handle serialization and deserialization (very useful!).

Ok, let's start by adding the dependencies into our `Cargo.toml` file:

```
toml = "0.4"
serde = "1.0"
serde_derive = "1.0"
```

Good, now let's write our `Config` struct:

```
pub struct Config {
    // fields...
}
```

So what should we put in there? The port and address the server should listen on to start, maybe?

```
pub struct Config {
    pub server_port: Option<u16>,
    pub server_addr: Option<String>,
}
```

Done. We also talked about handling authentication. Why not adding it as well? We'll need a new `struct` for users. Let's call it `User` (yay for originality!):

```
pub struct User {
    pub name: String,
    pub password: String,
}
```

Now let's add the users into the `Config` struct:

```
pub struct Config {
    pub server_port: Option<u16>,
    pub server_addr: Option<String>,
    pub users: Vec<User>,
    pub admin: Option<User>,
}
```

To make these two `struct` work with `serde`, we'll have to add the following tags:

```
#[derive(Deserialize, Serialize)]
```

And because we'll need to clone `Config`, we'll add `Debug` into the tags, which gives us:

```
#[derive(Clone, Deserialize, Serialize)]
pub struct Config {
    pub server_port: Option<u16>,
    pub server_addr: Option<String>,
    pub admin: Option<User>,
    pub users: Vec<User>,
}

#[derive(Clone, Deserialize, Serialize)]
pub struct User {
    pub name: String,
    pub password: String,
}
```

Ok, we're now ready to implement the reading:

```
use std::fs::File;
use std::path::Path;
use std::io::{Read, Write};

use toml;

fn get_content<P: AsRef<Path>>(file_path: &P) -> Option<String> {
    let mut file = File::open(file_path).ok()?;
    let mut content = String::new();
    file.read_to_string(&mut content).ok()?;
    Some(content)
}

impl Config {
    pub fn new<P: AsRef<Path>>(file_path: P) -> Option<Config> {
        if let Some(content) = get_content(&file_path) {
            toml::from_str(&content).ok()
        } else {
            println!("No config file found so creating a new one in
                    {}",file_path.as_ref().display());
            // In case we didn't find the config file,
                we just build a new one.
            let config = Config {
                server_port: Some(DEFAULT_PORT),
                server_addr: Some("127.0.0.1".to_owned()),
                admin: None,
                users: vec![User {
                    name: "anonymous".to_owned(),
                    password: "".to_owned(),
                }],
```

```
                    };
                    let content =
        toml::to_string(&config).expect("serialization failed");
                    let mut file =
        File::create(file_path.as_ref()).expect("couldn't create
                    file...");
                    writeln!(file, "{}", content).expect("couldn't fulfill
        config file...");
                    Some(config)
                }
            }
        }
```

Let's go through the `Config::new` method's code:

```
    if let Some(content) = get_content(&file_path) {
        toml::from_str(&content).ok()
    }
```

Thanks to `serde`, we can directly load the configuration file from a `&str` and it'll return our `Config` struct fully set. Amazing, right?

For information, the `get_content` function is just a `utility` function that allows the return of the content of a file, if this file exists.

Also, don't forget to add the `DEFAULT_PORT` constant:

```
    pub const DEFAULT_PORT: u16 = 1234;
```

In case the file doesn't exist, we can create a new one with some default values:

```
    else {
        println!("No config file found so creating a new one in {}",
                file_path.as_ref().display());
        // In case we didn't find the config file, we just build a new
    one.
        let config = Config {
            server_port: Some(DEFAULT_PORT),
            server_addr: Some("127.0.0.1".to_owned()),
            admin: None,
            users: vec![User {
                name: "anonymous".to_owned(),
                password: "".to_owned(),
            }],
        };
        let content = toml::to_string(&config).expect("serialization
    failed");
```

```
        let mut file =
    File::create(file_path.as_ref()).expect("couldn't create
        file...");
        writeln!(file, "{}", content).expect("couldn't fulfill config
    file...");
        Some(config)
    }
```

Now you might wonder, how will we actually be able to generate TOML from our `Config` struct using this code? With `serde`'s magic once again!

With this, our `config` file is now complete. Let get back to the `main.rs` one. First, we'll need to define a new constant:

```
    const CONFIG_FILE: &'static str = "config.toml";
```

Then, we'll need to update quite a few methods/functions. Let's start with the `main` function. Add this line at the beginning:

```
    let config = Config::new(CONFIG_FILE).expect("Error while loading
    config...");
```

Now pass the `config` variable to the `server` function:

```
    if let Err(error) = core.run(server(handle, server_root, config)) {
```

Next, let's update the `server` function:

```
    #[async]
    fn server(handle: Handle, server_root: PathBuf, config: Config) ->
    io::Result<()> {
        let port = config.server_port.unwrap_or(DEFAULT_PORT);
        let addr =
    SocketAddr::new(IpAddr::V4(config.server_addr.as_ref()
    .unwrap_or(&"127.0.0.1".to_owned())
                                            .parse()
                                            .expect("Invalid
    IpV4 address...")),
                                            port);
        let listener = TcpListener::bind(&addr, &handle)?;

        println!("Waiting clients on port {}...", port);
        #[async]
        for (stream, addr) in listener.incoming() {
            let address = format!("[address : {}]", addr);
            println!("New client: {}", address);
            handle.spawn(handle_client(stream, handle.clone(),
```

```
server_root.clone()));
        handle.spawn(handle_client(stream, handle.clone(),
server_root.clone(),
        config.clone()));
        println!("Waiting another client...");
    }
    Ok(())
}
```

Now, the server is started with the value from the Config struct. However, we still need the user list for each client in order to handle the authentication. To do so, we need to give a Config instance to each Client. In here, to make things simpler, we'll just clone.

Time to update the handle_client function now:

```
#[async]
fn handle_client(stream: TcpStream, handle: Handle, server_root:
PathBuf,
                config: Config) -> result::Result<(), ()> {
    await!(client(stream, handle, server_root, config))
        .map_err(|error| println!("Error handling client: {}",
error))
}
```

Let's update the client function now:

```
#[async]
fn client(stream: TcpStream, handle: Handle, server_root: PathBuf,
config: Config) -> Result<()> {
    let (writer, reader) = stream.framed(FtpCodec).split();
    let writer =
await!(writer.send(Answer::new(ResultCode::ServiceReadyForNewUser,
                                "Welcome to this FTP
server!")))?;
    let mut client = Client::new(handle, writer, server_root,
config);
    #[async]
    for cmd in reader {
        client = await!(client.handle_cmd(cmd))?;
    }
    println!("Client closed");
    Ok(())
}
```

The final step is updating the `Client` struct:

```
struct Client {
    cwd: PathBuf,
    data_port: Option<u16>,
    data_reader: Option<DataReader>,
    data_writer: Option<DataWriter>,
    handle: Handle,
    name: Option<String>,
    server_root: PathBuf,
    transfer_type: TransferType,
    writer: Writer,
    is_admin: bool,
    config: Config,
    waiting_password: bool,
}
```

The brand new `config` field seems logical, however what about `is_admin` and `waiting_password`? The first one will be used to be able to list/download/overwrite the `config.toml` file, whereas the second one will be used when the `USER` command has been used and the server is now expecting the user's password.

Let's add another method to our `Client` struct:

```
fn is_logged(&self) -> bool {
    self.name.is_some() && !self.waiting_password
}
```

Don't forget to update the `Config::new` method:

```
fn new(handle: Handle, writer: Writer, server_root: PathBuf,
config: Config) -> Client {
    Client {
        cwd: PathBuf::from("/"),
        data_port: None,
        data_reader: None,
        data_writer: None,
        handle,
        name: None,
        server_root,
        transfer_type: TransferType::Ascii,
        writer,
        is_admin: false,
        config,
        waiting_password: false,
    }
}
```

Ok, now here comes the huge update! But first, don't forget to add the `Pass` command:

```
pub enum Command {
    // variants...
    Pass(String),
    // variants...
}
```

Now the `Command::new` match:

```
b"PASS" => Command::Pass(data.and_then(|bytes|
String::from_utf8(bytes.to_vec()).map_err(Into::into))?),
```

Don't forget to also update the `AsRef` implementation!

Good, we're ready for the last (and very big) step. Let's head to the `Client::handle_cmd` method:

```
use config::{DEFAULT_PORT, Config};
use std::path::Path;

fn prefix_slash(path: &mut PathBuf) {
    if !path.is_absolute() {
        *path = Path::new("/").join(&path);
    }
}

#[async]
fn handle_cmd(mut self, cmd: Command) -> Result<Self> {
    println!("Received command: {:?}", cmd);
    if self.is_logged() {
        match cmd {
            Command::Cwd(directory) => return
Ok(await!(self.cwd(directory))?),
            Command::List(path) => return
Ok(await!(self.list(path))?),
            Command::Pasv => return Ok(await!(self.pasv())?),
            Command::Port(port) => {
                self.data_port = Some(port);
                return
Ok(await!(self.send(Answer::new(ResultCode::Ok,
                            &format!("Data port is now {}",
                            port))))?);
            }
            Command::Pwd => {
                let msg = format!("{}",
self.cwd.to_str().unwrap_or("")); // small
```

```
                        trick
                    if !msg.is_empty() {
                        let message = format!("\"{}\" ", msg);

                        return Ok(await!
(self.send(Answer::new(ResultCode::PATHNAMECreated,
                            &message)))?);
                    } else {
                        return
Ok(await!(self.send(Answer::new(ResultCode::FileNotFound,
                                "No such file or directory")))?);
                    }
                }
                Command::Retr(file) => return
Ok(await!(self.retr(file))?),
                Command::Stor(file) => return
Ok(await!(self.stor(file))?),
                Command::CdUp => {
                    if let Some(path) =
self.cwd.parent().map(Path::to_path_buf) {
                        self.cwd = path;
                        prefix_slash(&mut self.cwd);
                    }
                    return
Ok(await!(self.send(Answer::new(ResultCode::Ok, "Done")))?);
                }
                Command::Mkd(path) => return
Ok(await!(self.mkd(path))?),
                Command::Rmd(path) => return
Ok(await!(self.rmd(path))?),
                _ => (),
            }
        } else if self.name.is_some() && self.waiting_password {
            if let Command::Pass(content) = cmd {
                let mut ok = false;
                if self.is_admin {
                    ok = content ==
self.config.admin.as_ref().unwrap().password;
                } else {
                    for user in &self.config.users {
                        if Some(&user.name) == self.name.as_ref() {
                            if user.password == content {
                                ok = true;
                                break;
                            }
                        }
                    }
                }
```

```
            if ok {
                self.waiting_password = false;
                let name =
self.name.clone().unwrap_or(String::new());
                self = await!(
                    self.send(Answer::new(ResultCode::UserLoggedIn,
                                        &format!("Welcome {}",
name))))?;
            } else {
                self =
await!(self.send(Answer::new(ResultCode::NotLoggedIn,
                            "Invalid password")))?;
            }
            return Ok(self);
        }
    }
    match cmd {
        Command::Auth =>
            self =
await!(self.send(Answer::new(ResultCode::CommandNotImplemented,
                        "Not implemented")))?,
        Command::Quit => self = await!(self.quit())?,
        Command::Syst => {
            self = await!(self.send(Answer::new(ResultCode::Ok, "I
won't tell!")))?;
        }
        Command::Type(typ) => {
            self.transfer_type = typ;
            self = await!(self.send(Answer::new(ResultCode::Ok,
                        "Transfer type changed
successfully")))?;
        }
        Command::User(content) => {
            if content.is_empty() {
                self = await!
(self.send(Answer::new(ResultCode::InvalidParameterOrArgument,
                                    "Invalid username")))?;
            } else {
                let mut name = None;
                let mut pass_required = true;

                self.is_admin = false;
                if let Some(ref admin) = self.config.admin {
                    if admin.name == content {
                        name = Some(content.clone());
                        pass_required = admin.password.is_empty()
        == false;
                        self.is_admin = true;
```

```
                        }
                    }
                    // In case the user isn't the admin.
                    if name.is_none() {
                        for user in &self.config.users {
                            if user.name == content {
                                name = Some(content.clone());
                                pass_required =
user.password.is_empty() == false;
                                break;
                            }
                        }
                    }
                    // In case this is an unknown user.
                    if name.is_none() {
                        self =
await!(self.send(Answer::new(ResultCode::NotLoggedIn,
                                    "Unknown user...")))?;
                    } else {
                        self.name = name.clone();
                        if pass_required {
                            self.waiting_password = true;
                            self = await!(
self.send(Answer::new(ResultCode::UserNameOkayNeedPassword,
                                    &format!("Login OK, password
needed for {}",
                                        name.unwrap())))))?;
                        } else {
                            self.waiting_password = false;
                            self = await!
(self.send(Answer::new(ResultCode::UserLoggedIn,
                                &format!("Welcome {}!", content)))))?;
                        }
                    }
                }
            }
        Command::NoOp => self =
await!(self.send(Answer::new(ResultCode::Ok,
                                                        "Doing
nothing")))?,
        Command::Unknown(s) =>
            self =
await!(self.send(Answer::new(ResultCode::UnknownCommand,
                            &format!("\"{}\": Not implemented",
s))))?,
            _ => {
                // It means that the user tried to send a command while
they weren't
```

```
                    logged yet.
                    self =
    await!(self.send(Answer::new(ResultCode::NotLoggedIn,
                            "Please log first")))?;
              }
         }
        Ok(self)
    }
```

I told you it was huge! The main points in here are just the flow rework. The following commands only work when you're logged in:

- Cwd
- List
- Pasv
- Port
- Pwd
- Retr
- Stor
- CdUp
- Mkd
- Rmd

This command only works when you're not *yet* logged in and the server is waiting for the password:

- Pass

The rest of the commands work in any case. We're almost done in here. Remember when I talked about the security? You wouldn't want anyone to have access to the configuration file with the list of all users, I suppose.

Securing the config.toml access

This time, not much to do! We just need to add a check when a user wants to list, download, or overwrite the file. Which means that the three following commands have to be updated:

- List
- Retr
- Stor

Let's start with List. Before the first add_file_info function call, just wrap the add_file_info function call around this block:

```
if self.is_admin || entry.path() !=
self.server_root.join(CONFIG_FILE) {
```

Before the second one, add the following:

```
if self.is_admin || path != self.server_root.join(CONFIG_FILE)
```

Now let's update the retr function. Take the following condition:

```
if path.is_file() {
```

Replace it with this:

```
if path.is_file() && (self.is_admin || path !=
self.server_root.join(CONFIG_FILE)) {
```

Finally, let's update the stor function. Take the following condition:

```
if invalid_path(&path) {
```

Replace it with this:

```
if invalid_path(&path) || (!self.is_admin && path ==
self.server_root.join(CONFIG_FILE)) {
```

And we're done! You now have a configurable server that you can easily extend, following your needs.

Unit tests

A good software needs tests to ensure that it works in most cases. So, we will add tests to our FTP server by starting to write unit tests for the FTP `codec`.

Unit tests verify only a unit of the program, which may be a function. They are different from the integration tests, which we will see later, that test the software as a whole.

Let's go in the `codec` module and add a new inner module to it:

```
#[cfg(test)]
mod tests {
}
```

We are again using the `#[cfg]` attribute; this time, it only compiles the following module when running the tests. This is to avoid adding useless code in the final binary.

In this new module, we will add a few import statements that we will need later when writing the tests:

```
#[cfg(test)]
mod tests {
    use std::path::PathBuf;

    use ftp::ResultCode;
    use super::{Answer, BytesMut, Command, Decoder, Encoder,
FtpCodec};
}
```

As you can see, we use `super` to access some types from the parent module (`codec`): this is very frequent for unit tests because we usually test the code from the same file.

Let's now add a `test` function:

```
#[cfg(test)]
mod tests {
    // ...

    #[test]
    fn test_encoder() {
    }
}
```

In the `test_encoder()` function, we will write the code that will test that the `FtpCodec`, `Encoder` implementation works as intended.

We will first check that an `Answer` with a message produces the right output:

```
#[cfg(test)]
mod tests {
    // ...

    #[test]
    fn test_encoder() {
        let mut codec = FtpCodec;
        let message = "bad sequence of commands";
        let answer = Answer::new(ResultCode::BadSequenceOfCommands,
message);
        let mut buf = BytesMut::new();
        let result = codec.encode(answer, &mut buf);
        assert!(result.is_ok());
        assert_eq!(buf, format!("503 {}\r\n", message));
    }
}
```

Here, we start by creating the objects needed to call `Encode::encode`, for example, a `codec` and a buffer. Then, we call `codec.encode()`, since it is the method we actually want to test. After that, we check if the result is `Ok` and we check that the buffer was filled accordingly. To do so, we use some macros:

- `assert!`: This checks if the value is `true`. If it is `false`, it will panic and make the test fail.
- `assert_eq!`: This checks that both values are equal.

This a quite simple and effective test, but it does not test every path of the function. So, let's add more lines in this function to test the other possible path:

```
#[cfg(test)]
mod tests {
    // ...

    #[test]
    fn test_encoder() {
        // ...
        let answer =
Answer::new(ResultCode::CantOpenDataConnection, "");
        let mut buf = BytesMut::new();
        let result = codec.encode(answer, &mut buf);
        assert!(result.is_ok(), "Result is ok");
        assert_eq!(buf, format!("425\r\n"), "Buffer contains 425");
    }
}
```

Here, we test with an empty message. The rest is basically the same: we create the necessary objects and use the assert macros. But this time, we added a new parameter to the assert macros; this is an optional message to show when the test fails.

If we run the test with `cargo test`, we get the following result:

```
Compiling ftp-server v0.0.1 (file:///path/to/FTP-server-rs)
 Finished dev [unoptimized + debuginfo] target(s) in 1.29 secs
  Running target/debug/deps/ftp_server-452667ddc2d724e8

running 1 test
test codec::tests::test_encoder ... ok

test result: ok. 1 passed; 0 failed; 0 ignored; 0 measured; 0 filtered out
```

This shows the test that was run and that it passed.

Let's write a `test` function that fails:

```
#[test]
fn test_dummy() {
    assert!(false, "Always fail");
}
```

When we run `cargo test`, we see the following:

```
 Finished dev [unoptimized + debuginfo] target(s) in 1.30 secs
  Running target/debug/deps/ftp_server-452667ddc2d724e8

running 2 tests
test codec::tests::test_encoder ... ok
test codec::tests::test_dummy ... FAILED

failures:

---- codec::tests::test_dummy stdout ----
    thread 'codec::tests::test_dummy' panicked at 'Always fail',
src/codec.rs:102:8
note: Run with `RUST_BACKTRACE=1` for a backtrace.


failures:
    codec::tests::test_dummy
```

```
test result: FAILED. 1 passed; 1 failed; 0 ignored; 0 measured; 0 filtered
out

error: test failed, to rerun pass '--bin ftp-server'
```

We can see that the message we specified (`Always fail`) is shown. We also see that 1 test failed.

Backtraces

As mentioned in the output, we can set the environment variable RUST_BACKTRACE to 1 in order to get more information about where the test failed. Let's do so:

```
export RUST_BACKTRACE=1

Finished dev [unoptimized + debuginfo] target(s) in 0.0 secs
  Running target/debug/deps/ftp_server-452667ddc2d724e8

running 2 tests
test codec::tests::test_encoder ... ok
test codec::tests::test_dummy ... FAILED

failures:

---- codec::tests::test_dummy stdout ----
    thread 'codec::tests::test_dummy' panicked at 'Always fail',
src/codec.rs:102:8
note: Some details are omitted, run with `RUST_BACKTRACE=full` for a
verbose backtrace.
stack backtrace:
   0: std::sys::imp::backtrace::tracing::imp::unwind_backtrace
             at /checkout/src/libstd/sys/unix/backtrace/tracing/gcc_s.rs:49
   1: std::sys_common::backtrace::_print
             at /checkout/src/libstd/sys_common/backtrace.rs:68
   2: std::panicking::default_hook::{{closure}}
             at /checkout/src/libstd/sys_common/backtrace.rs:57
             at /checkout/src/libstd/panicking.rs:381
   3: std::panicking::default_hook
             at /checkout/src/libstd/panicking.rs:391
   4: std::panicking::rust_panic_with_hook
             at /checkout/src/libstd/panicking.rs:577
   5: std::panicking::begin_panic
             at /checkout/src/libstd/panicking.rs:538
   6: ftp_server::codec::tests::test_dummy
             at src/codec.rs:102
   7: <F as test::FnBox<T>>::call_box
```

```
          at /checkout/src/libtest/lib.rs:1491
          at /checkout/src/libcore/ops/function.rs:223
          at /checkout/src/libtest/lib.rs:142
     8: __rust_maybe_catch_panic
          at /checkout/src/libpanic_unwind/lib.rs:99


failures:
    codec::tests::test_dummy

test result: FAILED. 1 passed; 1 failed; 0 ignored; 0 measured; 0 filtered
out

error: test failed, to rerun pass '--bin ftp-server'
```

The important part here is the following:

```
6: ftp_server::codec::tests::test_dummy
          at src/codec.rs:102
```

This shows the file, function, and line where the code panicked.

This variable is useful even outside of testing code: when debugging a problem with a code that panics, we can use this variable as well.

Testing failures

Sometimes, we want to test that a function will panic. To do so, we can simply add the #[should_panic] attribute at the top of the test function:

```
#[should_panic]
#[test]
fn test_dummy() {
    assert!(false, "Always fail");
}
```

When doing so, the test now passes:

```
    Finished dev [unoptimized + debuginfo] target(s) in 1.30 secs
     Running target/debug/deps/ftp_server-452667ddc2d724e8

running 2 tests
test codec::tests::test_dummy ... ok
test codec::tests::test_encoder ... ok

test result: ok. 2 passed; 0 failed; 0 ignored; 0 measured; 0 filtered out
```

Ignoring tests

Sometimes, we have tests that take a lot of time, or we want to avoid running a specific test all the time. To avoid running a test by default, we can add the `#[ignore]` attribute above the function:

```
#[ignore]
#[test]
fn test_dummy() {
    assert!(false, "Always fail");
}
```

When we run the `test`, we'll see that the `test` function was not running:

```
    Finished dev [unoptimized + debuginfo] target(s) in 0.0 secs
     Running target/debug/deps/ftp_server-452667ddc2d724e8

running 2 tests
test codec::tests::test_dummy ... ignored
test codec::tests::test_encoder ... ok

test result: ok. 1 passed; 0 failed; 1 ignored; 0 measured; 0 filtered out
```

As you can see, the `test_dummy()` test function was ignored. To run it, we need to specify a command-line argument to the program running the tests (not to `cargo` itself):

```
cargo test -- --ignored
```

 Note: We specified `--` before `--ignored` to send the latter to the program running the tests (which is not `cargo`).

With that argument, we see that the test indeed runs:

```
    Finished dev [unoptimized + debuginfo] target(s) in 0.0 secs
     Running target/debug/deps/ftp_server-452667ddc2d724e8

running 1 test
test codec::tests::test_dummy ... FAILED

failures:

---- codec::tests::test_dummy stdout ----
    thread 'codec::tests::test_dummy' panicked at 'Always fail',
src/codec.rs:102:8
note: Run with `RUST_BACKTRACE=1` for a backtrace.
```

```
failures:
    codec::tests::test_dummy

test result: FAILED. 0 passed; 1 failed; 0 ignored; 0 measured; 1 filtered
out

error: test failed, to rerun pass '--bin ftp-server'
```

To end this section, let's write a unit test for the decoder:

```
#[cfg(test)]
mod tests {
    // ...

    #[test]
    fn test_decoder() {
        let mut codec = FtpCodec;
        let mut buf = BytesMut::new();
        buf.extend(b"PWD");
        let result = codec.decode(&mut buf);
        assert!(result.is_ok());
        let command = result.unwrap();
        assert!(command.is_none());
```

Here, we test that None is returned in the case when more input is needed:

```
        buf.extend(b"\r\n");
        let result = codec.decode(&mut buf);
        assert!(result.is_ok());
        let command = result.unwrap();
        assert_eq!(command, Some(Command::Pwd));
```

And here, we add the missing output to check that the command was parsed correctly:

```
        let mut buf = BytesMut::new();
        buf.extend(b"LIST /tmp\r\n");
        let result = codec.decode(&mut buf);
        assert!(result.is_ok());
        let command = result.unwrap();
        assert_eq!(command,
    Some(Command::List(Some(PathBuf::from("/tmp"))))));
    }
}
```

Finally, we test that parsing a command with an argument works. If we run `cargo test` again, we get the following output:

```
    Finished dev [unoptimized + debuginfo] target(s) in 1.70 secs
      Running target/debug/deps/ftp_server-452667ddc2d724e8

running 2 tests
test codec::tests::test_encoder ... ok
test codec::tests::test_decoder ... ok

test result: ok. 2 passed; 0 failed; 0 ignored; 0 measured; 0 filtered out
```

Integration tests

In the previous section, we checked that a part of our code works: now, we will check that the program as a whole works, by writing integration tests. These tests reside in the `tests/` directory, so we start by creating it:

```
mkdir tests
```

In this directory, we can create a new file, `tests/server.rs`, in which we'll put the following content:

```
extern crate ftp;

use std::process::Command;
use std::thread;
use std::time::Duration;

use ftp::FtpStream;
```

We import the `ftp` crate which is an FTP client; it will be useful to test our FTP server. We need to add it in `Cargo.toml` as well:

```
[dev-dependencies]
ftp = "^2.2.1"
```

Here we see a new section, `dev-dependencies`: it contains the dependencies that are needed outside the main crate itself, like in the integration tests. By putting the dependency here and not in `[dependencies]`, it won't be available in the main crate, which is what we want.

Let's go back to the file `tests/server.rs` and add a `test` function:

```
#[test]
fn test_pwd() {
    let child =
        Command::new("./target/debug/ftp-server")
            .spawn().unwrap();
    let mut controller = ProcessController::new(child);

    thread::sleep(Duration::from_millis(100));
    assert!(controller.is_running(), "Server was aborted");

    let mut ftp = FtpStream::connect("127.0.0.1:1234").unwrap();

    ftp.quit().unwrap();
}
```

Here, we don't need to put the code in an inner `tests` module because the integration tests are compiled separately. Since our crate is a binary, we need to run it with the `Command` object. We give the child process to a `ProcessController` that we will create later.

 Note: If our crate was a library, we would add an `extern crate` for it, and we would be able to call functions from it directly.

We then call `thread::sleep()` to give some time for our server to start. After that, we use the `ftp` crate to connect to our server, and then we quit.

Teardown

In the Rust test framework, there's no `setup()` and `teardown()` functions like there are in the test frameworks of many other languages. And here, we need to run some code when the test is done: we need to kill our FTP server. So, we need some kind of `teardown` function. We cannot simply say `child.kill()` at the end of the function because, if the test panics before that, the FTP server will continue running after the test ends. To make sure the cleanup code is always called, no matter how the function ended, we'll have to use the `RAII` pattern that we discovered in `Chapter 6`, *Implementing the Engine of the Music Player*.

Let's write a simple `teardown` structure:

```
struct ProcessController {
    child: Child,
}
```

The structure contains the child process that will be killed in the destructor. So, if the test panics, this destructor will be called. It will also be called if the function ends normally.

We'll also create a constructor and the `utility` method that we used in the `test` function:

```
impl ProcessController {
    fn new(child: Child) -> Self {
        ProcessController {
            child,
        }
    }

    fn is_running(&mut self) -> bool {
        let status = self.child.try_wait().unwrap();
        status.is_none()
    }
}
```

The function `is_running()` is used to ensure that the FTP server we launched is actually running; if another instance of the application is already running, our instance will not run. That's why we used an assert in the test function.

Finally, we need to create a destructor:

```
impl Drop for ProcessController {
    fn drop(&mut self) {
        let _ = self.child.kill();
    }
}
```

We're now ready to write the `test` function:

```
#[test]
fn test_pwd() {
    // ...

    let mut ftp = FtpStream::connect("127.0.0.1:1234").unwrap();

    let pwd = ftp.pwd().unwrap();
    assert_eq!("/", pwd);
```

```
ftp.login("ferris", "").unwrap();

ftp.cwd("src").unwrap();
let pwd = ftp.pwd().unwrap();
assert_eq!("/src", pwd);

let _ = ftp.cdup();
let pwd = ftp.pwd().unwrap();
assert_eq!("/", pwd);

ftp.quit().unwrap();
}
```

In this function, we issue some FTP commands and make sure the server state is correct by calling the assert_eq!() macro. When we run cargo test, we see the following output:

```
Finished dev [unoptimized + debuginfo] target(s) in 0.0 secs
  Running target/debug/deps/ftp_server-47386d9089111729

running 2 tests
test codec::tests::test_decoder ... ok
test codec::tests::test_encoder ... ok

test result: ok. 2 passed; 0 failed; 0 ignored; 0 measured; 0 filtered out

  Running target/debug/deps/server-1b5cda64792f5f82

running 1 test
Waiting clients on port 1234...
New client: [address : 127.0.0.1:43280]
Waiting another client...
Received command: Pwd
Received command: User("ferris")
Received command: Cwd("src")
Received command: Pwd
Received command: CdUp
Received command: Pwd
Received command: Quit
test test_pwd ... ok

test result: ok. 1 passed; 0 failed; 0 ignored; 0 measured; 0 filtered out
```

A new section is added for our integration test.

Print output to stdout

Let's see what happens when we add a call to `println!()` in our test (for debug purposes, for instance):

```
#[test]
fn test_pwd() {
    println!("Running FTP server");

    // ...
}
```

It will not be printed to the terminal. In order to see it, we need to pass another parameter to the test runner. Let's run `cargo test` this way to see the output to `stdout`:

```
cargo run -- --nocapture
```

This time, we see the following output:

```
...

    Running target/debug/deps/server-1b5cda64792f5f82

running 1 test
Running FTP server
Waiting clients on port 1234...
New client: [address : 127.0.0.1:43304]
Waiting another client...
Received command: Pwd
Received command: User("ferris")
Received command: Cwd("src")
Received command: Pwd
Received command: CdUp
Received command: Pwd
Received command: Quit
test test_pwd ... ok

test result: ok. 1 passed; 0 failed; 0 ignored; 0 measured; 0 filtered out
```

Documentation

Another very important aspect of a software is documentation. It is useful to describe how to use a project, giving some examples and detailing the complete public API: let's see how we can document a crate in Rust.

Documenting a crate

Documentation is written in comments, but these doc-comments start with a special symbol. We use the token /// to document the item following the comment, and //! to document the item from within this item. Let's start by seeing an example of the latter.

At the top of our crate's root (specifically, in the file main.rs), we'll add the following comment:

```
//! An FTP server, written using tokio and futures-await.
```

Here, we use the //! form because we cannot write a comment before a crate; we can only write a comment from within the crate.

Documenting a module

Documenting a module is very similar: we add a comment of the form //! at the top of a module's file. Let's add the following doc-comment in codec.rs:

```
//! FTP codecs to encode and decode FTP commands and raw bytes.
```

Headers

The doc-comments are written in Markdown, so let's look at some Markdown formatting syntax. We can write headers by starting a line with a #. The more #'s, the smaller the title.

For example:

```
/// Some introduction text.
///
/// # Big Title
///
/// ## Less big title
///
/// ### Even less big title.
///
/// #### Small title
///
/// ...
```

I think you get it at this point!

Here is a list of common headers:

- Examples
- Panics
- Failure

Code blocks

The code we write in doc-comments must be inserted between two pairs of ` ``` `. Usually, the code blocks are written under an `Examples` header. Let's see an example using all of these syntactic elements for a function that convert bytes to uppercase:

```
/// Convert a sequence of bytes to uppercase.
///
/// # Examples
///
/// ```
/// let mut data = b"test";
/// to_uppercase(&mut data);
/// ```
fn to_uppercase(data: &mut [u8]) {
    for byte in data {
        if *byte >= 'a' as u8 && *byte <= 'z' as u8 {
            *byte -= 32;
        }
    }
}
```

Here, we start with a short description of the function. Then, we show a code example.

It's recommended to add comments in the code if needed, to help users understand it more easily, so don't hesitate to add some!

Documenting an enumeration (or any type with public fields)

When we want to document an enumeration, we want not only to document the type, but also each variant. To do so, we can simply add a doc-comment before each variant. The same applies for a structure, for its fields.

Let's see an example for the Command type:

```
/// An FTP command parsed by the parser.
#[derive(Clone, Debug, PartialEq)]
pub enum Command {
    Auth,
    /// Change the working directory to the one specified as an
argument.
    Cwd(PathBuf),
    /// Get a list of files.
    List(Option<PathBuf>),
    /// Create a new directory.
    Mkd(PathBuf),
    /// No operation.
    NoOp,
    /// Specify the port to use for the data channel.
    Port(u16),
    /// Enter passive mode.
    Pasv,
    /// Print current directory.
    Pwd,
    /// Terminate the connection.
    Quit,
    /// Retrieve a file.
    Retr(PathBuf),
    /// Remove a directory.
    Rmd(PathBuf),
    /// Store a file on the server.
    Stor(PathBuf),
    Syst,
    /// Specify the transfert type.
    Type(TransferType),
    /// Go to the parent directory.
    CdUp,
    Unknown(String),
    User(String),
}
```

We see that the enum itself has a doc-comment and most of the variants also have documentation.

Generating the documentation

We can easily generate the documentation by running the following command:

```
cargo doc
```

This will generate the documentation in the directory `target/doc/ftp_server`. Here is how it looks:

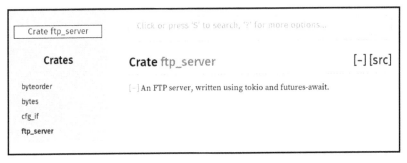

Figure 10.5

Warning about public items without documentation

When writing a library, it is very easy to forget to write the documentation about every item. But, we can use the help of the tools at our disposal. By adding the `#[warn(missing_docs)]` attribute in our crate's root, the compiler will warn us when public items do not have a doc-comment. In such a case, it will print something like this:

```
warning: missing documentation for crate
  --> src/main.rs:9:1
    |
9   | / #![feature(proc_macro, conservative_impl_trait, generators)]
10  | | #![warn(missing_docs)]
11  | | 
12  | | extern crate bytes;
... |
528 | |     }
529 | | }
    | |_^
    |
note: lint level defined here
  --> src/main.rs:10:9
    |
10  | #![warn(missing_docs)]
    |            ^^^^^^^^^^^^
    |
```

Hiding items from the documentation

Sometimes, we intentionally do not want to have a public item show up in the documentation. In this case, we can use the `#[doc(hidden)]` attribute:

```
#[doc(hidden)]
#[derive(Clone, Copy, Debug, PartialEq)]
pub enum TransferType {
    Ascii,
    Image,
    Unknown,
}
```

For instance, this can be useful for something that is used by a macro of the crate but is not intended to be used directly by the user.

Documentation tests

Writing documentation is a great thing. Showing code in your documentation is even better. However, how can you be sure that the code you're showing is still up to date? That it won't break when users copy/paste it to test it out? Here comes another wonderful feature from Rust: `doc tests`.

Tags

First, any code blocks in documentation comments will be tested by default if they don't have `ignore` or any non-recognized tag. So, for example:

```
/// ```ignore
/// let x = 12;
/// x += 1;
/// ```
```

This block code won't be tested (luckily, because it wouldn't compile!). A few other examples:

```
/// # Some text
///
/// ```text
/// this is just some text
/// but it's rendered inside a code block
/// nice, right?
/// ```
///
/// # Why not C?
///
/// ```c-language
/// int strlen(const char *s) {
///     char *c = s;
///
///     for (; *c; ++c);
///     return c - s;
/// }
/// ```
///
/// # Or an unknown language?
///
/// ```whatever
/// 010010000110100100100001
/// ```
```

A few other instructions might come in handy for you. Let's start with `ignore`!

ignore

Just like this flag name states, `ignore` makes the block code ignored. As simple as that. It'll still get the Rust syntax color once rendered in the documentation. For example:

```
/// ```ignore
/// let x = 0;
/// ```
```

However, once rendered, it'll have a graphical notification about the fact that this block code isn't tested:

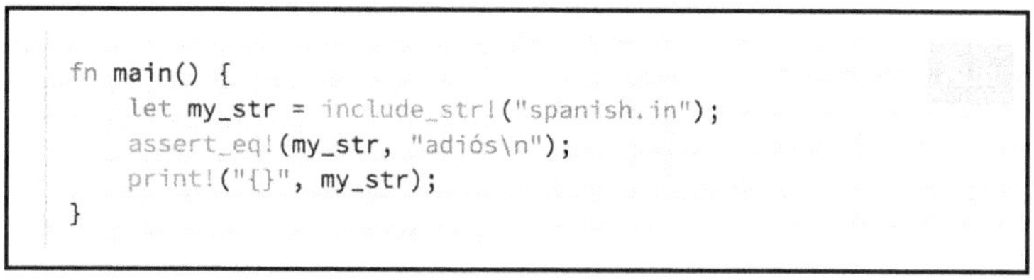

```
fn main() {
    let my_str = include_str!("spanish.in");
    assert_eq!(my_str, "adiós\n");
    print!("{}", my_str);
}
```

Figure 10.6

And when you hover over the ☺ sign:

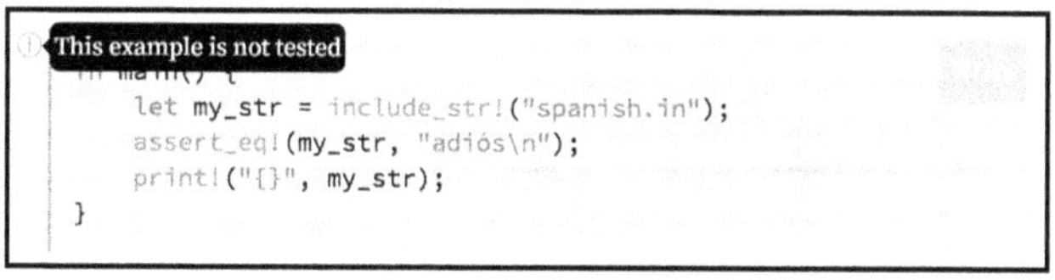

```
This example is not tested
    let my_str = include_str!("spanish.in");
    assert_eq!(my_str, "adiós\n");
    print!("{}", my_str);
}
```

Figure 10.7

Now let's continue with `compile_fail`!

compile_fail

The `compile_fail` flag ensures that the given code blocks don't compile. As simple as that. It's mostly used when you're showing bad code and demonstrating why it is bad. For example:

```
/// ```compile_fail
/// let x = 0;
/// x += 2; // Damn! `x` isn't mutable so you cannot update it...
/// ```
```

Then you just write a small explanation about what went wrong and show a working example. It's very common in tutorials, to help users understand why it's wrong and how to fix it.

In addition to this, please note that there will be a graphical indication that this block is supposed to fail at compilation:

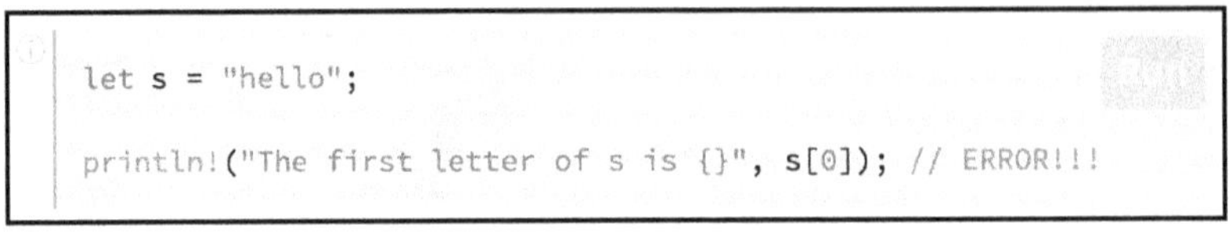

```
let s = "hello";

println!("The first letter of s is {}", s[0]); // ERROR!!!
```

Figure 10.8

And when you hover over the ⓘ sign:

```
ⓘ This example deliberately fails to compile
let s = "hello";

println!("The first letter of s is {}", s[0]); // ERROR!!!
```

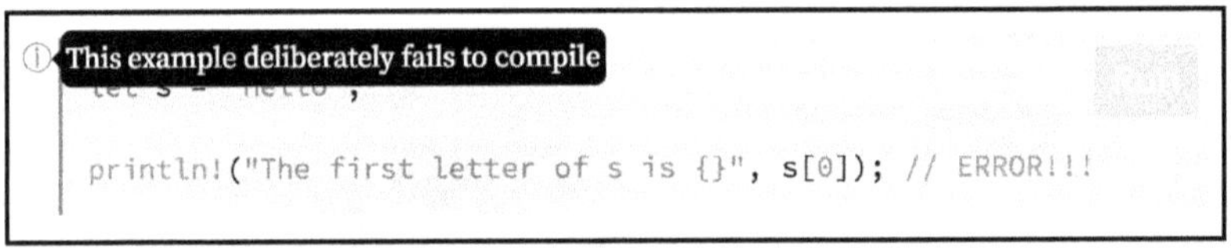

Figure 10.9

Let's continue with no_run!

no_run

The no_run flag tells rustdoc to only check if the code block compiles (and therefore, not to run it). It's mostly used in cases involving external resources (such as files). For example:

```
/// ```no_run
/// use std::fs::File;
///
/// let mut f = File::open("some-file.txt").expect("file not
found...");
/// ```
```

If you run this test, it's very likely (but not certain, since there is a possibility that some funny user decided to suddenly add a some-file.txt file) to fail at execution. However, the code is perfectly fine so it'd be a shame to just ignore it, right?

Now, let's see what to do if you *want* the test to fail:

should_panic

The `should_panic` flag ensures that your block code panics at execution. If it doesn't, then the test fails. Let's take the previous code block:

```
/// ```should_panic
/// use std::fs::File;
///
/// let mut f = File::open("some-file.txt").expect("file not
found...");
/// ```
```

Once again, the test should succeed (unless, again, you have a funny user who added the file). Quite useful if you want to show some *bad* behavior.

Combining flags?

It's actually possible to combine flags, although it's not really useful. For example:

```
/// ```rust,ignore
/// let x = 0;
/// ```
```

You could just have written this as follows:

```
/// ```ignore
/// let x = 0;
/// ```
```

For now, it's not really useful, but who knows what will happen in the future? At least now you know!

About the doc blocks themselves

I suppose you noticed that we never added a function or anything. So how does it actually work?

Well first, it checks if the `main` function is defined. If not, it'll wrap the code into one. Observe the following code:

```
/// ```
/// let x = 0;
/// ```
```

When you write the preceding code, it gets transformed into this:

```
/// ```
/// fn main() {
///     let x = 0;
/// }
/// ```
```

Also, you can use all the public items defined in your crate in your code blocks. No need to import the crate with an `extern crate` (however, you still have to import the item!).

One last (very) important point remains to be talked about: hiding code blocks lines.

Hiding code blocks lines

If you want to use ?, you'll have to do it inside a function returning an `Option` or a `Result`. But still, inside a function. However, you don't necessarily want to show those lines to the user in order to focus on what you're trying to explain.

To put it simply, you just need to add a # at the beginning of the line. As simple as that. As always, let's show it with a small example:

```
/// ```
/// # fn foo() -> std::io::Result<()> {
/// let mut file = File::open("some-file.txt")?;
/// write!(file, "Hello world!")?;
/// # Ok(())
/// # }
/// ```
```

The user will only see the following:

```
let mut file = File::open("some-file.txt")?;
write!(file, "Hello world!")?;
```

However, if they click on the **Run** button, they'll see the following:

```
fn main() {
use std::fs::File;
use std::io::prelude::*;

fn foo() -> std::io::Result<()> {
let mut file = File::open("some-file.txt")?;
write!(file, "Hello world!")?;
Ok(())
}
}
```

(Don't forget that the `main` function is added as well!).

That's it for the doc tests. With all this knowledge, you should be able to write a nice API documentation which will always be up to date and tested (hopefully)!

Fuzzing tests

There is another type of test that is very useful but is not integrated into the Rust standard library: fuzzing tests.

A fuzzing test will test a function's automatically generated input with the sole purpose of crashing this function or making it behave incorrectly. Fuzzing tests can be used to complement tests that are written manually because they can generate way more input than we can possibly write by hand. We will use `cargo-fuzz` to test our command parser.

First, we need to install it:

```
cargo install cargo-fuzz
```

Next, we will use the new `cargo fuzz` command to create a new fuzz test crate in our FTP server crate:

```
cargo fuzz init
```

This generated a few files. The most important of them and the one we will modify, is `fuzz/fuzz_targets/fuzz_target_1.rs`. Let's replace its content with the following:

```
#![no_main]
#[macro_use] extern crate libfuzzer_sys;

mod error {
    include!("../../src/error.rs");
}

include!("../../src/cmd.rs");

fuzz_target!(|data: &[u8]| {
    let _ = Command::new(data.to_vec());
});
```

Since our crate is a binary instead of a library, we cannot directly import functions from it. So, we use this little trick to get access to the functions we want:

```
mod error {
    include!("../../src/error.rs");
}

include!("../../src/cmd.rs");
```

The `mod error` is needed because our `cmd` module depends on it. With that sorted, we include the `cmd` module with a macro. This macro will expand to the content of the file, similarly to the `#include` preprocessor directive in C. Finally, we have our `test` function:

```
fuzz_target!(|data: &[u8]| {
    let _ = Command::new(data.to_vec());
});
```

Here, we just create a new command from the random input we receive. We ignore the result since there's no way we can possibly check if it is right, except by listing all possibilities (which would make a great unit test). So, if there's a bug in our command parser that causes a panic, the fuzzer could find it.

To run the fuzzer, issue the following command:

```
cargo fuzz run fuzz_target_1
```

```
        Fresh arbitrary v0.1.0
        Fresh cc v1.0.3
        Fresh libfuzzer-sys v0.1.0
(https://github.com/rust-fuzz/libfuzzer-sys.git#737524f7)
    Compiling ftp-server-fuzz v0.0.1 (file:///path/to/FTP-server-rs/fuzz)
      Running `rustc --crate-name fuzz_target_1
fuzz/fuzz_targets/fuzz_target_1.rs --crate-type bin --emit=dep-info,link -C
debuginfo=2 -C metadata=7eb012a2948092cc -C extra-
filename=-7eb012a2948092cc --out-dir /path/to/FTP-server-
rs/fuzz/target/x86_64-unknown-linux-gnu/debug/deps --target x86_64-unknown-
linux-gnu -L dependency=/path/to/FTP-server-rs/fuzz/target/x86_64-unknown-
linux-gnu/debug/deps -L dependency=/path/to/FTP-server-
rs/fuzz/target/debug/deps --extern libfuzzer_sys=/path/to/FTP-server-
rs/fuzz/target/x86_64-unknown-linux-
gnu/debug/deps/liblibfuzzer_sys-44f07aaa9fd00b00.rlib --cfg fuzzing -
Cpasses=sancov -Cllvm-args=-sanitizer-coverage-level=3 -Zsanitizer=address
-Cpanic=abort -L native=/path/to/FTP-server-rs/fuzz/target/x86_64-unknown-
linux-gnu/debug/build/libfuzzer-sys-b260d147c5e0139d/out`
    Finished dev [unoptimized + debuginfo] target(s) in 1.57 secs
        Fresh arbitrary v0.1.0
        Fresh cc v1.0.3
        Fresh libfuzzer-sys v0.1.0
(https://github.com/rust-fuzz/libfuzzer-sys.git#737524f7)
        Fresh ftp-server-fuzz v0.0.1 (file:///path/to/FTP-server-rs/fuzz)
    Finished dev [unoptimized + debuginfo] target(s) in 0.0 secs
      Running `fuzz/target/x86_64-unknown-linux-gnu/debug/fuzz_target_1 -
artifact_prefix=/path/to/FTP-server-rs/fuzz/artifacts/fuzz_target_1/
/path/to/FTP-server-rs/fuzz/corpus/fuzz_target_1`
INFO: Seed: 1369551667
INFO: Loaded 0 modules (0 guards):
Loading corpus dir: /path/to/FTP-server-rs/fuzz/corpus/fuzz_target_1
INFO: -max_len is not provided, using 64
INFO: A corpus is not provided, starting from an empty corpus
#0   READ units: 1
#1   INITED cov: 389 corp: 1/1b exec/s: 0 rss: 23Mb
#4   NEW    cov: 393 corp: 2/4b exec/s: 0 rss: 23Mb L: 3 MS: 3 ShuffleBytes-
InsertByte-InsertByte-
#5   NEW    cov: 412 corp: 3/62b exec/s: 0 rss: 23Mb L: 58 MS: 4
ShuffleBytes-InsertByte-InsertByte-InsertRepeatedBytes-
#7   NEW    cov: 415 corp: 4/121b exec/s: 0 rss: 23Mb L: 59 MS: 1
InsertByte-
#21 NEW    cov: 416 corp: 5/181b exec/s: 0 rss: 23Mb L: 60 MS: 5 ChangeBit-
InsertByte-ChangeBinInt-ChangeByte-InsertByte-
#707    NEW    cov: 446 corp: 6/241b exec/s: 0 rss: 23Mb L: 60 MS: 1
ChangeBit-
#710    NEW    cov: 447 corp: 7/295b exec/s: 0 rss: 23Mb L: 54 MS: 4
```

```
ChangeBit-InsertByte-EraseBytes-InsertByte-
#767    NEW    cov: 448 corp: 8/357b exec/s: 0 rss: 23Mb L: 62 MS: 1 CMP-
DE: "\x01\x00"-
#780    NEW    cov: 449 corp: 9/421b exec/s: 0 rss: 23Mb L: 64 MS: 4
CopyPart-InsertByte-ChangeByte-CrossOver-
#852    NEW    cov: 450 corp: 10/439b exec/s: 0 rss: 23Mb L: 18 MS: 1
CrossOver-
#1072   NEW    cov: 452 corp: 11/483b exec/s: 0 rss: 23Mb L: 44 MS: 1
InsertRepeatedBytes-
#85826  NEW    cov: 454 corp: 12/487b exec/s: 85826 rss: 41Mb L: 4 MS: 5
ChangeBit-InsertByte-InsertByte-EraseBytes-CMP- DE: "NOOP"-
#92732  NEW    cov: 456 corp: 13/491b exec/s: 92732 rss: 43Mb L: 4 MS: 1
CMP- DE: "PASV"-
#101858 NEW    cov: 477 corp: 14/495b exec/s: 50929 rss: 46Mb L: 4 MS: 2
ChangeByte-CMP- DE: "STOR"-
#105338 NEW    cov: 497 corp: 15/499b exec/s: 52669 rss: 47Mb L: 4 MS: 2
ShuffleBytes-CMP- DE: "LIST"-
#108617 NEW    cov: 499 corp: 16/503b exec/s: 54308 rss: 48Mb L: 4 MS: 1
CMP- DE: "AUTH"-
#108867 NEW    cov: 501 corp: 17/507b exec/s: 54433 rss: 48Mb L: 4 MS: 1
CMP- DE: "QUIT"-
#115442 NEW    cov: 503 corp: 18/511b exec/s: 57721 rss: 50Mb L: 4 MS: 1
CMP- DE: "SYST"-
#115533 NEW    cov: 505 corp: 19/515b exec/s: 57766 rss: 50Mb L: 4 MS: 2
ChangeBinInt-CMP- DE: "CDUP"-
#123001 NEW    cov: 513 corp: 20/518b exec/s: 61500 rss: 52Mb L: 3 MS: 5
PersAutoDict-EraseBytes-ChangeByte-ChangeBinInt-CMP- DE: "\x01\x00"-"RMD"-
#127270 NEW    cov: 515 corp: 21/521b exec/s: 63635 rss: 54Mb L: 3 MS: 4
EraseBytes-ChangeByte-InsertByte-CMP- DE: "PWD"-
#131072 pulse  cov: 515 corp: 21/521b exec/s: 65536 rss: 55Mb
#148469 NEW    cov: 527 corp: 22/525b exec/s: 49489 rss: 59Mb L: 4 MS: 3
ChangeBit-ChangeBit-CMP- DE: "USER"-
#151237 NEW    cov: 528 corp: 23/529b exec/s: 50412 rss: 60Mb L: 4 MS: 1
CMP- DE: "TYPE"-
#169842 NEW    cov: 536 corp: 24/532b exec/s: 56614 rss: 65Mb L: 3 MS: 1
ChangeByte-
#262144 pulse  cov: 536 corp: 24/532b exec/s: 52428 rss: 90Mb
#274258 NEW    cov: 544 corp: 25/535b exec/s: 54851 rss: 94Mb L: 3 MS: 2
ChangeBit-CMP- DE: "MKD"-
#355992 NEW    cov: 566 corp: 26/539b exec/s: 50856 rss: 116Mb L: 4 MS: 1
InsertByte-
#356837 NEW    cov: 575 corp: 27/558b exec/s: 50976 rss: 116Mb L: 19 MS: 1
InsertRepeatedBytes-
#361667 NEW    cov: 586 corp: 28/562b exec/s: 51666 rss: 117Mb L: 4 MS: 1
PersAutoDict- DE: "MKD"-
thread '<unnamed>' panicked at 'index out of bounds: the len is 0 but the
index is 0', fuzz/fuzz_targets/../../src/cmd.rs:85:46
note: Run with `RUST_BACKTRACE=1` for a backtrace.
```

```
==10969== ERROR: libFuzzer: deadly signal
    #0 0x55e90764cf73  (/path/to/FTP-server-rs/fuzz/target/x86_64-unknown-
linux-gnu/debug/fuzz_target_1+0x110f73)
    #1 0x55e9076aa701  (/path/to/FTP-server-rs/fuzz/target/x86_64-unknown-
linux-gnu/debug/fuzz_target_1+0x16e701)
    #2 0x55e9076aa64b  (/path/to/FTP-server-rs/fuzz/target/x86_64-unknown-
linux-gnu/debug/fuzz_target_1+0x16e64b)
    #3 0x55e907683059  (/path/to/FTP-server-rs/fuzz/target/x86_64-unknown-
linux-gnu/debug/fuzz_target_1+0x147059)
    #4 0x7f4bda433d9f  (/usr/lib/libpthread.so.0+0x11d9f)
    #5 0x7f4bd9e8789f  (/usr/lib/libc.so.6+0x3489f)
    #6 0x7f4bd9e88f08  (/usr/lib/libc.so.6+0x35f08)
    #7 0x55e9076c2b18  (/path/to/FTP-server-rs/fuzz/target/x86_64-unknown-
linux-gnu/debug/fuzz_target_1+0x186b18)

NOTE: libFuzzer has rudimentary signal handlers.
      Combine libFuzzer with AddressSanitizer or similar for better crash
reports.
SUMMARY: libFuzzer: deadly signal
MS: 2 CopyPart-InsertByte-; base unit:
6e9816a8e9d0388eecdb52866188c04e75e4b1b3
0x54,0x59,0x50,0x45,0x20,
TYPE
artifact_prefix='/path/to/FTP-server-rs/fuzz/artifacts/fuzz_target_1/';
Test unit written to /path/to/FTP-server-
rs/fuzz/artifacts/fuzz_target_1/crash-601e8dbb61bd6c7d63cff0bd3f749f7cb5392
2bc
Base64: VF1QRSA=
==10969==LeakSanitizer has encountered a fatal error.
==10969==HINT: For debugging, try setting environment variable
LSAN_OPTIONS=verbosity=1:log_threads=1
==10969==HINT: LeakSanitizer does not work under ptrace (strace, gdb, etc)
MS: 2 CopyPart-InsertByte-; base unit:
6e9816a8e9d0388eecdb52866188c04e75e4b1b3
0x54,0x59,0x50,0x45,0x20,
TYPE
artifact_prefix='/path/to/FTP-server-rs/fuzz/artifacts/fuzz_target_1/';
Test unit written to /path/to/FTP-server-
rs/fuzz/artifacts/fuzz_target_1/crash-601e8dbb61bd6c7d63cff0bd3f749f7cb5392
2bc
Base64: VF1QRSA=
```

There's actually a bug in our parser! We can see where, thanks to this line:

```
thread '<unnamed>' panicked at 'index out of bounds: the len is 0 but the
index is 0', fuzz/fuzz_targets/../../src/cmd.rs:85:46
```

The corresponding line in the source code is:

```
match TransferType::from(data?[0]) {
```

And indeed, if the data is empty, this will panic. Let's fix that:

```
impl Command {
    pub fn new(input: Vec<u8>) -> Result<Self> {
        // ...
        let command =
            match command.as_slice() {
                // ...
                b"TYPE" => {
                    let error = Err("command not implemented for
that
                        parameter".into());
                    let data = data?;
                    if data.is_empty() {
                        return error;
                    }
                    match TransferType::from(data[0]) {
                        TransferType::Unknown => return error,
                        typ => {
                            Command::Type(typ)
                        },
                    }
                },
                // ...
            };
        Ok(command)
    }
}
```

The fix is simple: we check if the data is empty, in which case we return an error.

Let's try the fuzzer to see if it can find another bug. Here's the output:

```
INFO: Seed: 81554194
INFO: Loaded 0 modules (0 guards):
Loading corpus dir:
/home/bouanto/Ordinateur/Programmation/Rust/Projets/FTP-server-
rs/fuzz/corpus/fuzz_target_1
INFO: -max_len is not provided, using 64
#0   READ units: 27
#27 INITED cov: 595 corp: 23/330b exec/s: 0 rss: 28Mb
#21494  NEW    cov: 602 corp: 24/349b exec/s: 0 rss: 28Mb L: 19 MS: 2
ShuffleBytes-CMP- DE: "STOR"-
#21504  NEW    cov: 606 corp: 25/354b exec/s: 0 rss: 28Mb L: 5 MS: 2
```

```
InsertByte-PersAutoDict- DE: "STOR"-
#24893  NEW    cov: 616 corp: 26/359b exec/s: 0 rss: 29Mb L: 5 MS: 1 CMP-
DE: "TYPE"-
#25619  NEW    cov: 620 corp: 27/365b exec/s: 0 rss: 29Mb L: 6 MS: 2
PersAutoDict-InsertByte- DE: "TYPE"-
#25620  NEW    cov: 621 corp: 28/379b exec/s: 0 rss: 29Mb L: 14 MS: 3
PersAutoDict-InsertByte-CMP- DE: "TYPE"-"\x00\x00\x00\x00\x00\x00\x00\x00"-
#32193  NEW    cov: 628 corp: 29/398b exec/s: 0 rss: 31Mb L: 19 MS: 1 CMP-
DE: "CWD"-
#34108  NEW    cov: 662 corp: 30/417b exec/s: 0 rss: 31Mb L: 19 MS: 1 CMP-
DE: "USER"-
#35745  NEW    cov: 666 corp: 31/421b exec/s: 0 rss: 31Mb L: 4 MS: 3
ShuffleBytes-EraseBytes-PersAutoDict- DE: "CWD"-
#36518  NEW    cov: 673 corp: 32/426b exec/s: 0 rss: 32Mb L: 5 MS: 1
PersAutoDict- DE: "USER"-
#36634  NEW    cov: 685 corp: 33/433b exec/s: 0 rss: 32Mb L: 7 MS: 2 CMP-
CMP- DE: "\xff\xff"-"RETR"-
#37172  NEW    cov: 688 corp: 34/437b exec/s: 0 rss: 32Mb L: 4 MS: 5
EraseBytes-ChangeBinInt-InsertByte-ChangeBit-CMP- DE: "RETR"-
#39248  NEW    cov: 692 corp: 35/442b exec/s: 0 rss: 32Mb L: 5 MS: 1
PersAutoDict- DE: "RETR"-
#65735  NEW    cov: 699 corp: 36/492b exec/s: 65735 rss: 39Mb L: 50 MS: 3
InsertRepeatedBytes-ChangeBit-CMP- DE: "LIST"-
#69797  NEW    cov: 703 corp: 37/497b exec/s: 69797 rss: 40Mb L: 5 MS: 5
ChangeByte-CopyPart-CopyPart-EraseBytes-PersAutoDict- DE: "LIST"-
#131072 pulse  cov: 703 corp: 37/497b exec/s: 65536 rss: 55Mb
#217284 NEW    cov: 707 corp: 38/511b exec/s: 54321 rss: 75Mb L: 14 MS: 2
CMP-ShuffleBytes- DE: "LIST"-
#219879 NEW    cov: 708 corp: 39/525b exec/s: 54969 rss: 76Mb L: 14 MS: 2
ChangeByte-ChangeBit-
#262144 pulse  cov: 708 corp: 39/525b exec/s: 52428 rss: 86Mb
#524288 pulse  cov: 708 corp: 39/525b exec/s: 52428 rss: 148Mb
#1048576    pulse  cov: 708 corp: 39/525b exec/s: 52428 rss: 273Mb
#2097152    pulse  cov: 708 corp: 39/525b exec/s: 51150 rss: 522Mb
#4194304    pulse  cov: 708 corp: 39/525b exec/s: 50533 rss: 569Mb
#8388608    pulse  cov: 708 corp: 39/525b exec/s: 50533 rss: 569Mb
#12628080   NEW    cov: 835 corp: 40/530b exec/s: 50311 rss: 570Mb L: 5 MS:
3 ChangeBit-ChangeBinInt-ShuffleBytes-
#12628883   NEW    cov: 859 corp: 41/540b exec/s: 50314 rss: 570Mb L: 10
MS: 1 CopyPart-
#12628893   NEW    cov: 867 corp: 42/604b exec/s: 50314 rss: 570Mb L: 64
MS: 1 CrossOver-
#12643279   NEW    cov: 868 corp: 43/608b exec/s: 50371 rss: 570Mb L: 4 MS:
2 EraseBytes-EraseBytes-
#12670956   NEW    cov: 871 corp: 44/652b exec/s: 50281 rss: 570Mb L: 44
MS: 4 EraseBytes-InsertByte-ChangeBinInt-ChangeBinInt-
#12671130   NEW    cov: 872 corp: 45/697b exec/s: 50282 rss: 570Mb L: 45
MS: 3 ChangeBit-CMP-InsertByte- DE: "\xff\xff\xff\xff"-
```

```
#12671140    NEW      cov: 873 corp: 46/750b exec/s: 50282 rss: 570Mb L: 53
MS: 3 ChangeBinInt-CMP-CopyPart- DE: "\x00\x00\x00\x00\x00\x00\x00\x00"-
#12671906    NEW      cov: 874 corp: 47/803b exec/s: 50285 rss: 570Mb L: 53
MS: 4 ChangeBit-ChangeByte-PersAutoDict-ShuffleBytes- DE: "CWD"-
#12687428    NEW      cov: 875 corp: 48/856b exec/s: 50346 rss: 574Mb L: 53
MS: 1 ShuffleBytes-
#12699014    NEW      cov: 945 corp: 49/862b exec/s: 50392 rss: 574Mb L: 6 MS:
2 InsertByte-ChangeBit-
#13319888    NEW      cov: 946 corp: 50/869b exec/s: 50074 rss: 579Mb L: 7 MS:
1 InsertByte-
#13424473    NEW      cov: 1015 corp: 51/878b exec/s: 50091 rss: 580Mb L: 9
MS: 1 CopyPart-
#13432333    NEW      cov: 1018 corp: 52/888b exec/s: 50120 rss: 580Mb L: 10
MS: 1 CopyPart-
#13651748    NEW      cov: 1019 corp: 53/901b exec/s: 50006 rss: 582Mb L: 13
MS: 1 CopyPart-
#13652268    NEW      cov: 1020 corp: 54/920b exec/s: 50008 rss: 582Mb L: 19
MS: 1 CopyPart-
#13652535    NEW      cov: 1025 corp: 55/978b exec/s: 50009 rss: 582Mb L: 58
MS: 3 InsertRepeatedBytes-ChangeBit-InsertByte-
#13662779    NEW      cov: 1028 corp: 56/997b exec/s: 50046 rss: 582Mb L: 19
MS: 2 ChangeBit-ShuffleBytes-
#16777216    pulse    cov: 1028 corp: 56/997b exec/s: 48913 rss: 589Mb
#33554432    pulse    cov: 1028 corp: 56/997b exec/s: 46154 rss: 589Mb
#67108864    pulse    cov: 1028 corp: 56/997b exec/s: 45343 rss: 589Mb
#134217728   pulse    cov: 1028 corp: 56/997b exec/s: 44325 rss: 589Mb
#268435456   pulse    cov: 1028 corp: 56/997b exec/s: 43819 rss: 589Mb
^C==16792== libFuzzer: run interrupted; exiting
```

So, we ran the fuzzer for a very long time and it didn't find a panic, so we ended it with *Ctrl* + *C*. We cannot be certain that there's no bug left, but we are more confident thanks to all these tests.

Summary

In this chapter, we finalized our FTP server. Then, we learned how to do different types of tests. We saw how we can test a single function or type by writing unit tests. We learned how to test a program as a whole by writing integration tests. We also learned about documentation and fuzzing tests to make sure our examples are up to date and to find even more bugs in our application.

In the next and ultimate chapter, we will learn about Rust's good practice and common idioms.

Rust Best Practices

Rust is a powerful language, but a few things easily avoidable with practice can make your life really hard when starting. This chapter aims to show you some good practices and tips.

We will cover the following topics in this chapter:

- Best practices
- API tips and improvements
- Usage tips
- Code readability

Now let's go!

Rust best practices

Let's start with some basics (and maybe obvious) things.

Slices

First, a little recap; a slice is a constant view over an array, and `&[T]` is the constant view of a `Vec<T>`, whereas `&str` is the constant view of a `String` (just like `Path` is the constant view of a `PathBuf` and `OsStr` is the constant view of an `OsString`). Now that you have this in mind, let's continue!

When a function expects a constant argument of type `Vec` or `String`, then always write them as follows:

```rust
fn some_func(v: &[u8]) {
    // some code...
}
```

Instead of:

```rust
fn some_code(v: &Vec<u8>) {
    // some code
}
```

And:

```rust
fn some_func(s: &str) {
    // some code...
}
```

Instead of:

```rust
fn some_func(s: &String) {
    // some code...
}
```

You might be wondering why this is the case. So, let's imagine your function displays your `Vec` as ASCII characters:

```rust
fn print_as_ascii(v: &[u8]) {
    for c in v {
        print!("{}", *c as char);
    }
    println!("");
}
```

And now you just want to print a part of your `Vec`:

```rust
let v = b"salut!";

print_as_ascii(&v[2..]);
```

Now, if the `print_as_ascii` only accepted references on `Vec`, you'd have to make a (useless) allocation, as follows:

```rust
let v = b"salut!";

print_as_ascii(&v[2..].to_vec());
```

API tips and improvements

When writing a public API (either for you or other users), a few tips can really make everyone's life easier. This is where generics kick in. Let's start with Option arguments:

Explaining the Some function

Generally, when a function expects an Option argument, it looks like this:

```
fn some_func(arg: Option<&str>) {
    // some code
}
```

And you call it as follows:

```
some_func(Some("ratatouille"));
some_func(None);
```

Now, what if I told you that you could get rid of the Some? Nice, right? Well, this is actually pretty easy:

```
fn some_func<'a, T: Into<Option<&'a str>>>(arg: T) {
    // some code
}
```

And you can now call it as follows:

```
some_func(Some("ratatouille")); // If you *really* like to write
"Some"...
some_func("ratatouille");
some_func(None);
```

Better! However, to make users' lives easier, it'll require a bit more code for whoever's writing the function. You can't use arg as it is; you need to add an extra step. Before, you'd just do this:

```
fn some_func(arg: Option<&str>) {
    if let Some(a) = arg {
        println!("{}", a);
    } else {
        println!("nothing...");
    }
}
```

Now, you'll need to add an `.into` call before being able to use `arg`:

```
fn some_func<'a, T: Into<Option<&'a str>>>(arg: T) {
    let arg = arg.into();
    if let Some(a) = arg {
        println!("{}", a);
    } else {
        println!("nothing...");
    }
}
```

And that's it. As we said before, it doesn't require much and makes users' lives easier, so why not do it?

Using the Path function

Just like the previous section, this will show you some tips to make your API more comfortable to use by *auto-converting* it into a `Path`.

So, let's take an example with a function receiving a `Path` as an argument:

```
use std::path::Path;

fn some_func(p: &Path) {
    // some code...
}
```

There's nothing new in here. You can call this function just like this:

```
some_func(Path::new("tortuga.txt"));
```

The annoying thing, here, is that you have to build the `Path` yourself before sending it to the function. This is way too annoying, but we can do better!

```
fn some_func<P: AsRef<Path>>(p: P) {
    // some code...
}
```

And that's it... You can now call the function as follows:

```
some_func(Path::new("tortuga.txt")); // If you *really* like to
build the "Path" by yourself...
some_func("tortuga.txt");
```

And just like for the `Into` trait, you need to add one line of code in order to make it work:

```
fn some_func<P: AsRef<Path>>(p: P) {
    let p: &Path = p.as_ref();
    // some code...
}
```

And that's it! Now, as long as the given type implements `AsRef<Path>`, you can just send it like that. For information, here's a (non-exhaustive) list of types implementing this trait:

- `OsStr` / `OsString`
- `&str` / `String`
- `Path` (yes, `Path` implements `AsRef<Path>` as well!) / `PathBuf`
- `Iter`

This is already quite a lot, so you should be able to do it pretty easily!

Usage tips

Now that you've seen few examples about how some small tips can make users' code more beautiful, how about we see some others things that might make *your* code better?

Builder pattern

A builder pattern is meant to be able to *build* a final object through multiple calls that can be chained. An excellent example is the `OpenOptions` type in the Rust standard library.

It's strongly recommended you use `OpenOptions` when you need to play with `File`!

```
use std::fs::OpenOptions;

let file = OpenOptions::new()
                        .read(true)
                        .write(true)
                        .create(true)
                        .open("foo.txt");
```

To make such APIs, you have two ways:

- Playing with mutable borrows
- Playing with moves

Let's start with the mutable borrows!

Playing with mutable borrows

The first one works just like OpenOptions:

```
struct Number(u32);

impl Number {
    fn new(nb: u32) -> Number {
        Number(nb)
    }

    fn add(&mut self, other: u32) -> &mut Number {
        self.0 += other;
        self
    }

    fn sub(&mut self, other: u32) -> &mut Number {
        self.0 -= other;
        self
    }

    fn compute(&self) -> u32 {
        self.0
    }
}
```

If you wonder about self.0, just remember that it's how you access a tuple field.

And then you can call it as follow:

```
let nb = Number::new(0).add(10).sub(5).add(12).compute();
assert_eq!(nb, 17);
```

This is the first way to do it.

You'll note that you need to add an *ending* method so that you can transform your mutable borrow into an object (otherwise, you'll have a borrow issue).

Let's now take a look at the second way to do it!

Playing with moves

Instead of taking `&mut` every time, we'll directly take the object's ownership every time:

```
struct Number(u32);

impl Number {
    fn new(nb: u32) -> Number {
        Number(nb)
    }

    fn add(mut self, other: u32) -> Number {
        self.0 += other;
        self
    }

    fn sub(mut self, other: u32) -> Number {
        self.0 -= other;
        self
    }
}
```

Then, there's no more need for the *ending* method:

```
let nb = Number::new(0).add(10).sub(5).add(12);
assert_eq!(nb.0, 17);
```

I generally prefer this way of doing builder patterns but it's more of a personal opinion than a thoughtful decision. Pick whichever seems to fit the best in your situation!

Code readability

We'll now talk about Rust's syntax itself. A few things can improve the code readability and are important to know. Let's start with big numbers.

Big number formatting

It's not uncommon to see huge constant numbers in code, such as this:

```
let x = 1000000000;
```

However, this is quite difficult to read for us (human brains aren't very efficient at parsing such numbers). In Rust, you can insert _ characters into numbers without any problem:

```
let x = 1_000_000_000;
```

A lot better, right?

Specifying types

The Rust compiler can automatically detect the type of a variable in most cases. However, for people reading the code, it's not always obvious what a code returns. An example? Sure!

```
let x = "a 10 11 coucou 12 14".split(' ')
                    .filter_map(|e|
e.parse::<u32>().ok())
                    .filter(|x| x % 2 == 0)
                    .map(|s| format!("{}", s))
                    .collect::<Vec<_>>()
                    .join("::");
```

After reading the code carefully, you'll guess that x is a String. However, you needed to read all those closures to get it and even then, are you really sure of the type?

In such cases, it's strongly recommended to just add the type annotation:

```
let x: String = "a 10 11 coucou 12 14".split(' ')
                    .filter_map(|e|
e.parse::<u32>().ok())
                    .filter(|x| x % 2 == 0)
                    .map(|s| format!("{}", s))
                    .collect::<Vec<_>>()
                    .join("::");
```

It doesn't cost much and allows readers (including you) to go through the code so much faster.

Matching

It's common to use pattern matching through `match` blocks in Rust. However, it's often a better solution to use `if let` conditions. Let's take a simple example:

```
enum SomeEnum {
    Ok,
    Err,
    Unknown,
}
```

Now let's say you want to perform an action only when you get `Ok`. With a `match`, you would do this:

```
let x = SomeEnum::Err;

match x {
    SomeEnum::Ok => {
        // Huge code doing a lot of things...
    }
    _ => {}
}
```

Not really an issue, right? Now let's see it with an `if let`:

```
let x = SomeEnum::Err;

if let SomeEnum::Ok = x {
    // Huge code doing a lot of things...
}
```

And that's it. It basically makes the code a little shorter, while improving readability a lot. Whenever you just need to get one value, it's often a better solution to use `if let` instead of `match`.

Summary

With this last chapter, you should have a good overview of good practices in Rust. Keep in mind that good code is easy to read and well commented. Even complex features can be a lot simpler to understand with well-made documentation.

Other Books You May Enjoy

If you enjoyed this book, you may be interested in these other books by Packt:

Learning Rust
Paul Johnson, Vesa Kaihlavirta

ISBN: 978-1-78588-430-6

- Set up Rust for Windows, Linux, and OS X
- Write effective code using Rust
- Expand your Rust applications using libraries
- Interface existing non-Rust libraries with your Rust applications
- Use the standard library within your applications
- Understand memory management within Rust and speed efficiency when passing variables
- Create more complex data types
- Study concurrency in Rust with multi-threaded applications and sync threading techniques to improve the performance of an application problem

Mastering Rust

Vesa Kaihlavirta

ISBN: 978-1-78588-530-3

- Implement unit testing patterns with the standard Rust tools
- Get to know the different philosophies of error handling and how to use them wisely
- Appreciate Rust's ability to solve memory allocation problems safely without garbage collection
- Get to know how concurrency works in Rust and use concurrency primitives such as threads and message passing
- Use syntax extensions and write your own
- Create a Web application with Rocket
- Use Diesel to build safe database abstractions

Leave a review - let other readers know what you think

Please share your thoughts on this book with others by leaving a review on the site that you bought it from. If you purchased the book from Amazon, please leave us an honest review on this book's Amazon page. This is vital so that other potential readers can see and use your unbiased opinion to make purchasing decisions, we can understand what our customers think about our products, and our authors can see your feedback on the title that they have worked with Packt to create. It will only take a few minutes of your time, but is valuable to other potential customers, our authors, and Packt. Thank you!

Index

A

API tips, Rust
    Path function, using 422
    some function, explaining 421
application
    improving 161
arrays
    about 31
    for loops 32
    slices 31
asynchronous IO
    advantages 329
    disadvantages 330
asynchronous user interface 239

B

binary project
    creating 330, 331, 334
builder pattern
    about 423
    moves, playing 425
    mutable borrows, playing 424
built-in data types
    about 13
    Boolean type 14
    character type 14
    floating-point types 14
    integer types 14
bytes codec
    about 360
    data bytes, decoding 360
    data bytes, encoding 361

C

cargo 48

Cargo.toml file 50
child widget
    adding 246, 248
    dialogs 254
    methods 256
    one-way data binding 249
    post-initialization of view 250, 251, 253
chunks of commands
    basics 299, 304
    implementation 297, 301
clients
    handling 344
code blocks 402
code readability, Rust
    big number formatting 425
    matching 427
    types, specifying 426
commands implementation
    about 307
    CDUP command, implementation 322
    CWD command, implementation 318
    LIST command, implementation 312, 322
    MKD command, implementation 325
    NOOP command, implementation 310
    PWD command, implementation 311
    RMD command, implementation 326
    SYST command, implementation 307
    TYPE command, implementation 311
    USER command, implementation 308
commands
    handling 345, 349
config.toml access
    securing 388
configuration 376, 377, 378, 380, 382, 387
containers
    about 171
    box container 172

types 171
control flow
  about 15
  condition, writing 15
  copy types 20
  mutable references 21
  while loops, creating 15
cover
  displaying 186
CPU usage
  condition variable 220
  improving 219
crate
  documenting 401
  reference link 48
current directory
  changing 352, 354, 355
  managing 351
  printing 351
custom widgets
  creating 239

D

dependencies
  installing 190
  installing, on Linux 190
  installing, on Mac 190
  installing, on Windows 190
dialogs 254
directories
  creating 362
  removing 363
doc blocks
  about 410
  code blocks lines, hiding 410
docs.rs documentation
  about 49
  Cargo.toml file 50
documentation
  about 400
  generating 403
  tags 405
  testing 405
drawing
  about 56

features, playing 67
images, loading 66
images, playing 68
options, playing 62
solution 63

E

enumeration
  about 23
  documenting 402
error handling
  about 336
  error type 337
  unwrapping 336
error type
  ? operator, revisited 341
  about 337
  composing 339
  displaying 339
  error, displaying 337
event loop
  about 197
  atomic reference counting 198
  lock-free data structures 199
  mutual exclusion 199
  Resource Acquisition Is Initialization (RAII) 204
  send trait 199
  sync trait 199

F

file
  downloading 371, 373
  formatted data, reading 76
  handling 71
  high scores, loading 74
  high scores, saving 74
  iterators 74
  listing 365, 367, 368, 370
  opening, with file dialog 183
  uploading 374, 375
fonts
  installing, on Linux 145
  installing, on OS X 145
  loading 146, 148, 149, 151

system/package manager 145
FTP 296
FTP codec 346
FTP commands
  decoding 347
  encoding 348
FTP protocol
  about 295
  chunks of commands, implementation 297
  commands implementation 307
  testing 327
functions
  creating 16
futures
  using 336

G

game map
  interacting 102, 103, 104
game mechanisms
  about 133
  fonts 144
  rendering UI 133
generics
  about 30
  option type 30
gstreamer
  used, for playback 232, 234, 235
GTK+
  installing, on Linux 154
  installing, on Mac 154
  installing, on Windows 154

H

headers 401
high scores
  loading 74, 117
  overwriting 117
  saving 74

I

ID3
  MP3 metadata 182
images

SDL2_image, installing on Linux 66
SDL2_image, installing on Mac 66
integration tests
  about 396
  output, printing to stdout 400
  teardown 397, 399
interior mutability 208, 209, 211, 213, 215
irrefutable patterns 26
items
  hiding, from documentation 405
iterators 74

L

level 113, 116
lines sent 113, 116
LIST command 315

M

macros
  about 34
  multiple pattern rules 35
  repetitions 36
messages 243
methods
  about 21, 256
  constructors 22
model 242
model parameter 259, 261, 262, 264
module
  documenting 401
MP3 decoder
  implementing 191, 192, 194
MP3 files
  decoding 191
  dependencies, adding 191
  frame samples 195
  opening 180
Multiple-Producers-Single-Consumer (MPSC) 283
music player
  using 206
music
  event loop 197
  mutex guard 204
  playing 196, 202, 275, 277, 280, 281, 285

MVC pattern 176

O

one-way data binding 249

P

passive mode
  bytes codec 360
  entering 357, 358, 359
PASV command
  implementation 312
pattern matching
  about 24
  irrefutable patterns 26
playlist
  about 258
  adding 174
  loading 226, 229, 231
  model parameter 259, 261, 262, 264
  MVC pattern 176
  saving 226
post-initialization of view 250, 251, 253
prerequisite
  GTK+, installing on Linux 154
  GTK+, installing on Mac 154
  GTK+, installing on Windows 154
  installing 153
public items
  warning, without documentation 404

Q

quitting 361

R

reference-counting pointer 181
references
  about 18, 19
  clone types 19
relm widget
  adding 265
  data binding 291, 292
relm
  asynchronous user interface 239
  custom widgets, creating 239

Rust nightly, installing 241
  state mutation 238
  used, instead of gtk-rs directly 238
  used, on stable Rust 289
  window, creating 240
rendering 137
rendering initialization 134, 135, 137
repetitions, macros
  optional quantifier 38
Rust crates 41
Rust nightly
  installing 241
Rust project
  cargo 47
  crates.io 47
  docs.rs documentation 49
  setting up 46
Rust's modules 51
Rust
  about 8
  API tips 421
  best practices 419
  code readability 425
  improvements 421
  installation, testing 11
  installing 9
  Linux/Mac 9
  main function 12
  references 12
  slices 419
  usage tips 423
  variables 12
  Windows 9

S

score 113
SDL events 105, 107, 109, 111, 112
SDL2
  installing 41
  installing, on Linux 41
  installing, on Windows 42
  Windows (MinGW) 44
  Windows (MSVC) 45
  Windows, with Build 42
SDL2_image

installing, on Windows 67

Semantic Versioning (SemVer) 47

server
  about 342
  clients, handling 344
  commands, handling 345
  FTP codec 346

slices 420

song duration
  computing 285, 287

song
  current time, displaying 222, 223, 225
  deleting 185
  pausing 207
  progression, displaying 215, 217
  resuming 207

stable Rust
  relm, used 289

state mutation 238

structures
  creating 16

T

tags, documentation
  compile_fail 407
  flags, combining 409
  ignore 406
  no_run 408
  should_panic 409

tests
  fuzzing 411, 412, 415

tetrimino
  about 82, 83, 85
  creating 86, 88, 89, 90, 92
  generating 92, 94
  rotating 94, 95, 97

tetris 53

tetris struct 98, 99, 100, 101

Tetris
  writing 81

Tokio event loop 341

Tokio
  event loop 336
  using 335

tool button events

adding 164
  lifetime 166, 168, 169
  ownership 170

toolbar
  creating 158
  stock item 160

traits
  about 26
  associated types 28
  default methods 28
  rules 29

transfer type
  setting 355

tuples 23

U

unit tests
  about 389, 390
  backtraces 392
  failures, testing 393
  tests, ignoring 394, 395

unwrapping 336

usage tips, Rust
  builder pattern 423

V

view
  about 244
  code generation 245
  events 244
  properties 244

W

widget
  about 242
  communicating 266
  emit 267
  message, sending to relm widget 271
  messages 243
  messages, handling from relm widget 270
  method 268
  model 242
  update function 245
  view 243

widgets
  communicating 266
Window
  creating 154, 157

window
  creating 54
Window
  creating, with relm 240
  default behavior, preventing of an event 158